SUPPLY CHAIN & BUSINESS PROCESSES

— — —

SAP SCM
A COMPLETE MANUAL

YOGI KALRA

ACKNOWLEDGMENTS

I am very thankful foremost to my clients and their employees who have given me the opportunity to work on their SAP systems, always learning from them and their Businesses; notable among them being, Stericycle, Shred-it, Kemira, Johnson & Johnson, BELL Industries, Chevron Phillips, Freightliner and many more. Without their support and my learning their Business Processes, this manual would not have been possible.

I am grateful to my family for tolerating my absence while I composed this manual ignoring them most of the time. I will have to make up to them one day! I am thankful to my wife Michelle for helping me edit the proof of this manual and finding it's numerous errors.

Finally, and not the least, I am grateful to you, the reader for selecting this book among the thousands available, never an easy choice and I hope it met or exceeded your expectations. . I am happy to answer any questions you may have on the topic or if, for better learning, you would like access to the demo system on which this book was written – ykalra@shefaria.com. The author will be grateful for your review and feedback on the public fora if the book helped you increase your understanding of the subject.

CONTENTS

SUPPLY CHAIN MANAGEMENT

At the time of writing, there is no formal module called Supply Chain Management in SAP as we have Finance or Sales and Distribution or Materials Management. Supply Chain is a process and flow of activities that touch all these three primary areas plus (at least) Production and Quality management. The target audience of this book is the users in organizations and SAP consultants though the book is very exhaustive and is of use to practically anyone interested in SCM. This Supply Chain manual will involve all functions across this entire spectrum. It will not go into configurations of each module but will stay with the important transactional functions relating to the entire Order to cash, Requisition to Pay, General Ledger & the daily and periodic financial activities in any organization. This manual has been written keeping standard Business processes proposed by SAP. In writing this book, I have stayed away from all frills and concentrated on providing only useful subject matter with tips and tricks based on over my years of experience in SAP implementations and consulting. This book is not a result of overnight arrangement but a composition of several years of training and understanding of Business processes across multiple industries in various disciplines. I believe it is as comprehensive as any book can be for users new and old, to conducting Supply Chain functions on SAP. This manual will be very useful to someone trying to make an entry into the field of SAP as a user, to companies already implementing or running SAP and consultants wanting to explore the user side better to become more comfortable with the Business lingo.

For New users: One of the primary learning curves in SAP is navigation. The data in SAP is so well organized that first time users are often astonished to see the integrative nature of this ERP system. It is no exaggeration to say that everything you need to know in SAP is at one, two or maximum three clicks away. Mastering navigation in SAP is half the battle won. It would be very worth the while to spend time on navigation on the different screens and get familiar with them as for the most part, there is a commonality in the way SAP is structured across different areas in terms of screen layouts. For some tips, read the section short cuts in Navigation towards the end of this book, before starting on the chapters. To get an even better understanding of Navigation in a structured form, read the author's book SAP Navigation & General Components. Use the F1 key for help liberally – it will help you wade through the screens understanding everything thoroughly. As is the case with all seemingly multifaceted structures, the base is very simple. In spite of SAP's complexity as an ERP system, it's edifice is built on very elementary processes as you will notice while going through this book. Processes that are uniform, scalable and easily comprehensible. One of SAP's masterstrokes is the Transaction code and the philosophy that drives it. Usually a 4 alpha-numeric or alpha code (but can be often longer, especially in Finance reporting), it is used to invoke a program which will guide you through the entire process. Thus, a user need only to remember this transaction code for the function to be performed and entering it in the transaction window to begin your activity. This manual endeavors to cover over 300 such transactions; bear in mind, each of them will perform a related and unique business function. Further, to simplify learning, a transaction code is usually suffixed as 01, 02 or 03 signifying create, change or display respectively. Thus, VA01., VA02 and VA03 become Create Sales Order, Change Sales Order and

Display sales order, respectively. Yet, to keep more uniformity, as a general rule, Sales related transactions begin with a 'V', Materials with a 'M', Finance with 'F', Production with 'P', Quality with 'Q' etc. A glossary of terms and transaction codes at the end of this book will serve as a short cut to finding your way out in the text. Also, for the most part, for transaction codes and for configurable objects (a finite list that can be chosen from, a concept you will discover once you start learning), SAP is case insensitive i.e. VA01 is same as va01.

For SAP Users and Process Owners: This book covers over 250 standard business processes in depth with easily understandable language and only relevant screen shots. It is unlikely that any organization will be required to call upon any other substantial transactions other than these in its normal functioning. Care has been taken to keep a logical flow of information while going back to Accounting here and there to explain the import of the posting or the operation being executed. Towards the end, the book also touches on some cross application components, which if you have access to, will simplify your work in SAP tremendously. Anyone new to the SAP world is advised to read the chapter on 'Variants' after getting a good feel of the first couple of transactions while leaving the rest to the end. Again, for users new to SAP, the best and perhaps fastest way to learn from this book is to think of what you do or did in your legacy system and look up this manual on how to perform the same process in SAP. I have called this book a manual as it is a step by step guide on how to run your regular business transactions in SAP by referring to the relevant section in the Table of Contents.

For Consultants: Though this book is not about configuration, the processes covered are very exhaustive. They will help you understand how SAP has been configured behind the process, and using that, explore IMG and make changes. The screens will also help you understand the challenges users face; often, over time, users become more accomplished than us when it comes to running transactions.

Most importantly, you will learn a lot by diving into the details of the transactions as explained in this book and that will help you face the users more confidently. I can't recount the number of times I was embarrassed in my early days at client's sites when the experienced users explained to me navigation on the screens I did not even know myself!

Your inputs and criticism are very welcome. If there is anything the author can do to help you understand the subject better or guide you in any way, please feel free to drop an email to shefariaentinc@gmail.com noting the name of the book and topic in the subject of the email. Obviously there will be some errors and omissions in the book. I will be very grateful for your comments and responses if you find them or even otherwise give your suggestions since they will work to make the next edition better.

GENERAL LEDGER IN SAP

A Company Code (CC) is the highest object in SAP. Every SAP implementation begins with setting up a CC. All transactions in SAP are conducted in the CC and P&L and Balance sheet generated for a CC.

A Chart of Accounts (CoA) is a set of General Ledger accounts (see next chapter) that a company uses to post entries to.

The General ledger, henceforth, G/L Accounts in SAP is simply a list and G/L accounts are 'buckets' in which amounts pertaining to different activities or balances are held. The G/L accounts usually belong to a Chart of Accounts and a CoA may be repeated over multiple Company Codes, thereby indirectly assigning the G/L account to a CC. However, the G/L accounts then also need to be created/extended to the CC itself for postings to actually occur in that CC. This uniformity allows the multinational companies to do reporting more easily and efficiently as revenue and costs across different CCs can be totaled up effortlessly..

A G/L account can be set up directly also i.e. while not being a part of a CoA, it can still be assigned to a CC for the purpose of journal entries. This is called setting up the G/L account 'centrally'.

There are 3 different types of G/L accounts in SAP:

1. Accounts to which we must post via transactions i.e. no direct journal entries (JE) are possible to these accounts. Typically, these entries are posted from a different module like Sales & Distribution (SD) posts revenues/receivables and Materials Management (MM) posts purchases/payables. No direct entry to these accounts is possible. Instead, the entries emanate from a sub ledger – there are also reconciliation accounts which fall in this definition.
2. Direct entry accounts like direct purchases e.g. some consumption accounts, accounts reserved for manual postings and adjustments etc
3. Indirect accounts where postings take place as a part of a different posting – typically a tax account will be like that where the taxes are a certain % of the revenue or expense and get posted accordingly

Alternatively, we can set up G/L accounts in a CoA and later extend them to the CCs we wish to. The G/L account must exist in the CC to enable postings to take place to the account.

G/L accounts are best explained by creating one to represent different business activities or balances. For the sake of brevity, we will set them up in 2 major groups that represent the P & L and a Balance sheet.

We have a specific numbering sequence for both for identification:

New Entries: Overview of Added Entries

Field status

Chrt/Accts	Acct Group	Name	From acct	To account
SFE	BS	Balance Sheet Accounts	100000	399999
SFE	PL	Profit & Loss Accounts	400000	999999

Figure 1: *New Entries: Overview of Added Entries*

G/L accounts generally are set up by the people running the accounting and finance areas in the organization. Let us set up the above accounts and understand the significance of each field in this set up which users must know. The transaction to set up a G/L account is in a menu called FS00 or we can follow the below path on the transactional SAP menu:

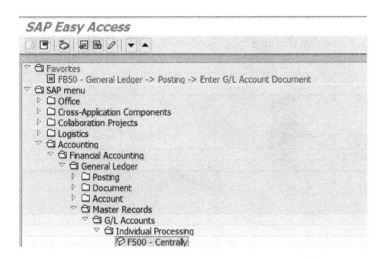

Figure 2: *Create G/L Account Centrally*

Enter the G/L account and conpany code in the transaction window Let's create a revenue account 451010 as in figure 3:

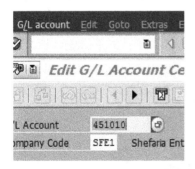

Figure 3: *GL Account – Account Number*

Enter the Account # and CC as above, and Go to Create:

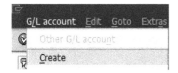

Figure 4: *GL Account - Create*

Select PL as we know this is a P&L Account based on it's number:

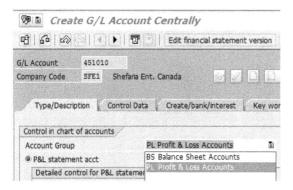

Figure 5: *Create GL Account Centrally*

To enable reporting for functional areas, we can assign the G/L account to a relevant functional area e.g. this is a Revenue account we defined for Business Division 1, so we can link it to Functional Area 4000 as in figure 6:

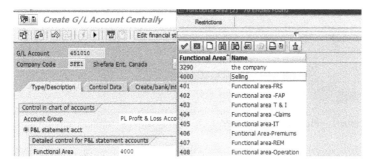

Figure 6: *Create GL Account Centrally - Functional Area*

Give it the appropriate description as in figure 7:

Description	
Short Text	Revenue Stream 1
G/L Acct Long Text	Revenue from Furniture Division

Consolidation data in chart of accounts

Figure 7: *Create GL Account Centrally- Description*

On the next tab, the main field is currency which should auto populate from the CC currency which is set up in configuration. See figure 8.

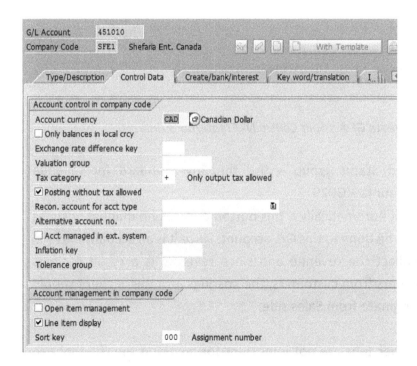

Figure 8: *Create GL Account Centrally- Control Data*

- Tax category – in SAP the output taxes (on sales) and input taxes (on purchases) are different categories. Since this is a revenue account, it makes sense to mark it as Output

- Posting w/o tax allowed – as a general rule, keep this checked in case you have nontaxable customers.
- Line item display – keep this checked as a general rule. This will provide reporting on line items of the transaction instead of clubbing them together
- Sort Key – this enables the reporting sequence. Usually 000 is the preferred one as it gives the listing in sequential of the transaction # (assignment #)

Click on the Create/Bank/Interest tab: See figure 9

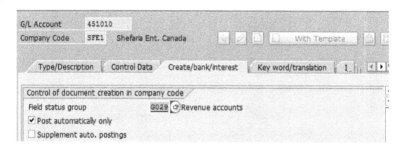

Figure 9: *Create GL Account Centrally- Create/bank/interest*

- Field Status group – use the SAP standard for revenue accounts – G029
- Post automatically – this button ensures no manual postings can be done to this G/L account. Since it is an account that will collect the revenue and since revenue is a result of sales orders from customers, the postings into this account should originate from Sales side.

The other tabs are not important for anything specific that can affect the postings.

Save the account and a message appears at the bottom:

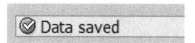

POSTING G/L ENTRIES

At this point, we assume we have the following set up for our learning:

1. Our company code and its CoA
2. A few G/L accounts, some allow direct postings, some not
3. Employee tolerances which determine how much an employee can post, both in absolute terms of a manual JE and in relative terms as a % or $ difference from the original transaction document.

While there are some more configurations like tax codes for accounts that mandatorily require taxes in the amounts to be posted, we will for the moment, proceed with minimal and simplest posting to see how it is done.

When G/L entries are done, every entry must have a debit and credit side to it and both must balance else SAP will not allow the posting to take place. Thus, 2 or more different accounts are needed to make one posting in the system. SAP allows till 999 line items for every document.

The books in SAP are posted to from the point of view of the corporation. The accounting rules that drive them are:

1. To increase the value of an expense or asset account, we post a debit entry to it
2. To decrease the value of the expense or asset account, we post a credit entry to it
3. To increase the value of a revenue or liability account, we post a credit entry to it
4. To decrease the value of a revenue or liability account, we post a debit entry to it

Posting Keys

Before we actually post any entries, we need to look at the concept of posting keys in SAP. Posting keys control the line item posting and the underlying data in a document.

> A/c Type (A-assets, D-customer, K-vendor and S-GL)
> Transaction Type and
> Nature of the Transaction (debit/credit)

A unique combination of these 3 elements is a different posting key. Just by knowing the # of the posting key, one can identify what kind of transaction it is. It facilitates daily work when posting manual JEs.

They are categorized into 4 groups:

Customer (01 to 20)
Vendor (21-39)
GL (40&50)
Asset (70&75)

For G/L postings, depending on what we are going, we use 40 or 50 or SAP self-determines them based on what we actually did.

| 40 | Debit entry | Debit | G/L account |
| 50 | Credit entry | Credit | G/L account |

Thus, a direct debit entry to a G/L account will use a posting key 40 while a credit one will use 50.

Making an entry via a transaction will make the usage of posting keys more clear. The t-code to make an entry directly is FB50 or follow the path:

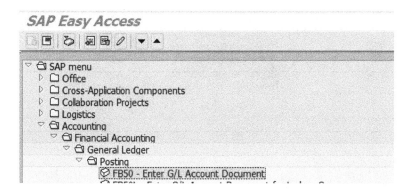

Figure 1: *Enter G/L Accounts Document*

The transaction took us directly to post into CC SFE1 because we have been working in it, SAP holds that data in its memory.

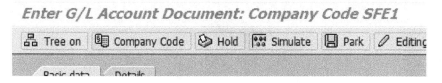

Figure 2: *Enter G/L Account Document - Company Code*

If, however, it does not show up as 'default', it can be made so by clicking on the option

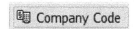

Figure 3: *Company Code*

Then choose your co code from the drop down list or enter it directly as in figure 4:

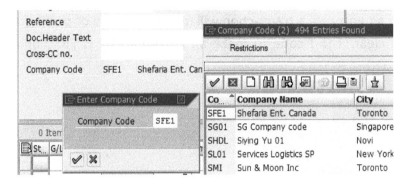

Figure 4: *Company Code List*

Let us try to purchase goods and thereby increase the inventory. A typical journal entry (JE) will require this information as in figure 5:

Figure 5: *Enter G/L Account Document – Required information*

Enter the dates and texts to give the JE a meaning.

In the lower part of the screen, let's try the first line item, debiting the purchase account as in figure 6:

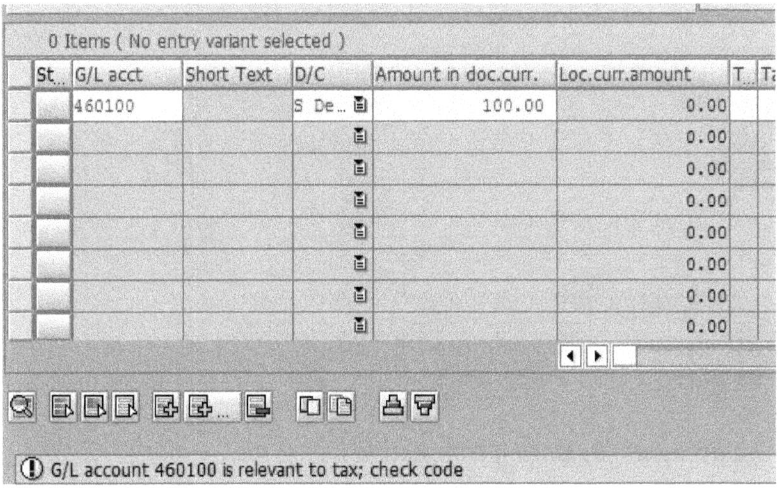

Figure 6: *G/L account – Debit transaction*

On the 2nd line, enter the corresponding inventory account to credit it – an asterisk in the amount column will 'copy' the amount from the 1st line, thereby preventing the need to manually enter and make any mistake:

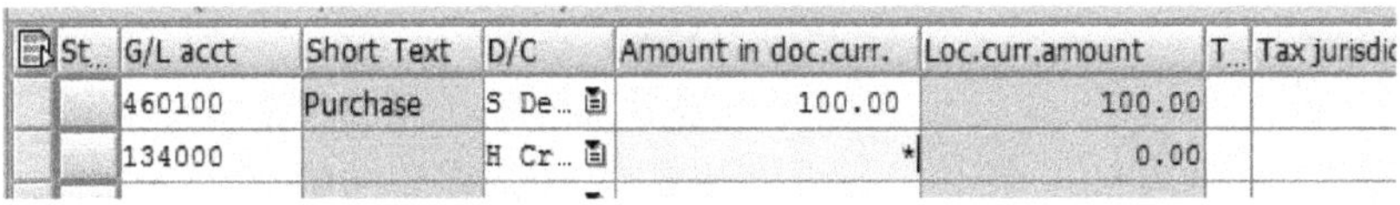

Figure 7: *G/L account – Credit transaction*

As in figure 8, a message in yellow may appear if the G/L account is set up to reflect taxes in it. However entry of taxes is not mandatory as there may not be any taxes to pay/collect.

Figure 8: *G/L account – message relevant to tax*

Hit Enter and the data screen changes to a balancing sign at the top right in Amount Information section in Green.

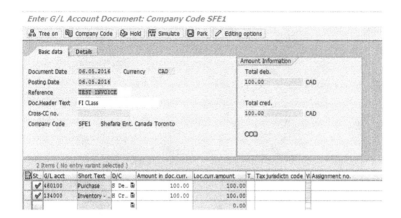

Figure 9: *G/L account – Balancing transaction*

As we know, SAP will allow to make an entry only if the credit and debit balance match as they do in this case. If the amounts don't match, the screen would display the red light:

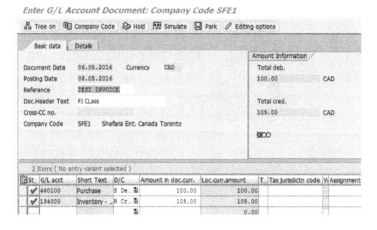

Figure 10: *G/L account – Red light*

For multiple line entries, it is also possible to 'simulate' to ensure everything is in sync and correct before posting. Click on the tab:

Figure 11: *Simulate button*

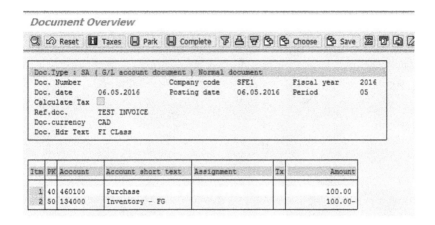

Figure 12: *G/L account – Simulation screen*

The above posting keys 40 and 50 were self-determined by SAP based on the G/L transaction that is being posted.

At this point, we have the option to Park or Post the document or to go back and make changes. Let us post this document by clicking on the Save button.

As in figure 13, a message appears at the bottom informing the document was posted:

Figure 13: *G/L account – Posting message*

RECLASSING ENTRIES

Occasionally mistakes occur in which a posting to be made manually or automatically in a certain G/L account is inadvertently made to another G/L. Balances can be moved around from one G/L to another using transaction F-02:

Enter the data as necessary relating to the G/L you made the incorrect entry to. E.g. we need to move some amount from G/L 460100 to 460300:

Enter data in F-02 - credit 460100 with the amount as in figure 1.

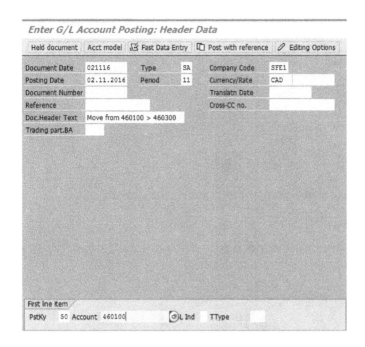

Figure 1: *Enter G/L account Posting – Header Data*

Hit Enter and on the next screen enter the amount and the account to be debited:

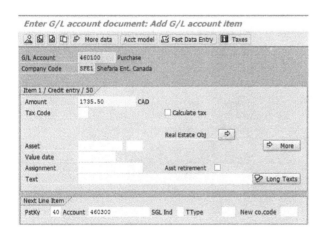

Figure 2: *Enter G/L Account Document –Account to be credited*

Hit Enter again and on the following screen copy the amount to be debited using * as in figure 3 or entering it:

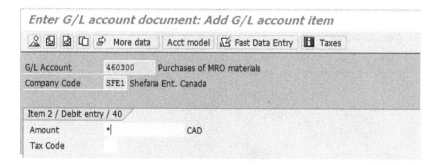

Figure 3: *Enter G/L Account Document –Account to be debited*

Now you can simulate the document to see the effects of your changes:

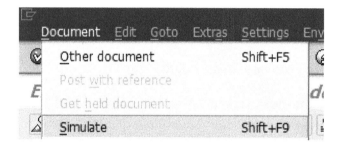

Figure 4: *Enter G/L Accounts Document – Simulate function*

Enter G/L account document: Display Overview

Document Date	02.11.2016	Type	SA	Company Code	SFE1
Posting Date	02.11.2016	Period	11	Currency	CAD
Document Number	INTERNAL	Fiscal Year	2016	Translatn Date	02.11.2016
Reference				Cross-CC no.	
Doc.Header Text	Move from 460100 > 460300			Trading part.BA	

Items in document currency

PK	BusA	Acct		CAD Amount	Tax amnt
001 50		0000460100 Purchase		1,735.50-	
002 40		0000460300 Purchase - MRO		1,735.50	

Figure 5: *Enter G/L Accounts Document – Simulation*

And post:

Document 100000176 was posted in company code SFE1

DISPLAYING BALANCES IN G/L ACCOUNTS

If you are new to the world of SAP, then at this point, you will be well served to read the chapter on Variants towards the end of this book under Cross-application and General and then come back to this section.

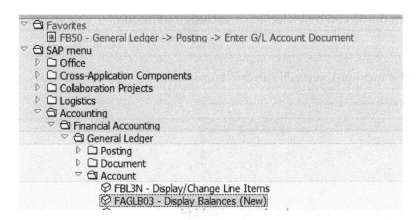

Figure 1: *G/L Account Balance Display*

FAGLB03 will be a transaction any SAP FI user will use often. It is used to check G/L Balances. On the main screen, enter the G/L account, CC (since in a common CoA, a G/L account can be across several CCs) and the year you wish to look up in. See figure 2

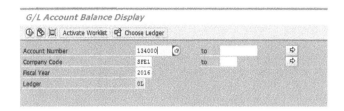

Figure 2: *G/L Account Balance Display*

Multiple G/L accounts can be entered at the same time by clicking on the button 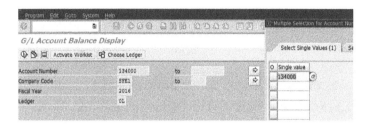 and in the screen that comes up:

Figure 3: *G/L Account Balance Display – Account number*

G/L accounts can be included or excluded as needed in the above tabs.

For the moment, we will run this transaction for the G/L 134000.

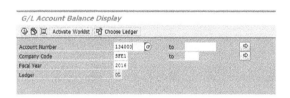

Figure 4: *G/L Account Balance Display – Execute*

Click on the Execute button ⊕ or hit F8. A new screen comes up giving the balances as in the different months as in figure 5:

| Document Currency | Document Currency | Document Currency | Document Currency | | Individual Account |

Account Number	134000	Inventory - FG
Company Code	SFE1	Shefaria Ent. Canada
Fiscal Year	2016	

Display More Chars

| All Documents in Currency | * | Display Currency | CAD | Company code currenc |

Period	Debit	Credit	Balance	Cumulative balance
Bal.Carryfor.				
1				
2				
3				
4				
5		100.00	100.00-	100.00-
6				100.00-
7				100.00-

Figure 5: *Balance Display*

As we notice above, the amount is the G/L entry we did in an earlier section in FB50 in the current month in the account 134000 as a credit entry which is reflected here. A debit entry would have reflected in the first column.

If we double click on the highlighted line below we can find more details about the balances. Depending on which cell/column you click (Debit or credit or balance), you can see either only the debit, or only the credit or all the postings in that G/L as in figure 6.

Account Number	134000	Inventory - FG
Company Code	SFE1	Shefaria Ent. Canada
Fiscal Year	2016	

Display More Chars

| All Documents in Currency | * | Display Currency | CAD | Company code currenc |

Period	Debit	Credit	Balance	Cumulative balance
Bal.Carryfor.				
1				
2				
3				
4				
5		100.00	100.00-	100.00-

Figure 6: *Balance Display for Account Number*

We will find the actual documents relating to those postings as in figure 39, all the cleared and open items all together when we click on the balance column as in figure 7:

```
G/L Account Line Item Display G/L View
H  ◀  ▶  H  |  ⟨⟩ ⊘ 몴  |  ⌧ ⌧  |  ⏴ ⌧ ⌧  |  ⊞ ⊕ ⊕  |  ⌧ % ⌧ ⌧  |  ⊞ ⎗  Select
```

	St	Assignment		DocumentNo	BusA	Typ	Doc. Date	PK	Amount in local cur.	LCurr	A
☐	✓			100000000		SA	06.05.2016	50	100.00-	CAD	
*	✓								100.00-	CAD	
**	Account 134000								100.00-	CAD	
***									100.00-	CAD	

G/L Account   134000   Inventory - Finished Goods
Company Code   SFE1
Ledger   0L

Figure 7: *G/L Account Line Item Display*

A very neat way of looking at this table to sort the data is by switching the layout mode in Settings>Switch List (figure 8):

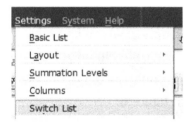

Figure 8: *Switch List*

A more pleasing Excel type layout emerges as in figure 9:

```
G/L Account Line Item Display G/L View
⟨⟩ ⊘ 몴 ⌧ | ⏴ ⌧ | ⏴ ⌧ ⌧ | ⊞ ⊕ ⊕ | ⌧ % ⌧ ⌧ | ⊞ ⊕  Selections
```

G/L Account   134000 Inventory - Finished Goods
Company Code   SFE1
Ledger   0L

	S	Assignment		Document	BusA	Ty	Doc. Date	PK	Σ	Amount in local cur.	LCurr		Amount
	✓			100000000		SA	06.05.2016	50		100.00-	CAD		
	⟁								•	100.00-	CAD		
		Account 134000							⟁ • •	100.00-	CAD		
	⟁								• • •	100.00-	CAD		

Figure 9: *G/L Account Line Item Display - layout*

DISPLAYING LINE ITEMS

Line items in SAP are the individual entries that were posted in a document. To view them in the accounting document, the path is:

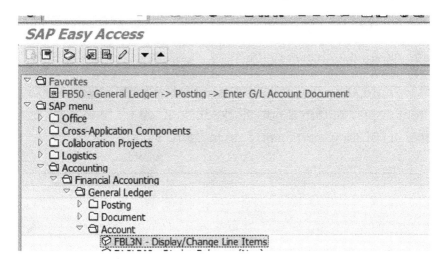

Figure 1: *G/L Account Line Item Display*

Or use transaction FBL3N.

Line item display is only possible for the G/L accounts which are set up so in the account setup under the Control tab:

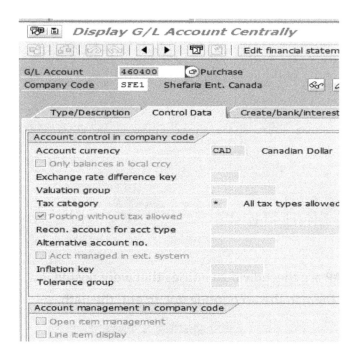

Figure 2: *Display G/L Account Centrally*

As we note, this account 460400 is not set up for line item display (line item display button is not checked), so if we try to look up its balances in FBL3N, we get an error as in figure 3

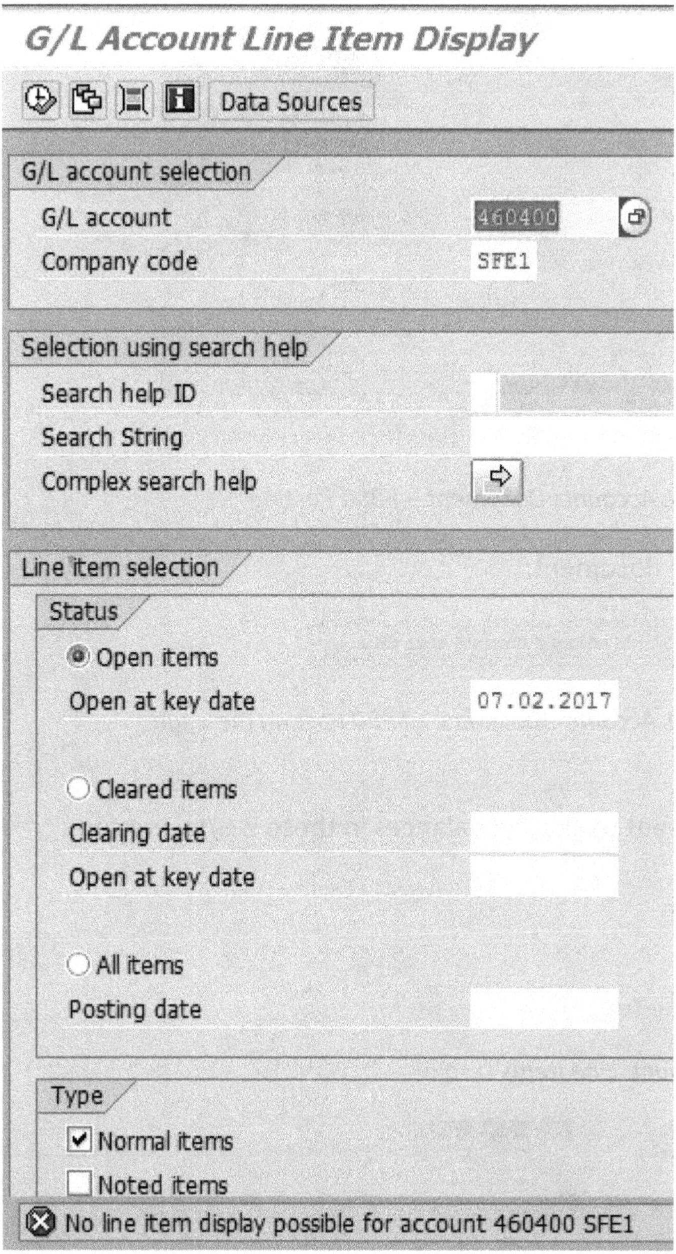

G/L Account Line Item Display

🔽 📑)=(ℹ️ Data Sources

G/L account selection

G/L account   460400   🔲

Company code   SFE1

Selection using search help

Search help ID

Search String

Complex search help   ⇨

Line item selection

Status

◉ Open items

  Open at key date   07.02.2017

○ Cleared items

  Clearing date

  Open at key date

○ All items

  Posting date

Type

☑ Normal items

☐ Noted items

❌ No line item display possible for account 460400 SFE1

Figure 3: G/L Account Line Item Display – message error

Let us now post in FB50 a G/L entry for accounts that support line item reporting. Let us credit Labor inventory (external labor bought) and debit Purchases account as in figure 4.

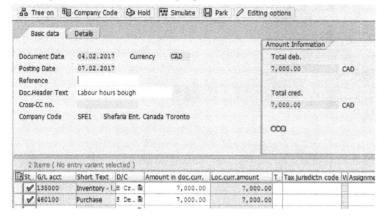

Figure 4: *Enter G/L Accounts Document – FB50 Posting*

And post the document:

Figure 5: *Enter G/L Account Document – FB50 Posting message*

Now, if we want to see the balances in these 2 G/Ls, we can:

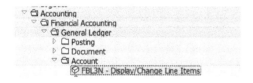

Figure 6: *G/L Account Line Items Display*

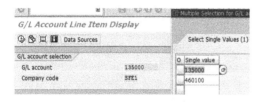

Figure 7: *G/L Account Line Item Display – G/L Account selection*

We can now see all our entries at line item level in this report:

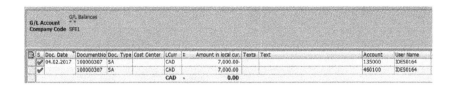

Figure 8: *Entries at Line Item Level*

This is because both the G/L accounts allow for a <u>line item display</u>:

Figure 9: *Control Data – Line Item Display*

Again the list can be seen in a different form also, in settings:

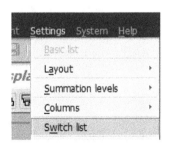

Figure 10: *Settings – Switch List*

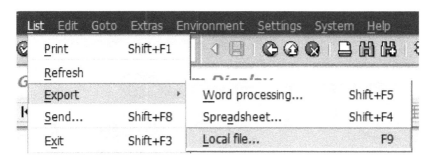

Figure 11: *Line Item Display - Layout*

We can also export it on our desktop to work with it; this is especially useful when there are many entries to be analyzed.

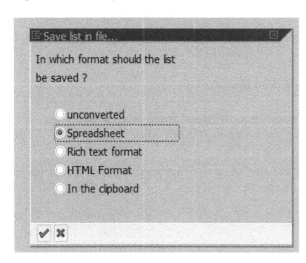

Figure 12: *List Export menu*

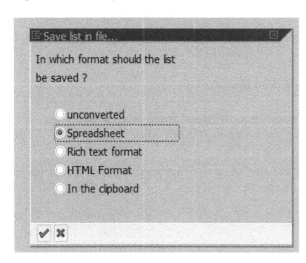

Figure 13: *Export - Options*

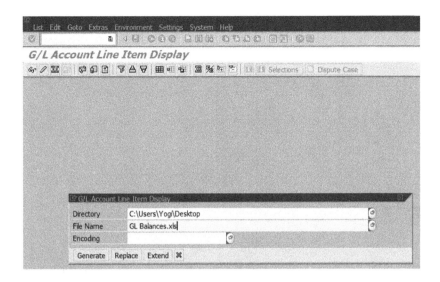

Figure 14: *Export – File Name*

This downloading of data from reports will be a common recurring process throughout and users often use it all the time. For the most part, the process is standard across entire SAP.

REVERSING ACCOUNTING ENTRIES

A document number once used up can't be cancelled or deleted in accounting. This is to ensure a complete audit trail. However, it can be reversed. The path to do that is:

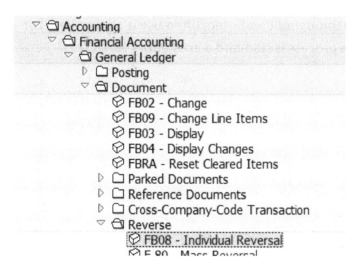

Figure 1: *Reverse Document*

Or t-code FB08:

Enter the document # you need to reverse and give the reason thereof which is mandatory:

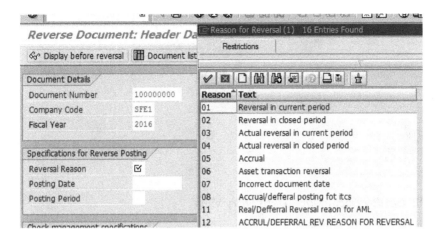

Figure 2: *Reverse Document – Reason options*

One can define our own reasons also via configuration though it is unnecessary and one of standard SAP ones will work fine, like 01 above.

You can also give a different date if the original posting date belonged to a period which is now closed:

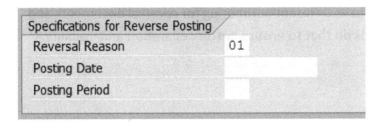

Figure 3: *Specification for Reverse Posting*

Before reversing, you can also look at the original document if you need to for confirmation:

Figure 4: *Display before reversal button*

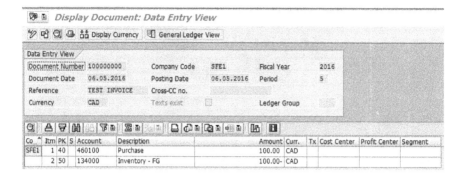

Figure 5: Display Document – Data Entry View

Save and a message is displayed at the bottom:

Figure 6: Reverse Document Posting

Note that it took the next available number from the same series. It is possible to have different numbering for reversal documents and often companies do that to ensure better separation and visibility.

When we run the report again, we find the reversal entries have appeared together under the documents that posted them as in figure 7:

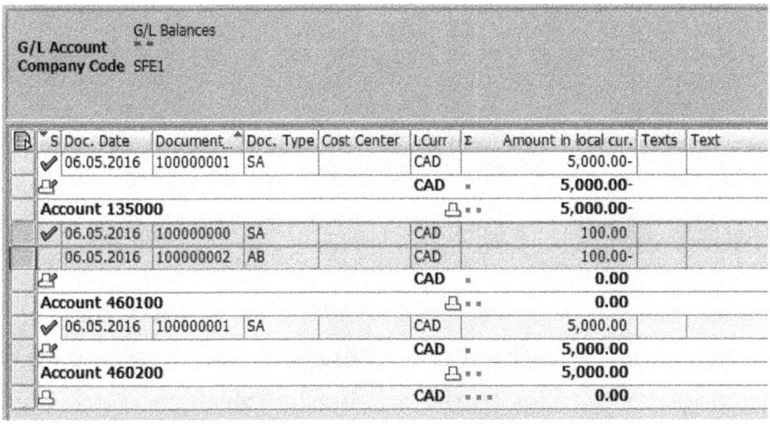
G/L Balances

G/L Account **

Company Code SFE1

S	Doc. Date	Document...	Doc. Type	Cost Center	LCurr	Σ	Amount in local cur.	Texts	Text
✓	06.05.2016	100000001	SA		CAD		5,000.00-		
					CAD	•	**5,000.00-**		
Account 135000						••	**5,000.00-**		
✓	06.05.2016	100000000	SA		CAD		100.00		
	06.05.2016	100000002	AB		CAD		100.00-		
					CAD	•	**0.00**		
Account 460100						••	**0.00**		
✓	06.05.2016	100000001	SA		CAD		5,000.00		
					CAD	•	**5,000.00**		
Account 460200						••	**5,000.00**		
					CAD	•••	**0.00**		

Figure 7: *Reversal Entries*

PARKING A DOCUMENT

Occasionally, we have situations where we may be expecting more information or changes to the postings in which case we can park the document till we are ready to post it. Documents may also be required to park if there is an informal process of getting authorizations before making postings directly to the G/L. Parking the document has the same effect as posting in terms of obtaining a document number except that it does not update the balances. To park a document, we can either go via the same route of FB50:

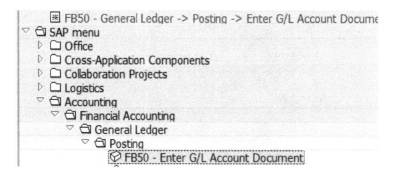

Figure 1: *Enter G/L Accounts Document*

And choose the option to park instead of post:

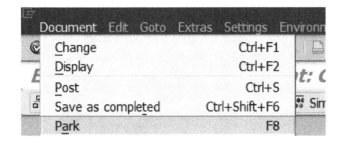

Figure 2: *Park Document*

Or go directly to t-code FV50:

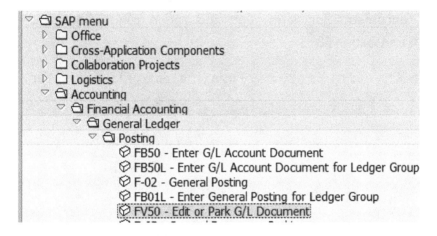

Figure 3: *Enter G/L Accounts Document*

The screens look similar but are not same. FB50, because it is the transaction to post when saved, it will by default, post the document but gives the option to park also:

Figure 4: *Enter G/L Account Document – FB50 (Post by default)*

FV50, because it is the transaction to park, will by default, park the document when saved, but gives the option to post also:

Figure 5: *Enter G/L Account Document -– FV50 (Park by default)*

Saving as completed and parking are the same things. A list of parked documents for verification and action can be obtained through transaction FBV3.

Let us try and park a document using the same process as earlier.

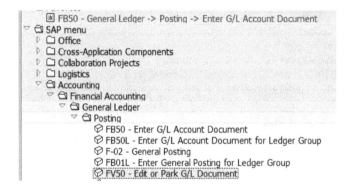

Figure 6: *Enter G/L Account Document – Edit or Park G/L Document*

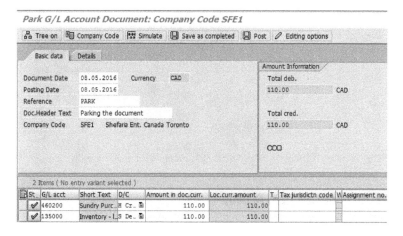

Figure 7: *Park G/L Account Document*

Save the document and SAP will give a number at the bottom:

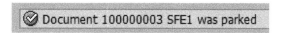

Figure 8: *Park Document message*

 The difference between this and the posted document is that this number will not show up in G/L line balances when we run the report for these 2 G/L accounts

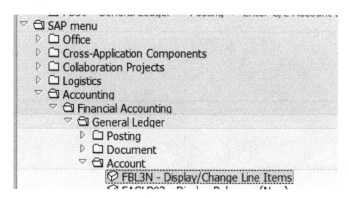

Figure 9: *G/L Account Line Item Display*

G/L Account Line Item Display

⊕ 🅑 ⊐ 🅗 Data Sources   🗗 Multiple Selection for G/L account

G/L account selection				
G/L account	460100	to		🖪
Company code	SFE1	to		⇨

Select Single Values   Selec

O	Single value
	135000
	460200	

Selection using search help	
Search help ID	
Search String	
Complex search help	⇨

Line item selection

Figure 10: *G/L Account Line Item Display*

On executing the report for these 2 G/Ls, we see other numbers but not the parked one as in figure 11:

S	Doc. Date	Document	Doc. Type	Cost Center	LCurr	Σ	Amount in local cur.	Texts	Text
✓	06.05.2016	100000001	SA		CAD		5,000.00-		
					CAD	▪	5,000.00-		
Account 135000						🖨 ▪▪	5,000.00-		
✓	06.05.2016	100000001	SA		CAD		5,000.00		
					CAD	▪	5,000.00		
Account 460200						🖨 ▪▪	5,000.00		
					CAD	▪▪▪	0.00		

Figure 11: *Line Item Display for accounts*

However, if you do want to see them, check on the box in the previous selection screen:

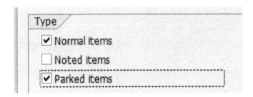

Type
- ✓ Normal items
- ☐ Noted items
- ✓ Parked items

Figure 12: *Type menu for FBL3N*

It now appears along with the other actual postings too as in figure 13:

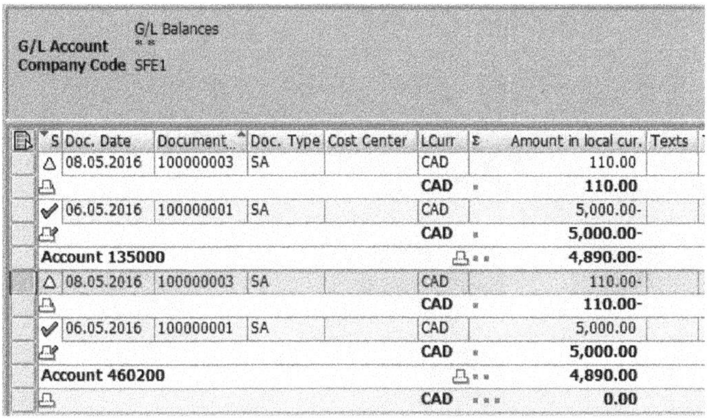

S	Doc. Date	Document	Doc. Type	Cost Center	LCurr	Σ	Amount in local cur.	Texts
△	08.05.2016	100000003	SA		CAD		110.00	
					CAD	▪	110.00	
✓	06.05.2016	100000001	SA		CAD		5,000.00-	
					CAD	▪	5,000.00-	
Account 135000							4,890.00-	
△	08.05.2016	100000003	SA		CAD		110.00-	
					CAD	▪	110.00-	
✓	06.05.2016	100000001	SA		CAD		5,000.00	
					CAD	▪	5,000.00	
Account 460200							4,890.00	
					CAD	▪▪▪	0.00	

Figure 13: *Line Item Display for Park Document*

The Yellow upward triangle symbol in the first column tells you it is a parked document:

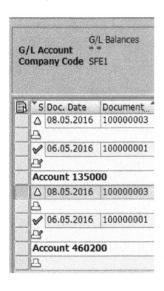

Figure 14: *Symbol for Park Document*

While Green means it is posted:

Figure 15: *Symbol for Posted Document*

To see just the list of parked postings by G/L for taking action on them, either un-select the Posted button:

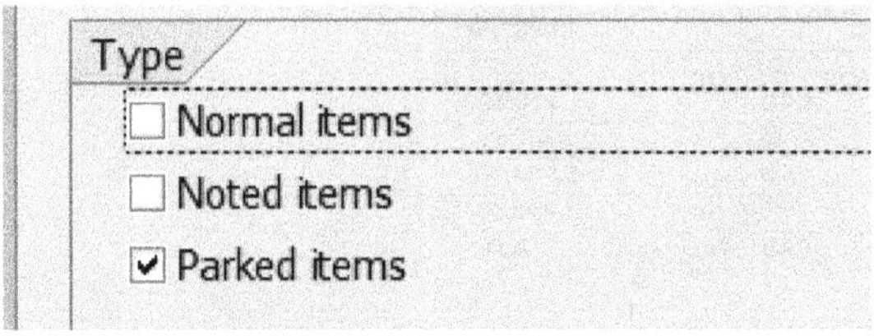

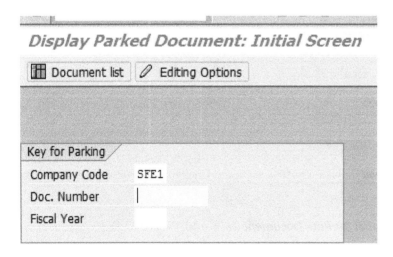

Figure 16: *Type menu for FBL3N*

Now re-run the report.

Alternatively, to just get a list of the parked documents, run the transaction FBV3:

Figure 17: *Display Parked Document – FBV3*

Enter the document # (figure 17) if you know and are specifically looking for it:

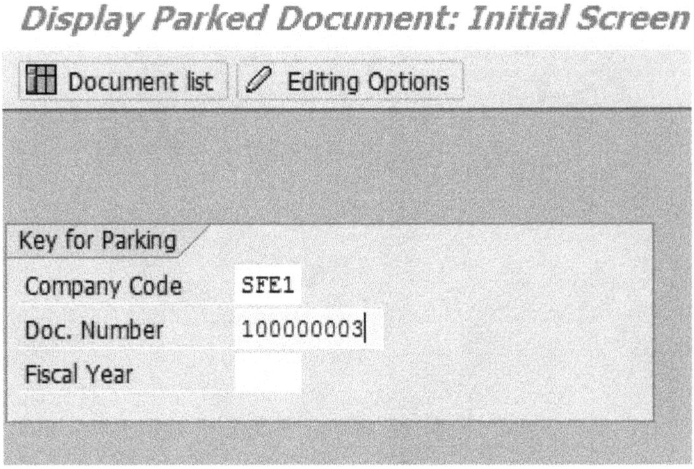

Display Parked Document: Initial Screen

⊞ Document list ⧄ Editing Options

Key for Parking

Company Code   SFE1

Doc. Number   100000003|

Fiscal Year

Figure 18: *Display Parked Document – Doc. Number*

The fiscal year will also be needed to be entered in case the same document number exists in multiple fiscal years. In our case since it is only in current year so that is not necessary.

If you do not know the document # and just want a list to work on, click on:

Figure 19: *Document List*

Now you have many options – you can run it open i.e. for the report to display all the parked documents in any or all CC/s.

Or restrict the selection to specific times, people (Entered by), dates etc:

List of Parked Documents

Company code	SFE1	to		⇨
Document number		to		⇨
Fiscal year	2016	to		⇨

General Selections

Posting date		to		⇨
Document date		to		⇨
Document type		to		⇨
Reference		to		⇨
Document header text		to		⇨
Entered by	IDES0164	to		⇨

Figure 20: *List of Park Document*

Executing it will display the parked documents that were entered by IDES0164 in CC SFE1 as in figure 21:

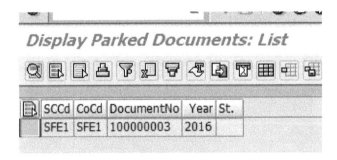

Figure 21: *Display Park Document List*

We saw this same document also appear in the G/L line item display earlier. See figure 22

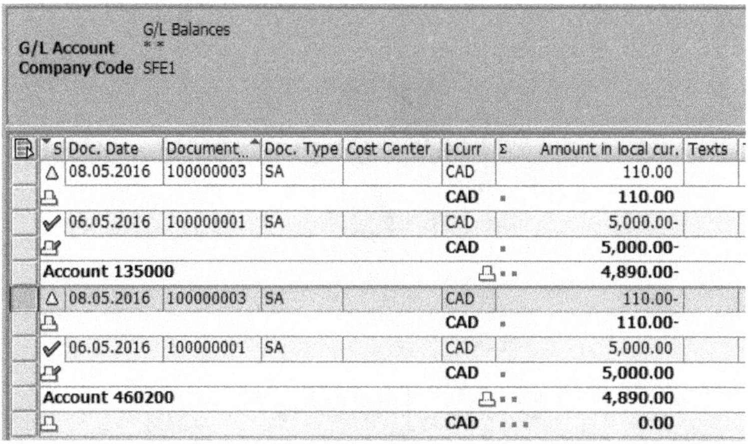

G/L Balances
G/L Account * *
Company Code SFE1

S	Doc. Date	Document	Doc. Type	Cost Center	LCurr	Σ	Amount in local cur.	Texts
△	08.05.2016	100000003	SA		CAD		110.00	
					CAD	▪	110.00	
✔	06.05.2016	100000001	SA		CAD		5,000.00-	
					CAD	▪	5,000.00-	
Account 135000						▪ ▪	4,890.00-	
△	08.05.2016	100000003	SA		CAD		110.00-	
					CAD	▪	110.00-	
✔	06.05.2016	100000001	SA		CAD		5,000.00	
					CAD	▪	5,000.00	
Account 460200						▪ ▪	4,890.00	
					CAD	▪ ▪ ▪	0.00	

Figure 22: *G/L Line Item Display*

45

POSTING PARKED DOCUMENTS

Once you have obtained all the information and/or authorizations needed, the parked documents can be posted in the system. This will change their status from parked to posted and update the database accordingly. To post a parked document, go to the menu:

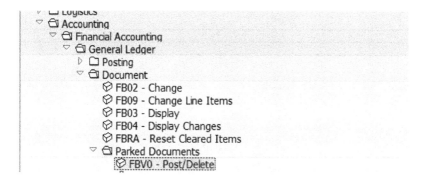

Figure 1: *Post Parked Document*

Or t-code FBV0

Enter the document #:

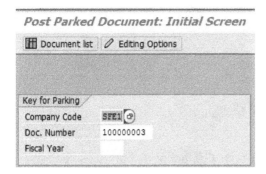

Figure 2: *Post Parked Document*

Hit Enter:

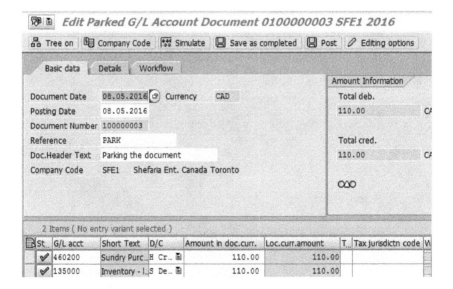

Figure 3: *Edit Parked G/L Account Document*

Post the document: See figure 4

Figure 4: *Post button*

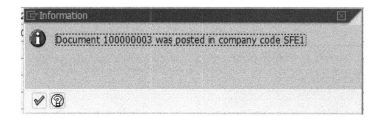

Figure 5: *Information posting message*

When we re-run the line items or G/L account balances reports, FBL3N, this document will change its status from Yellow to Green as in figure 6:

	S	Doc. Date	Document	Doc. Type	Cost Center	LCurr	Σ	Amount in local cur.	Texts	T
	✓	06.05.2016	100000001	SA		CAD		5,000.00-		
		08.05.2016	100000003	SA		CAD		110.00		
						CAD	▪	4,890.00-		
	Account 135000							4,890.00-		
	✓	06.05.2016	100000001	SA		CAD		5,000.00		
		08.05.2016	100000003	SA		CAD		110.00-		
						CAD	▪	4,890.00		
	Account 460200							4,890.00		
						CAD	▪▪▪	0.00		

G/L Balances
G/L Account ▪ ▪
Company Code SFE1

Figure 6: *G/L Balances Report*

Also, that document will no longer show up in the parked documents report FBV3: See figure 7

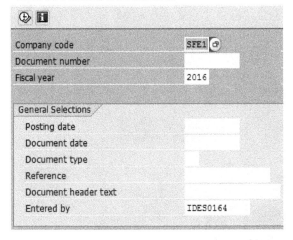

Figure 7: *List of Park Document*

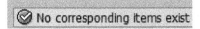

Figure 8: *Message for parked Document already posted*

CUSTOMER NOTED ITEM

Memorandum (Noted) Item Entries

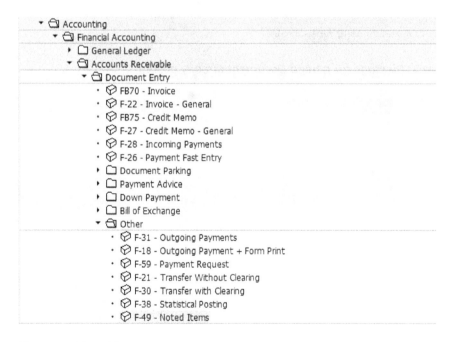

Figure 1: *Noted Items*

These can be used for recording Bank Guarantee or any other entries which we don't want to post in the customer Account and the general ledger A/c. It creates a one sided entry only. These entries will have no effect on the Financial Books. We use them only for the record purpose and after the purpose is over we can reverse the same

Create the transaction with the posting key as 09 or 19 using the following Special GL Indicator:

L : Letter of Credit
G: Bank Gurantee

Customer Account Number and Amount is to be filled.

Fill in the Bank Guarantee Due Dates so thatlater on, on the Maturity Date we can reverse the same later on.

E.g. Scenario : Customer provides bank gurantee Draft / Cheque. Now to get the payment encashed in the real world, it may take some time. In SAP we can record the transaction in a form of entry without impacting the book of accounts . This entry is just for information purposes.

In the following scren fill up the required details :

Account : Customer Account No.
Reference : We can put Sales Order no or Bank Gurantee Check No
Amount : Bank Gurantee Amount
Text : Free Field for Description

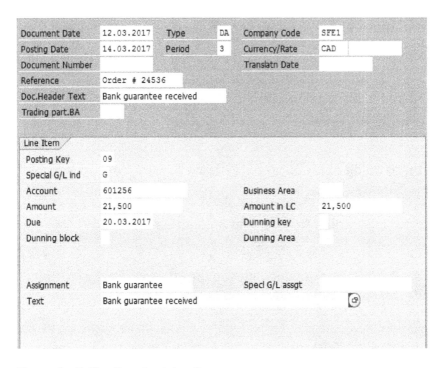

Figure 2: *F-49 – Required details*

Save:

Figure 3: *Noted Item posted*

System saved the entry as a NOTED Item :

We can also view the entry in Customers' receivables transaction FBL5N (will look at this in more detail in a late chapter) with choosing the option 'Noted Items'. See figure 4

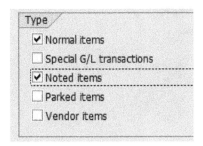

Figure 4: *FBL5N – Type*

S..	Assignment	DocumentNo	Ty..	Doc. Date	S	DD	Σ	Amount in local cur.	LCurr	Clrng doc.	Text
	0080015448	90036836	RV	13.03.2017				105.00-	CAD		
	Bank guarantee	1600000020	DA	12.03.2017	G			2.00	CAD		
	Bank guarantee	1600000021	DA	12.03.2017	G			21,500.00	CAD		Bank guarantee received

Customer 601256
Company Code SFE1
Name Showroom 1 for SFE1
City Toronto

Figure 5: *FBL5N – Noted Items for customer*

Reversal of Noted Item Entries

We generally use this option in order to cancel the initial entry/postings or those which are found to be incorrect. SAP provides the list of Reason code to be selected during reversal : we can choose as applicable as in Fig 6.

Reason	Text
01	Reversal in current period
02	Reversal in closed period
03	Actual reversal in current period
04	Actual reversal in closed period
05	Accrual
06	Asset transaction reversal
07	Incorrect document date
08	Accrual/defferal posting fot itcs
11	Real/Defferral Reversal reaon for AML
12	ACCRUL/DEFERRAL REV REASON FOR REVERSAL
13	ACCRUL/DEFERRAL REV REASON FOR REVERSAL
1R	Reversal, incorrect original date aml
1S	Accrual/defferal posting for soda
ER	Posting Error - C900
RE	Reversal, incorrect original date
WE	Wrong Entry

Figure 6: *Reversal reasons*

As normal documents are reversed we can in the same way, reverse the Noted Entries by using FB08.

Provide the Noted Item Document Number, Company Codes, Fiscal Year and Reversal Reason.

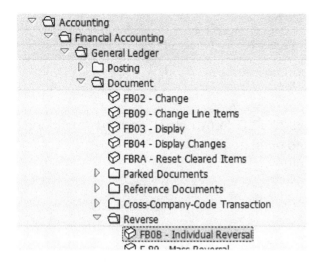

Figure 7: *Reverse Document*

Reverse Document: Header Data

| 👁 Display before reversal | 🏢 Document list | 🔠 Mass Reversal |

Document Details	
Document Number	1600000021
Company Code	SFE1
Fiscal Year	2017

Specifications for Reverse Posting	
Reversal Reason	01
Posting Date	
Posting Period	

Check management specifications	
Void reason code	

Figure 8: *Reverse Document – Header Data*

Select 💾 option to save / post the reversal entries. System confirms the posting displaying the following message :

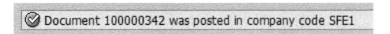

Figure 9: *Reversal entries posting message*

This will clear the old NOTED Item entries and the Customer Account will be left with no open items.

Figure 10: *Noted Item cleared*

The entry will disappear from FBL5N as in figure 11:

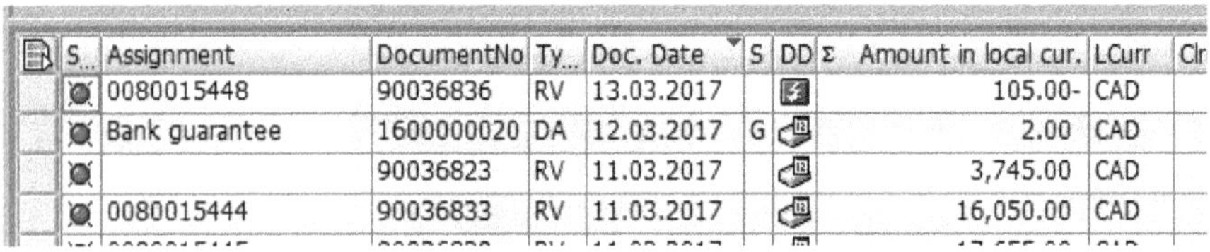

S	Assignment	DocumentNo	Ty	Doc. Date	S	DD	Σ	Amount in local cur.	LCurr	Clr
	0080015448	90036836	RV	13.03.2017				105.00-	CAD	
	Bank guarantee	1600000020	DA	12.03.2017	G			2.00	CAD	
		90036823	RV	11.03.2017				3,745.00	CAD	
	0080015444	90036833	RV	11.03.2017				16,050.00	CAD	

Figure 11: *Noted Item entries cleared from FBL5N*

MASTER DATA IN SAP

Master data in SAP refers to the most often repeated scenario in a transaction with a vendor or a customer, a material or works orders or any other data dependent transaction. To prevent redundancy and accuracy as well as relieve the users of non value added work, master data is created and stored in tables to be used at times of transactions. Since SAP is such an integrated system, it requires a lot of data to keep the flow of information going as well as ensuring the data integrity and validity. Master data can make or break a SAP implementation – there have been numerous instances where enough attention was not paid to master data in the initial stages causing the implementations to suffer badly. As we will see in the course of this manual, one transaction builds upon the previous one; as a result, it carries forward the data from the preceding document to the subsequent document. It is not uncommon that some data in the first document will have a role to play only when the entire business cycle is ending and if that data is not correct, the ending will not be happy. The solution to that, often is to unroll the entire transaction string one by one by cancelling or reversing them in the reverse chronological manner. Needless to say, it can be very frustrating. SAP is very unforgiving when it comes to valid master data. Thus for users and consultant, it can't be under stated how critical it is to understand the importance of certain fields in the customer, vendor and material masters at least from the Supply Chain perspective.

This master data is not cast in stone. For the most part, it is merely a composition of the most often repeated scenario for the transaction. E.g. if we have a vendor credit terms set to 30 days, it is not necessary that every PO must be of 30 days payment terms only. This 30 days will certainly default into the PO when that vendor # is inserted; however, the user for the most part, has the ability to over write it with anything else like 60 or 15 days. The idea merely is, to ensure the user does not have to waste time entering it every time a PO is created and since 30 will be the 'normal' terms anyway, the POs can generally be created with these payment terms in the 'master data'. The transactional data will always be paramount and trump the master data and can often be changed in most of the cases.

It is important to realize that a substantial part of this master data gets pulled into the PO for purchasing from the vendor and into the sales order for selling from the customer. It then gets transferred to the subsequent documents and in some cases may get its it's validity checked only in the subsequent document. Thus, one is well advised to pay good attention to the way customers and vendors are setup in the first place to prevent data integrity or non compliance issues.

VENDOR MASTER - FI PERSPECTIVE

We are now ready to create our first vendor. The t-code to create a vendor is XK01 centrally or, from a Finance perspective only, FK01. We can also follow the path on the SAP main menu:

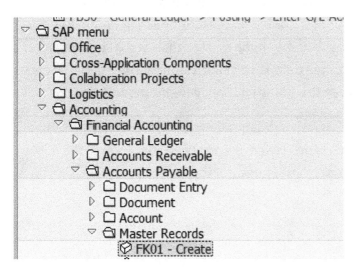

Figure 1: *Create Vendor*

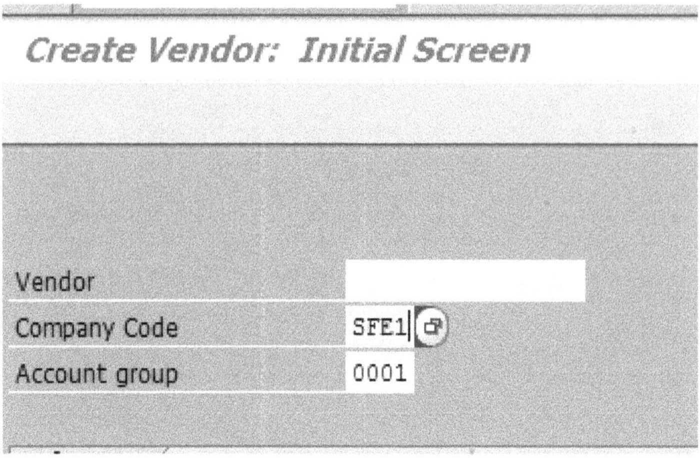

Create Vendor: Initial Screen

Vendor	
Company Code	SFE1
Account group	0001

Figure 2: *Create Vendor*

Hit Enter and the system takes you to the main address screen where you can enter the data as required. Toggle through the screens using the buttons  to fill up all the necessary data. Most fields are self-explanatory, a few important ones are defined below. There is a lot more to the vendor master than we will cover here; however, all that other data is relevant to purchasing departments and thus, is a part of the Material Management module and we will cover it later in this manual.

The field Search term is used as an abbreviated form of the name to 'search' for vendors in the huge database.

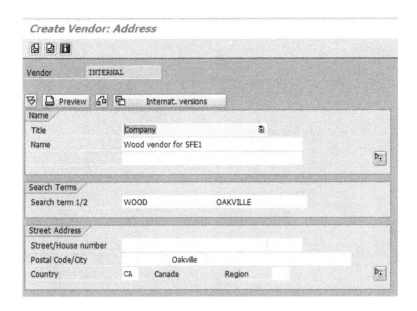

Figure 3: *Create Vendor – Address screen*

The Plus icon denotes that there are more fields that can be viewed and filled up by exploding this icon. On the above screen, they will relate mainly to the address. See figure 3.

Create Vendor: Control

⊟ ⊟ ℹ️ Tax categories

| Vendor | INTERNAL | Vendor for FI Class 2 |

Account control

| Customer | | ⊡ | Authorization | |
| Trading Partner | | | Corporate Group | |

Tax information

Tax Number 1		Tax number type		☐ Equalzatn tax
Tax Number 2		Tax type		☐ Sole Proprietr
Tax Number 3				☐ Sales/pur.tax
Tax Number 4				☐ Tax split
Fiscal address				
Tax Jur.		VAT Reg. No.		Other...
Tax office				
Tax Number				

Reference data

Location no. 1		Location no. 2		Check digit	
Industry					
SCAC		Car.freight grp		ServAgntProcGrp	
POD-relevant					
Actual QM sys.		QM system to			

Figure 4: *Create Vendor – Account Control*

Customer: If the vendor also happens to be a customer, enter its customer # here as in figure 4. This can also be used to adjust the payables against the receivables or vice versa once some other data settings are done.

The field trading partner is used to denote if it is an inter-company vendor by entering the trading partner number in it.

On the next screen define the vendor's banking information where payments can be made:

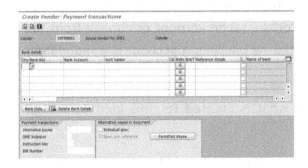

Figure 5: *Create Vendor –Banking information*

Alternative payee: If the vendor to be paid for the purchases is different from the current vendor #, enter that payee # here

On the next screen, 2 fields are mandatory and marked as such with a ☑

Create Vendor: Accounting information Accounting

| Vendor | INTERNAL | Wood vendor for SFE1 | Oakville |
| Company Code | SFE1 | Shefaria Ent. Canada | |

Accounting information

Recon. account	☑	Sort key	
Head office		Subsidy indic.	
Authorization		Cash mgmnt group	☑
		Release group	
Minority indic.		Certificatn date	

Interest calculation

Interest indic.		Last key date	
Interest freq.		Last interest run	

Withholding tax

W. Tax Code		Exemption number	
WH Tax Country		Valid until	
Recipient type		Exmpt.authority	

Reference data

Prev.acct no.		Personnel number	

Figure 6: *Create Vendor – Accounting Information*

A reconciliation account is the account to which the account payables or receivables are posted via the sub-ledger. The balance in the recon accounts at any time, is the current asset or current liability on the balance sheet. Enter the recon account or choose from the drop down or press F4 - the reconciliation account is a mandatory field.

Choose 211000 which is what is created for this kind of vendor (domestic):

Figure 7: *Create Vendor – Reconciliation Account*

The other field is Cash management group:

Cash mgmnt group ☑

Figure 8: *Create Vendor – Cash mgmnt group check box*

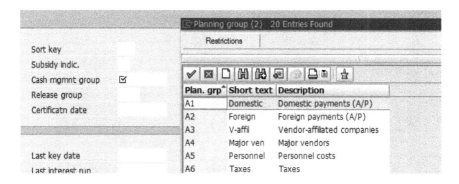

Figure 9: *Create Vendor – Cash mgmnt group options*

Let us say this will be handled by the domestic payments group and select A1 as in figure 9.

The next screen has payment related data:

Create Vendor: Payment transactions Accounting

| Vendor | INTERNAL | Wood vendor for SFE1 | Oakville |
| Company Code | SFE1 | Shefaria Ent. Canada | |

Payment data

Payt Terms	0003	Tolerance group	
Cr memo terms		Chk double inv.	✔
Chk cashng time			

Automatic payment transactions

Payment methods	CI	Payment block		Free for payment
Alternat.payee		House Bank		
Individual pmnt	☐	Grouping key		
B/exch.limit		CAD		
Pmt adv. by EDI	☐	Alt.payee(doc.)	☐	Permitted Payee

Invoice verification

| Tolerance group | |

Figure 10: *Create Vendor – Payment transactions accounting*

Enter the data as appropriate and always check the indicator – Chk double invoice. This drives that SAP will, at the time of doing invoice verification, ensure we do not book the same invoice from the same vendor for payment again.

The next screen has data relating to how to correspond with this vendor:

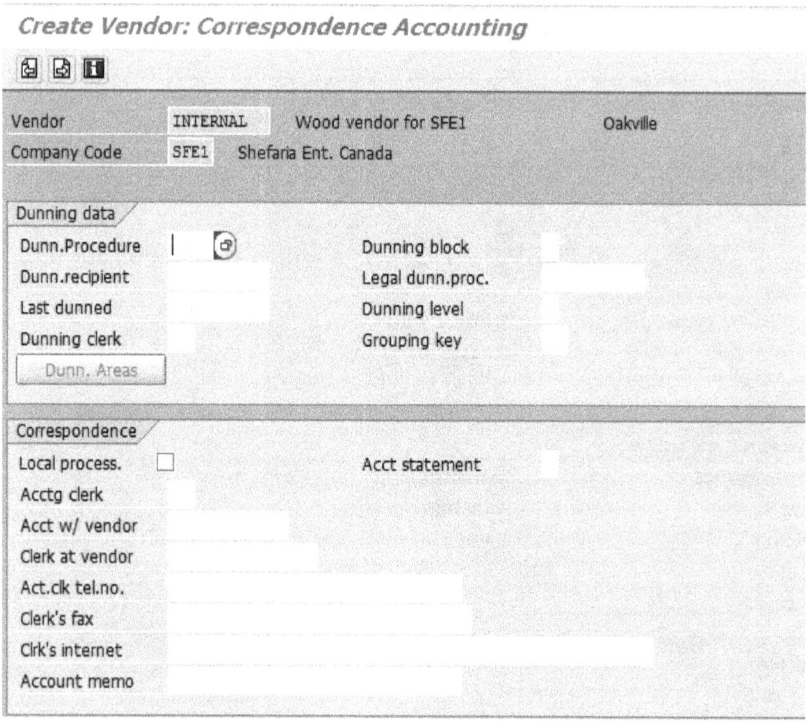

Figure 11: *Create Vendor – Correspondence Accounting*

Data like Acct clerk is used to provide visibility to the vendor. The acct clerk is a person or group responsible to make payments to this vendor and if we run reports for accounting clerks, we get the lists of vendors whose payments are due.

Now when we click on [icons], we get the message that the last screen has been reached:

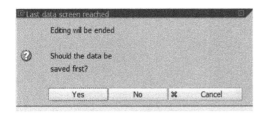

Figure 12: *Create Vendor –save message*

At this point, we have entered in all the data that the system needed on the screens we chose to set up. We now save this vendor by clicking on Yes and the message follows:

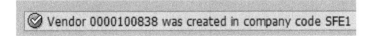

Figure 13: *Create Vendor – Creation message*

At various times over the learning cycle, we will come back to the vendor master to populate certain more data and see its effect on our transactions.

CUSTOMER MASTER - FI PERSPECTIVE

The path to create a customer from the Accounting/Finance perspective is

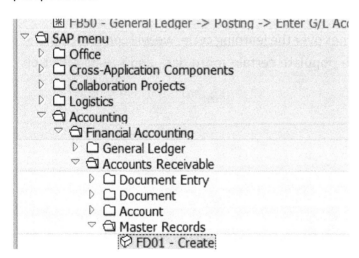

Figure 1: *Create Customer*

Or use t-code FD01.

Choose the account group 0001: See figure 2

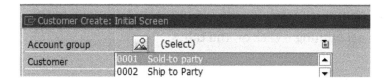

Figure 2: *Customer Create – Account group*

Leave the field Customer blank as SAP will auto generate the next available number. Enter your CC

Figure 3: *Customer Create – Initial screen, Required data*

Hit Enter:

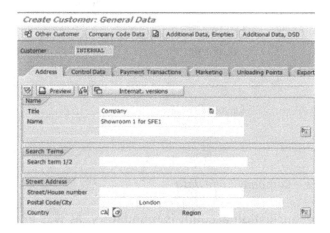

Figure 4: *Customer Create – General data*

The field Country is mandatory so we enter that – populate the data related to accounting – click on the tab:

Company Code Data

Figure 5: *Customer Create – Company Code Data button*

This view has a few screens:

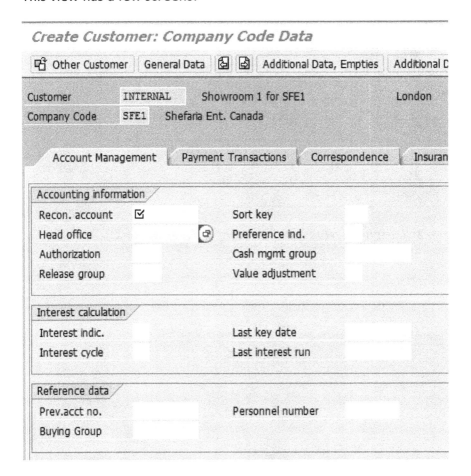

Figure 6: *Customer Create – Company Code data*

We see that the reconciliation account is mandatory, as was in the vendor master.

So let us enter the recon account as below:

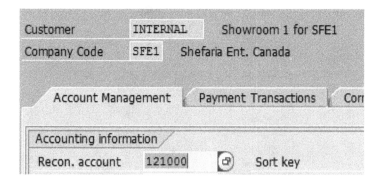

Figure 7: *Customer Create – Reconciliation Account*

On the next tab, payment Transactions we can enter the payment terms we have given the customer as well as the tolerance group which will, in turn, decide the flexibility the employees have in posting payments or write offs.

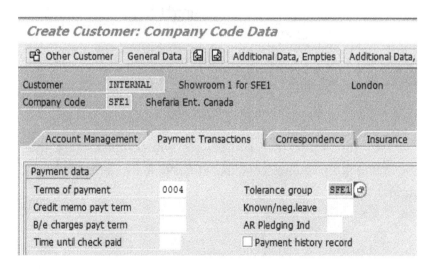

Figure 8: *Customer Create – Payment Transaction*

On the next tab, Correspondence , we find the field Accounting Clerk is mandatory (Fig 9):

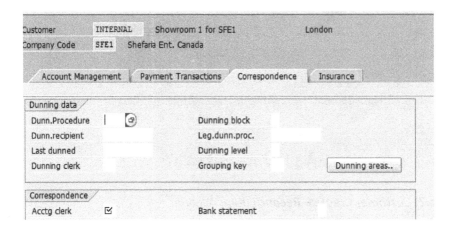

Figure 9: *Customer Create – Correspondence*

This is because we made it so in the configuration. The accounting clerk is a person or group responsible for making payments or collections from the account. Populate it with the accounting clerk (in our case, WR) and save.

Figure 10: *Customer Create – Create message*

At various times over the course, we will come back to the customer master to populate certain data and see its effect on our transactions.

POSTING CUSTOMER INVOICES IN FI

Under normal times, customer invoices will be created as a part of a transaction in which services and/or goods were provided. In SAP, invoicing is a function performed under Sales & Distribution module as they are a result of goods and/or services provided, however, in reality, it may be done by the Finance department as most non-SAP systems have billing as a part of the accounting function. Billing in SAP is a very generic term and encompasses invoicing, credit notes, cancellation documents etc. Every invoice in SAP generally leads up to an accounting document. Billing will be discussed in-depth later in this manual.

There are times when customers are invoiced directly in SAP and those transactions create accounting documents that show up in the AR reports of the customer. It is also common during data transfer of A/R from legacy systems into SAP when existing invoices are posted to create the AR. To create one such manual invoice, let us follow the path in figure 1:

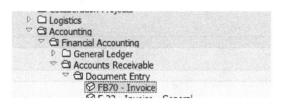

Figure 1: *Enter Customer Invoice*

Or transaction FB70:

Enter your CC if/when prompted to do so:

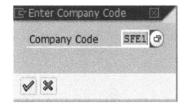

Figure 2: *Posting Customer Invoice – Enter Company Code*

Enter your data, at the minimum, the customer #, date and amount and Hit Enter:

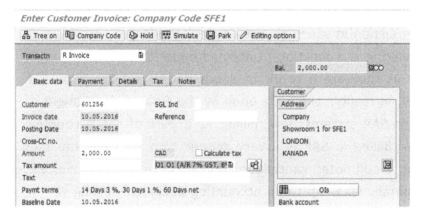

Figure 3: *Posting Customer Invoice – Basic Data*

If tax is applicable, check *Calculate tax*, else leave it unchecked.

Enter the revenue account you want to post this amount against:

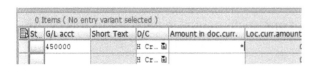

Figure 4: *Posting Customer Invoice – Revenue account entries*

The * will copy the amount from the main line.

While you are learning, it is always a good idea to simulate the entry first using the simulate button:

Figure 5: *Posting Customer Invoice – Simulate button*

St	G/L acct	Short Text	D/C	Amount in doc.curr.	Loc.curr.amount	T	T
	450000		H Cr… 🗎	2,000.00	0.00 01		
			H Cr… 🗎		0.00 01		
			H Cr… 🗎		0.00 01		
			H Cr… 🗎		0.00 01		

0 Items (No entry variant selected)

❌ Account 450000 can only be posted to internally in company code SFE1

Figure 6: *Posting Customer Invoice – Posting error message*

We get an error (figure 6) because the way the GL 450000 was defined prevents us from posting directly to it, only automatic postings (from Sales or Purchase) can be made. See figure 7 (G/L account setup in FS00).

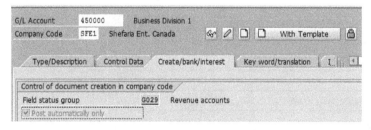

Figure 7: *Posting Customer Invoice – Post automatically only field*

This setting determines that postings to this account can come only from the sales side. So this would not work obviously. We should change the account to a revenue account that allows direct postings. Normally, companies keep an account or two only for these purposes i.e. to make direct JEs for revenues or expenses.

We have account 450300 for this purpose. Let us substitute 450000 with 450300 and try the posting again and also w/o any taxes to keep it simple:

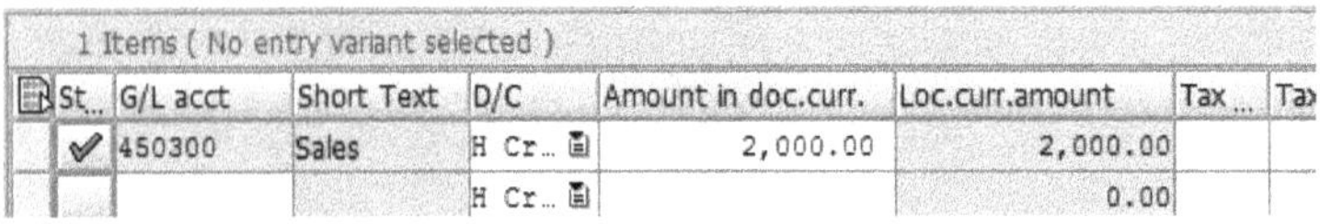

	St...	G/L acct	Short Text	D/C	Amount in doc.curr.	Loc.curr.amount	Tax...	Ta>
	✔	450300	Sales	H Cr.. 🔳	2,000.00	2,000.00		
				H Cr.. 🔳		0.00		

1 Items (No entry variant selected)

Figure 8: *Posting Customer Invoice – Revenue Account entries*

The simulation button gives no errors – only an Info (!) message that can be bypassed by hitting Enter:

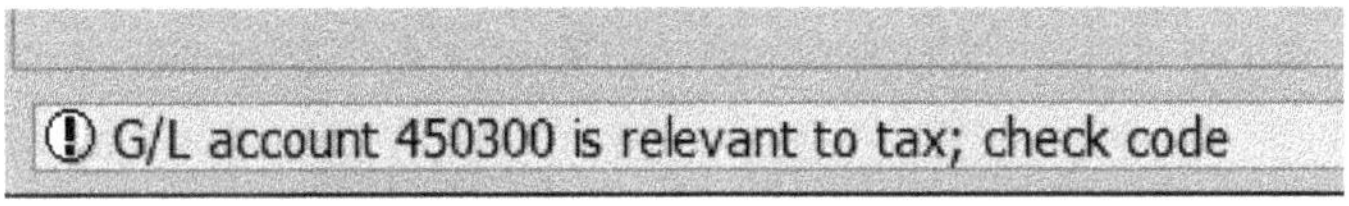

ⓘ G/L account 450300 is relevant to tax; check code

Figure 9: *Posting Customer Invoice – Posting information message*

Simulation screen tells us the customer is being debited and G/L account is being credit for the same amount:

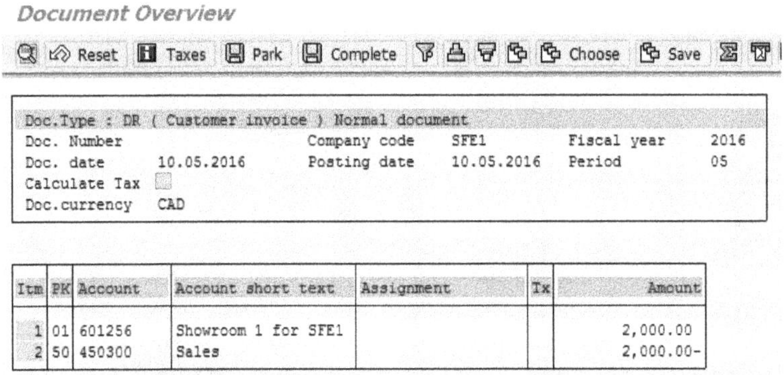

Document Overview

🔍 ✍ Reset | 🗎 Taxes | 💾 Park | 💾 Complete | ▽ 📇 🖨 📑 📑 Choose | 📑 Save | 📧 📃

```
Doc.Type : DR ( Customer invoice ) Normal document
Doc. Number                    Company code   SFE1        Fiscal year   2016
Doc. date       10.05.2016     Posting date   10.05.2016  Period        05
Calculate Tax  ☐
Doc.currency    CAD
```

Itm	PK	Account	Account short text	Assignment	Tx	Amount
1	01	601256	Showroom 1 for SFE1			2,000.00
2	50	450300	Sales			2,000.00-

Figure 10: *Posting Customer Invoice – Simulation view*

Since no errors were observed, we save this posting:

✅ Document 1800000000 was posted in company code SFE1

Figure 11: *Posting Customer Invoice – Posting message*

Note the numbering is yet another sequence. These numbers also tell us what kind of posting was made.

POSTING A VENDOR INVOICE IN FI

The process is exactly the same as posting a customer's invoice except for the G/L accounts and the debit and credit side so it is important to understand either one in depth. FB60 is used to post this entry or the path:

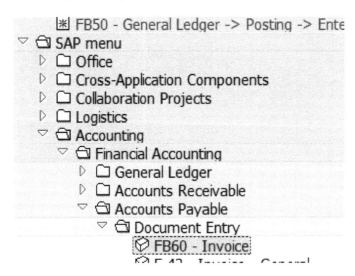

Figure 1: *Enter Vendor Invoice*

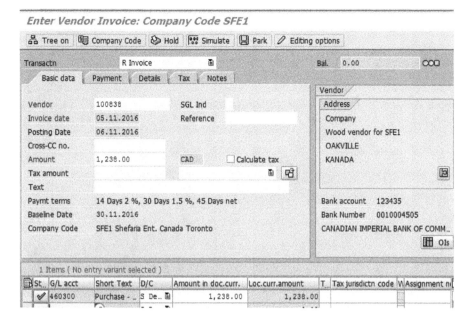

Enter Vendor Invoice: Company Code SFE1

Figure 2: *Enter Vendor Invoice*

Simulate:

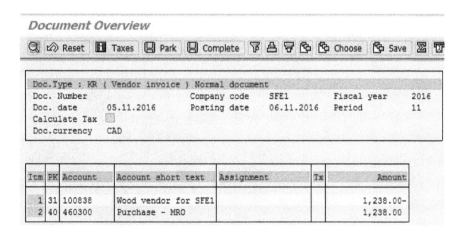

Figure 3: *Vendor Invoice – Document Overview*

Save (post) and the system gives us the document number:

Figure 4: *Vendor Invoice – Posting message*

DUPLICATE INVOICE CHECK

This functionality has been provided by SAP to ensure multiple bookings of invoices for the same purchases don't take place. To activate this, some configurations have been done already; from the vendor master data point of view, the indicator *Chk double inv.* needs to be checked (recall we did this in the vendor setup):

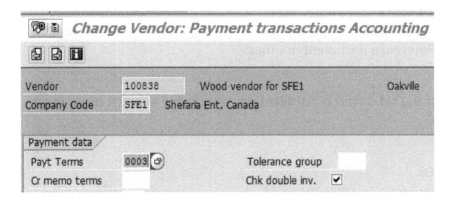

Figure 1: *Change Vendor – Payment transactions Accounting*

In the screen for posting a vendor invoice, there is a field called Reference:

Enter Vendor Invoice: Company Code SFE1

| Tree on | Company Code | Hold | Simulate | Park | Editing options |

| Transactn | R Invoice | | | Bal. | 0.00 | |

| Basic data | Payment | Details | Tax | Notes |

				Vendor
Vendor	100838	SGL Ind		Address
Invoice date	05.11.2016	Reference	109	Company
Posting Date	06.11.2016			Wood vendor for SFE1

Figure 2: *Enter Vendor Invoice – Reference field*

Though a free field that can be used for anything, most companies prefer to insert the vendor's invoice # in this field. At the time of checking for duplicates, SAP looks at the following fields for complete match in data:

CC
Vendor
Currency
Invoice Date
Reference document number

If the ref # field is not filled up, it looks for a match using these fields:

CC
Vendor
Currency
Invoice Date
Amount in document currency
i.e. it replaces the Reference Number with the amount for validation purpose.

Let us post a vendor invoice with the following data in FB60:

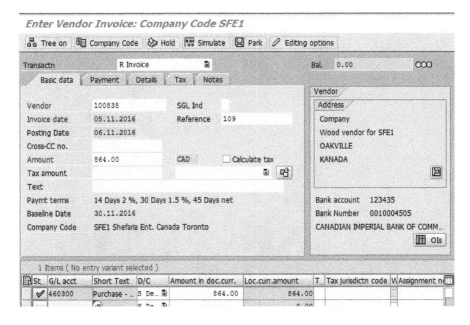

Figure 3: *Enter Vendor Invoice - Data*

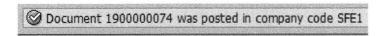

Figure 4: *Enter Vendor Invoice – Posting message*

Now if we attempt another posting with the same reference even if with a different amount we get the same message (Fig 5):

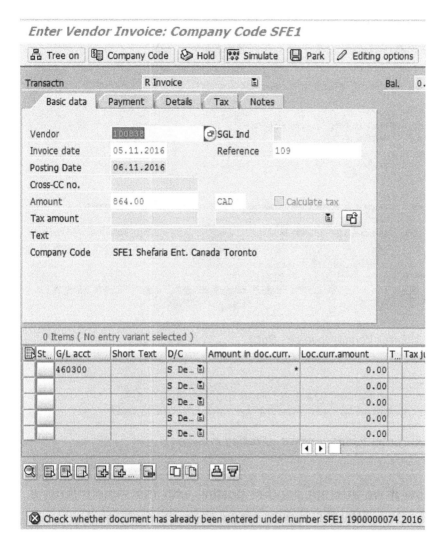

Figure 5: *Enter Vendor Invoice - Reference# error message*

We can post this 2nd invoice only if we remove the reference # from the field or change it to any other as below:

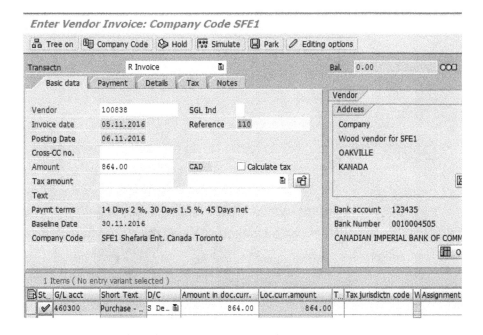

Figure 6: *Enter vendor Invoice – Reference # changed*

LOOKING UP PAYABLES & RECEIVABLES

PAYABLES. The items not yet paid are called open items or payables. These payables can be looked up using the transaction code FBL1N or follow the path:

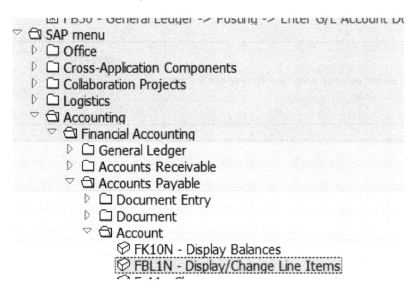

Figure 1: *Posting and Looking up Payables*

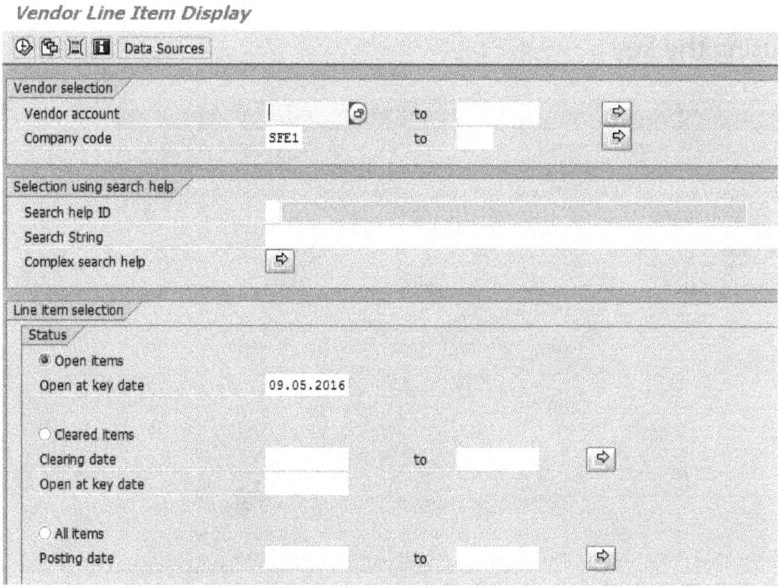

Vendor Line Item Display

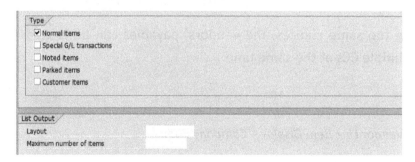

Figure 2: *Vendor Line Item Display*

Figure 3: *Vendor Line Item Display - Type*

This screen is almost identical to what you will see for receivables so let us understand the usage of most input fields here:

Vendor account: See figure 4

Figure 4: *Vendor Line Item Display – Vendor Account*

This is the actual vendor #. We can look up the payables by including or excluding a range of vendors, or individual multiple vendors using the key 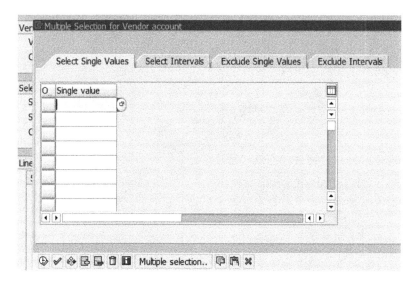 :

Figure 5: *Vendor Line Item Display – Multiple selection for Vendor account*

Using the same choices, the vendors' payables can be looked across multiple CCs at the same time:

Figure 6: *Vendor Line Item Display – Company Code*

The more data we give to restrict the inputs on this screen, the faster will be the results. For most people, when running day to day transactions, the selection key will be very useful. It further restricts the inputs to many more fields which are not available on the main screen:

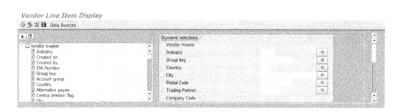

Figure 7: *Vendor Line Item Display - Selection*

Normally, one will be responsible for certain groups of vendors or certain vendors. That person can be made the accounting clerk for those vendors in the vendor's master data and when the report is run for that accounting clerk selected in the above screen, then only the A/P for those vendors that have this accounting clerk in their master data will show up in the report. This input data can be saved as a 'variant' and whenever the user wants to run this report, he/she can call for that variant. Let us consider an example:

We want to run this report for all vendors whose accounting clerk is as below:

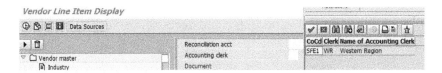

Figure 8: *Vendor Line Item Display – Accounting clerk option*

We select it and run the report:

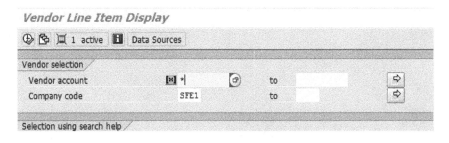

Figure 9: *Vendor Line Item Display – Vendor Account Selection*

It displays all balances payable to all vendors that have this as their accounting clerk:

	S	Document	Doc. Type	Doc. Date	Vendor	S	DD	Σ	Amount in doc. curr.	Curr.	Clrng doc.	PayT	Cu
		1900000017	KR	20.01.2016	100838				12,800.00-	CAD		0001	
		1900000019	KR	20.01.2016	100838				1,400.00-	CAD		0001	
		1900000020	KR	25.01.2016	100838				2,300.00-	CAD		0001	
		1900000021	KR	25.01.2016	100845				3,500.00-	CAD		0001	
		1900000022	KR	25.01.2016	100845				6,000.00-	CAD		0001	
		1900000023	KR	02.02.2016	100845				4,300.00-	CAD		0001	
		1900000024	KR	05.02.2016	100845				7,500.00-	CAD		0001	
		1900000025	KR	10.02.2016	100845				5,600.00-	CAD		0001	
		1900000026	KR	23.02.2016	100845				3,350.00-	CAD		0001	
		1900000027	KR	05.03.2016	100845				890.00-	CAD		0001	
		1900000029	KR	10.05.2016	100838				2,000.00-	CAD		0003	

Figure 10: *Vendor Line Item Display – Vendors Balance*

This link between the vendor and the accounting clerk is formed from the vendor master data.

TRANSFER AR BETWEEN CUSTOMERS

AR can be transferred from one customer to another. Situations like these can arise at the time of initial upload of data, re-alignment of customers, customer buyouts/takeover etc. The same can be achieved in the transaction code F-30. Choose the appropriate posting key for debiting/crediting the 2 customer numbers. Let's say the AR exists as below in Figure 1:

	S	Assignment	Document	Ty	Doc. Date	DD	E	Amount in local cur.	LCurr	Clrng doc.	Text
Customer											
Company Code SFE1											
Name											
City											
		0080015387	90036764	RV	10.09.2016			6,420.00	CAD		
			90036749	RV	23.09.2016			1.12	CAD	1400000080	
			1400000076	DZ	05.11.2016			99.00	CAD	1400000088	
			1400000077	DZ	05.11.2016			50.00	CAD	1400000089	
			90036720	RV	15.06.2016			10.50-	CAD	1400000111	
		0080015373	90036716	RV	11.06.2016			267.50	CAD	1400000111	
		0080015375	90036718	RV	11.06.2016			1,337.50	CAD	1400000111	
		0080015375	90036747	RV	19.09.2016			87.50-	CAD	1400000111	
			1400000070	DZ	05.11.2016			4.96	CAD	1400000118	
							*	8,082.33	CAD		
Account 601256								8,082.33	CAD		
			1800000034	DR	12.06.2016			80,000.00	CAD		
			1800000036	DR	13.06.2016			2,300.00	CAD	1400000116	
		0080015377	90036723	RV	18.06.2016			267.50	CAD	1400000116	
			1800000035	DR	13.06.2016			40,000.00	CAD	1400000120	
							*	122,567.50	CAD		
Account 601263								122,567.50	CAD		
							***	130,649.83	CAD		

Figure 1: *Vendor Line Item Display – Customer balance report*

If we want any AR from 601263 to 601256, debit the customer 601256 and credit the customer 601263 with this amount using the appropriate posting keys from the defined series.

In F-30:

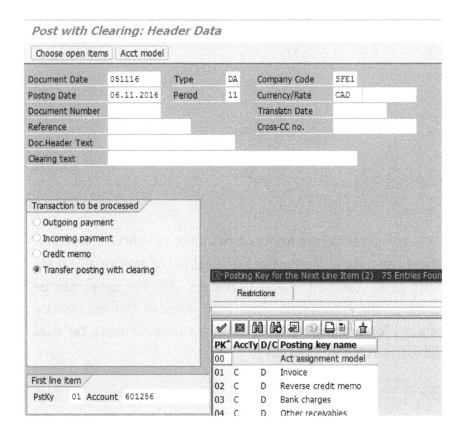

Figure 2: *Post with clearing*

On the next screen enter the offsetting data: See figure 3

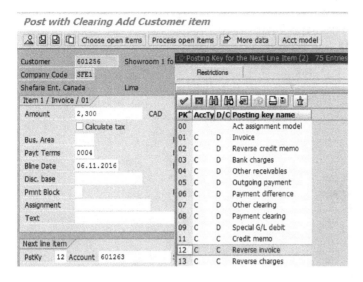

Figure 3: *Post with clearing – Posting key*

Hit Enter and on the next screen and copy the amount:

Post with Clearing Add Customer item

	🗐 🗐 🗐 🗐	Choose open items	Process open items	🖪 More data	Acct model	

Customer	601263	ALMAZ		G/L Acc	121000
Company Code	SFE1				
Shefaria Ent. Canada		TORONTO			

Item 2 / Reverse invoice / 12

Amount	*	CAD			
	☐ Calculate tax				
Bus. Area					
Payt Terms		Days/percent	/		/
Bline Date	05.11.2016	Disc. amount			
Disc. base					
Pmnt Block		Pmt Method			
Assignment					
Text					🖉 Long Texts

Next line item

PstKy	Account	SGL Ind	New co.code

Figure 4: *Post with clearing - Amount*

Simulate and/or save:

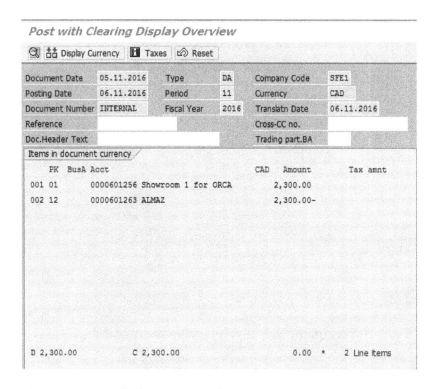

Figure 5: *Post with clearing - Simulation*

Figure 6: *Post with clearing – Posting message*

When you run FBL5N for the customers, the 2 offsetting entries will be available in the line items of the 2 customers as in figure 7:

S	Assignment	Document	Ty	Doc. Date	DD	Σ Amount in local cur.	LCurr	Clrng doc.	Text
		100000147	AB	21.09.2016		0.23-	CAD		
		1400000066	DZ	21.09.2016		2.50	CAD		
		1400000075	DZ	05.11.2016		2.02-	CAD		
	0080015387	90036764	RV	10.09.2016		6,420.00	CAD		
		90036749	RV	23.09.2016		1.12	CAD	1400000080	
		1400000076	DZ	05.11.2016		99.00	CAD	1400000088	
		1400000077	DZ	05.11.2016		50.00	CAD	1400000089	
		90036720	RV	15.06.2016		10.50-	CAD	1400000111	
	0080015373	90036716	RV	11.06.2016		267.50	CAD	1400000111	
	0080015375	90036718	RV	11.06.2016		1,337.50	CAD	1400000111	
	0080015375	90036747	RV	19.09.2016		87.50-	CAD	1400000111	
		1600000005	DA	05.11.2016		2,300.00	CAD	1400000115	
		1400000070	DZ	05.11.2016		4.96	CAD	1400000118	
					▪	10,382.33	CAD		
Account 601256					▪ ▪	**10,382.33**	**CAD**		
		1600000005	DA	05.11.2016		2,300.00-	CAD		
		1800000034	DR	12.06.2016		80,000.00	CAD		
		1800000036	DR	13.06.2016		2,300.00	CAD	1400000116	
	0080015377	90036723	RV	18.06.2016		267.50	CAD	1400000116	

Figure 7: *Post with clearing entries*

CLEARING RECEIVABLES & PARTIAL PAYMENTS

A customer invoice remains outstanding or open till it is paid or cancelled or re-adjusted in some other way. To clear a receivable we must first have an invoice. For this purpose we will use one of invoices we posted earlier.

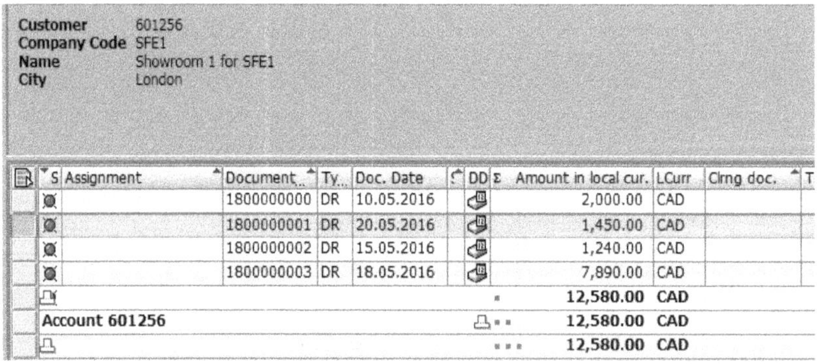

	S	Assignment	Document	Ty.	Doc. Date	DD	Σ	Amount in local cur.	LCurr	Clrng doc.	T
			1800000000	DR	10.05.2016			2,000.00	CAD		
			1800000001	DR	20.05.2016			1,450.00	CAD		
			1800000002	DR	15.05.2016			1,240.00	CAD		
			1800000003	DR	18.05.2016			7,890.00	CAD		
								12,580.00	CAD		
		Account 601256						12,580.00	CAD		
								12,580.00	CAD		

Customer 601256
Company Code SFE1
Name Showroom 1 for SFE1
City London

Figure 1: *Customer account balance*

Let's assume the customer is making only a part payment against the invoice highlighted above. F-28 is the transaction code or the path to clear open items as in figure 2:

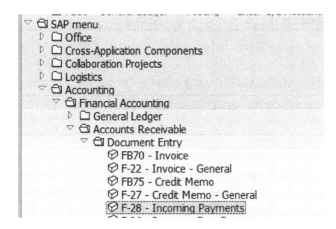

```
▽ 🗁 SAP menu
  ▷ 🗀 Office
  ▷ 🗀 Cross-Application Components
  ▷ 🗀 Collaboration Projects
  ▷ 🗀 Logistics
  ▽ 🗁 Accounting
    ▽ 🗁 Financial Accounting
      ▷ 🗀 General Ledger
      ▽ 🗁 Accounts Receivable
        ▽ 🗁 Document Entry
            ⊗ FB70 - Invoice
            ⊗ F-22 - Invoice - General
            ⊗ FB75 - Credit Memo
            ⊗ F-27 - Credit Memo - General
            ⊗ F-28 - Incoming Payments
```

Figure 2: *Post Incoming Payment*

A few fields are mandatory but one should try and fill in as much as known:

Post Incoming Payments: Header Data

Process open items				
Document Date	☑	Type	DZ	Company Code	SFE1
Posting Date	20.05.2016	Period	5	Currency/Rate	CAD
Document Number				Translatn Date	
Reference				Cross-CC no.	
Doc.Header Text				Trading part.BA	
Clearing text					

Bank data			
Account	☑	Business Area	
Amount		Amount in LC	
Bank charges		LC bank charges	
Value date		Profit Center	
Text		Assignment	

Open item selection			Additional selections	
Account			⦿ None	
Account Type	D	☐ Other accounts	○ Amount	
Special G/L ind		☑ Standard OIs	○ Document Number	
Pmnt advice no.			○ Posting Date	
☐ Distribute by age			○ Dunning Area	
☐ Automatic search			○ Others	

Figure 3: *Post Incoming Payment*

The document type DZ should be selected by default but if not, please enter DZ. The period should again be the current open posting period. It is possible your company may have a different document type in which case you will be told what to choose.

Document date is the date on which it is being entered, usually 'today'

Bank Data: Amount is the total amount on the check, Account is the Bank G/L account to which the posting will be made.

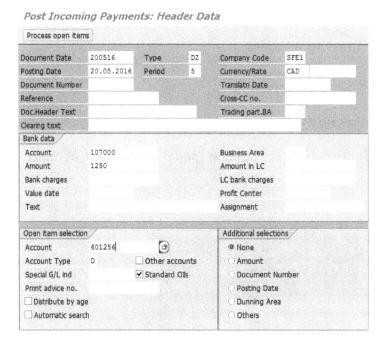

Figure 4: *Post incoming payment – Open Item Selection*

In the section Open Items selection, the Account is the customer #.

Enter data as above and click on Process open items or simply Press Enter.

The new window displays all the open items lying against that customer. These lines are the same as what we saw in the customer receivable report.

As we notice in the below print, there are cash discounts against invoices as the customer is paying on/before the date when it receives this discount for early payment. We will discuss the applicability of discounts later; here we simply adjust the amount that is being paid against the invoice. To do that we need to be able to 'isolate' the 2nd line from the rest.

First, deactivate all the line items by

(i)   selecting Select All button:

Figure 5: *Select option*

All lines will turn Blue:

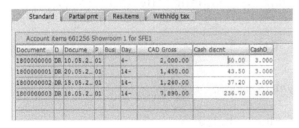

Standard		Partial pmt		Res.items		Withhldg tax		
Account items 601256 Showroom 1 for SFE1								
Document	D.	Docume	P.	Busi	Day	CAD Gross	Cash discnt	CashD
1800000000	DR	10.05.2...	01		4-	2,000.00	60.00	3.000
1800000001	DR	20.05.2...	01		14-	1,450.00	43.50	3.000
1800000002	DR	15.05.2...	01		14-	1,240.00	37.20	3.000
1800000003	DR	18.05.2...	01		14-	7,890.00	236.70	3.000

Figure 6: *Post incoming payment – Open Items*

(ii)   Next, click on Deactivate all items:

Figure 7: *Post incoming payment – Items option*

All lines will turn black:

Standard	Partial pmt	Res.items	Withhldg tax

Account items 601256 Showroom 1 for SFE1

Document	D	Docume.	P	Busi	Day	CAD Gross	Cash discnt	CashD
1800000000	DR	10.05.2..	01		4-	2,000.00	60.00	3.000
1800000001	DR	20.05.2..	01		14-	1,450.00	43.50	3.000
1800000002	DR	15.05.2..	01		14-	1,240.00	37.20	3.000
1800000003	DR	18.05.2..	01		14-	7,890.00	236.70	3.000

Figure 8: *Post incoming payment – Open items*

Position the cursor in the line to be adjusted:

Standard	Partial pmt	Res.items	Withhldg tax

Account items 601256 Showroom 1 for SFE1

Document	D	Docume..	P	Busi	Day	CAD Gross	Cash discnt	CashD..
1800000000	DR	10.05.2..	01		4-	2,000.00	60.00	3.000
1800000001	DR	20.05.2..	01		14-	1,450.00	43.50	3.000
1800000002	DR	15.05.2..	01		14-	1,240.00	37.20	3.000
1800000003	DR	18.05.2..	01		14-	7,890.00	236.70	3.000

Figure 9: *Post incoming payment – Open items*

And then activate the line item with the activate item key:

Figure 10: *Post incoming payment – Items option*

Only that line will turn blue as below.

Note: Alternatively, double clicking the actual amount also works the same way. Double clicking toggles between blue and black. It is not necessary to first make all of them inactive and then active...it merely depends on how many lines there are. E.g. if there are just 2 lines, double click on the one you want or don't want to select by toggling between Blue and Blank. As a general SAP process, Blue means active, Black means inactive. Practice this a few times to get a better understanding of it.

Since we are not allowing the cash discount on this payment, we simply clear out the amount in the cash discount column for this line as in figure 11.

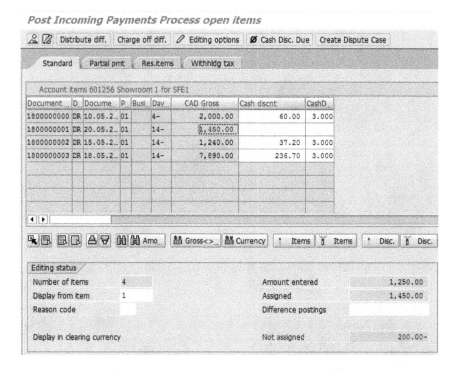

Figure 11: *Post incoming payment – Cash discount amount cleared out*

Note the difference between the invoice value and the payment as the Not Assigned amount at the bottom right. To balance it, we need to move this amount to the difference postings cell by double clicking in it:

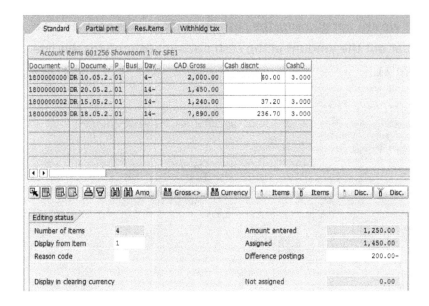

Figure 12: *Post incoming payment – Difference postings cell*

We can now either simulate this first or post directly. Simulation tells us:

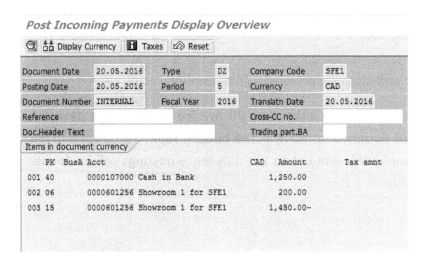

Figure 13: *Post incoming payment – Simulation*

The balance of the receivable will be automatically put back in the AR of the customer via the posting key 06 which is a unique combination of payment from a customer and a debit:

Usually, for the benefit of the auditors as well for our own memory, we put some notes. By double clicking on the line we find a spot to put this text in the notes:

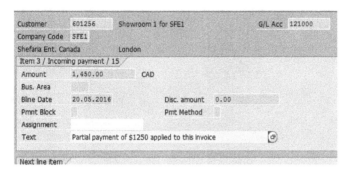

Figure 14: *Post incoming payment – Text*

If the above space is not sufficient for the notes, click on  and enter it there. Texts can be entered even after the document has been posted by going back to it in a 'change' mode. While the amounts, G/Ls etc can't be modified in an already posted document, the notes can always be altered.

Post the document and SAP gives us the posting #:

Document 1400000000 was posted in company code SFE1

Figure 15: P*ost incoming payment – Posting message*

When we look up the customers' receivables in FBL5N again, we find this invoice now has only the remaining balance:

	S	Assignment	Document	Ty	Doc. Date	DD	Σ Amount in local cur.	LCurr	Clrng doc.	Text
			1400000000	DZ	20.05.2016		200.00	CAD		
			1800000000	DR	10.05.2016		2,000.00	CAD		
			1800000002	DR	15.05.2016		1,240.00	CAD		
			1800000003	DR	18.05.2016		7,890.00	CAD		
							11,330.00	CAD		
	Account 601256						11,330.00	CAD		
							11,330.00	CAD		

Customer   601256
Company Code SFE1
Name   Showroom 1 for SFE1
City   London

Figure 16: *Customer Receivables – Remaining balance*

We can look up this document in transaction FB03:

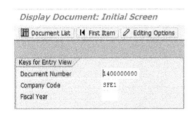

Display Document: Initial Screen

Document List | First Item | Editing Options

Keys for Entry View
Document Number   1400000000
Company Code   SFE1
Fiscal Year

Figure 17: *Display Document in FB03 view*

Display Document: Data Entry View

Display Currency   General Ledger View

Data Entry View
Document Number 1400000000   Company Code SFE1   Fiscal Year 2016
Document Date 20.05.2016   Posting Date 20.05.2016   Period 5
Reference   Cross-CC no.
Currency CAD   Texts exist   Ledger Group

Co	Itm	PK	S	Account	Description	Amount	Curr.	Tx	Cost Cent
SFE1	1	40		107000	Cash in Bank	1,250.00	CAD		
	2	06		601256	Showroom 1 for SFE1	200.00	CAD		
	3	15		601256	Showroom 1 for SFE1	1,450.00-	CAD		

Figure 18: *Display Document in FB03 view*

To see the notes, just double click the line that represents the full invoice:

Co	Itm	PK	S	Account	Description	Amount	Curr.	Tx	Cost
SFE1	1	40		107000	Cash in Bank	1,250.00	CAD		
	2	06		601256	Showroom 1 for SFE1	200.00	CAD		
	3	15		601256	Showroom 1 for SFE1	1,450.00-	CAD		

Figure 19: *Display Document in FB03 view*

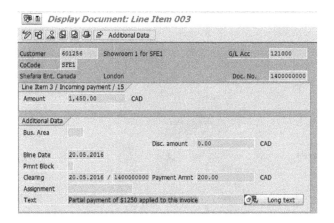

Figure 20: *Display Document - Line item*

To look up documents in FB03: If we don't know the document #, then click on Document List:

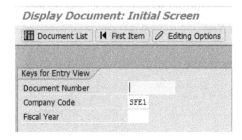

Figure 21: *Display Document – Document List*

Enter as much data as you can on the screen and click Execute:

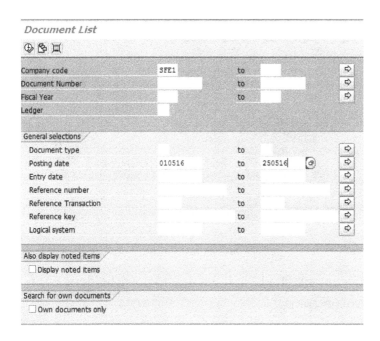

Figure 22: *Display Document – Data entries*

You can also ask it to display only those documents that you may have posted by clicking on:

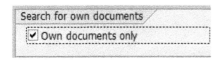

Figure 53: *FB03 view – Display own document only*

In the report that comes up, the document type DZ means a payment document:

Document List

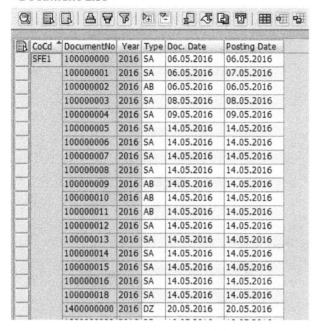

	CoCd ▲	DocumentNo	Year	Type	Doc. Date	Posting Date
	SFE1	100000000	2016	SA	06.05.2016	06.05.2016
		100000001	2016	SA	06.05.2016	07.05.2016
		100000002	2016	AB	06.05.2016	06.05.2016
		100000003	2016	SA	08.05.2016	08.05.2016
		100000004	2016	SA	09.05.2016	09.05.2016
		100000005	2016	SA	14.05.2016	14.05.2016
		100000006	2016	SA	14.05.2016	14.05.2016
		100000007	2016	SA	14.05.2016	14.05.2016
		100000008	2016	SA	14.05.2016	14.05.2016
		100000009	2016	AB	14.05.2016	14.05.2016
		100000010	2016	AB	14.05.2016	14.05.2016
		100000011	2016	AB	14.05.2016	14.05.2016
		100000012	2016	SA	14.05.2016	14.05.2016
		100000013	2016	SA	14.05.2016	14.05.2016
		100000014	2016	SA	14.05.2016	14.05.2016
		100000015	2016	SA	14.05.2016	14.05.2016
		100000016	2016	SA	14.05.2016	14.05.2016
		100000018	2016	SA	14.05.2016	14.05.2016
		1400000000	2016	DZ	20.05.2016	20.05.2016

Figure 24: *Display Document – Document type*

Double click on it to see more details as in figure 26:

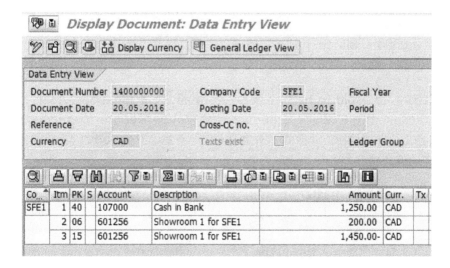

Figure 25: *Display Document – Document type details*

107

CUSTOMER MASTER - SD PERSPECTIVE

i) Customer Account groups

Customers in SAP are grouped into various grouping depending on their role vis-à-vis the vendor. A few are groups are:

a)   0001 - Sold to party – this is the highest level and the party regarded as the one with whom all the business transactions are done.

b)   0002- Ship to party – this is the customer where goods are shipped or services provided

c)   0003 - Payer – the one who will pay the invoice

d)   0004 - Bill to party – the one who will get the invoice (address)

In SAP, the sold to party can perform all the 4 functions. Apart from these 4, there can be other account groups like inter-company customers, one time customers, franchisees etc. New ones can be configured under Financial accounting configurations.

The customer master in standard SAP is a composition of 3 distinct categories:

*   General Data – this is the data specific to the customer and does not change whichever sales area the customer may be having business in.

- Company code data – this data stored information on the customer's banking records, who will be responsible for collections, payment methods, based on which the AR will post

- Sales area data – the most important data for Sales & Distribution (SD), which can vary by each sales area. It contains information relating to pricing, credit, shipping etc. A sales area is a *unique* combination of a sales organization (SO - the entity responsible for selling in SAP), a distribution channel (DC - like retail, wholesale etc) and a division (DIV - like lightning, machinery, tools etc)

We already saw how to create a customer wrt accounting in FD01. Now we will create a customer centrally. We can also create it only for the sales views in VD01. VD01+FD01=XD01. Transaction XD01 or follow the path:

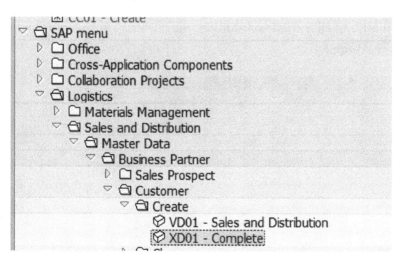

Figure 1: *Create Customer Centrally*

Enter SFE1-01-F1 in the sales area, enter the data as below and Hit Enter:

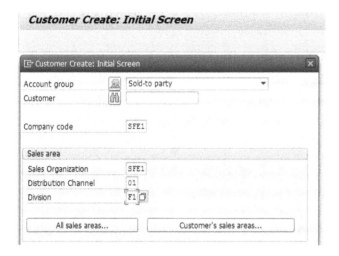

Figure 2: *Customer Create*

Alternatively, we can click on 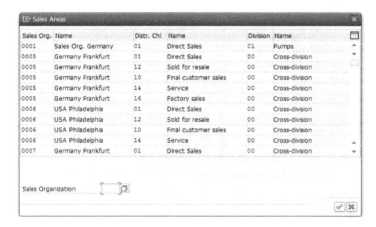 All sales areas... and select from among all the sales area that will come up in the window by double clicking on it:

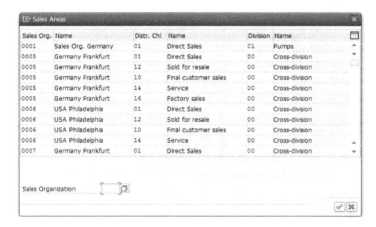

Figure 3: *Customer Create – Sales Area*

ii) General data

Give it a name and address:

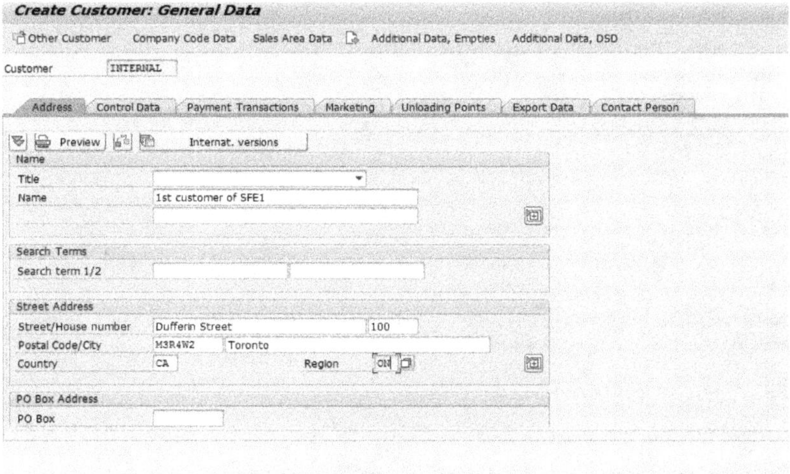

Figure 4: *Customer Create – General Data*

All the above different tabs belong to the general area data of the customer. In SAP one customer number can have only one address. For multiple customer locations we have to create multiple customers and assign them to the sold to customer number as ship to, or bill to or payer as the case may be.

iii) Sales Area Data

We can enter more data but since it is not necessary, we will proceed to the sales area data

See figure 5.

Create Customer: Sales Area Data

Other Customer General Data Company Code Data Additional Data, Empties Additional Data, DSD

Customer	INTERNAL	1st customer of SFE1	Toronto
Sales Org.	SFE1	Shefaria Sales Org	
Distr. Channel	01	Direct Sales	
Division	F1	Furniture	

Sales Shipping Billing Documents Partner Functions

Sales order

Sales district			Order probab.	100 %
Sales Office			AuthorizGroup	
Sales Group			Item proposal	
Customer group			Acct at cust.	
ABC class			UoM Group	
Currency	CAD	Canadian Dollar	Exch. Rate Type	
Switch off rounding			PP cust. proc.	
Product attributes				

Pricing/Statistics

Price group
Cust.pric.proc.
Price List
Cust.Stats.Grp

Figure 5: *Customer Create – Sales Area Data*

Note how the currency came in pre-populated. SAP could obtain it from the setup of the sales organization. Some fields here are very important for transactions to be done for the customer, notably Pricing procedure and sales office. Let us populate them with the available data by selecting using F4 or doing a drop down:

Sales Shipping Billing Documents Partner Functions

Sales order

Sales district			Order probab.	100 %
Sales Office	WEST		AuthorizGroup	
Sales Group	F01		Item proposal	
Customer group			Acct at cust.	
ABC class			UoM Group	
Currency	CAD	Canadian Dollar	Exch. Rate Type	
Switch off rounding			PP cust. proc.	
Product attributes				

Pricing/Statistics

Price group
Cust.pric.proc.
Price List
Cust.Stats.Grp

Figure 6: *Customer Create – Sales Area Data, Sales Tab*

On the Shipping tab, enter some data that will help in delivering the goods e.g. Plant and shipping conditions:

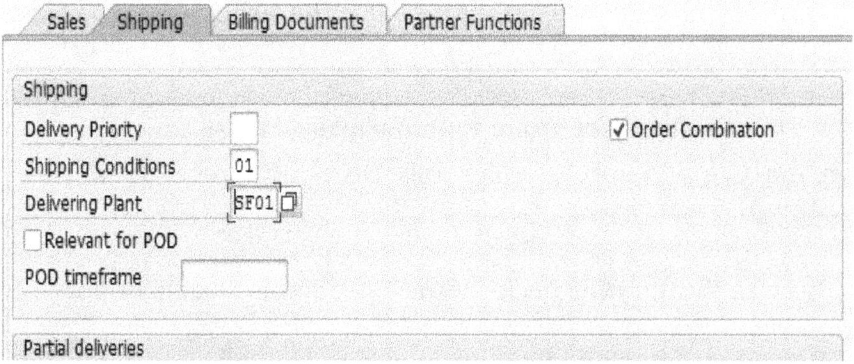

Figure 7: *Customer Create – Sales Area Data, Shipping Tab*

On the billing tab:

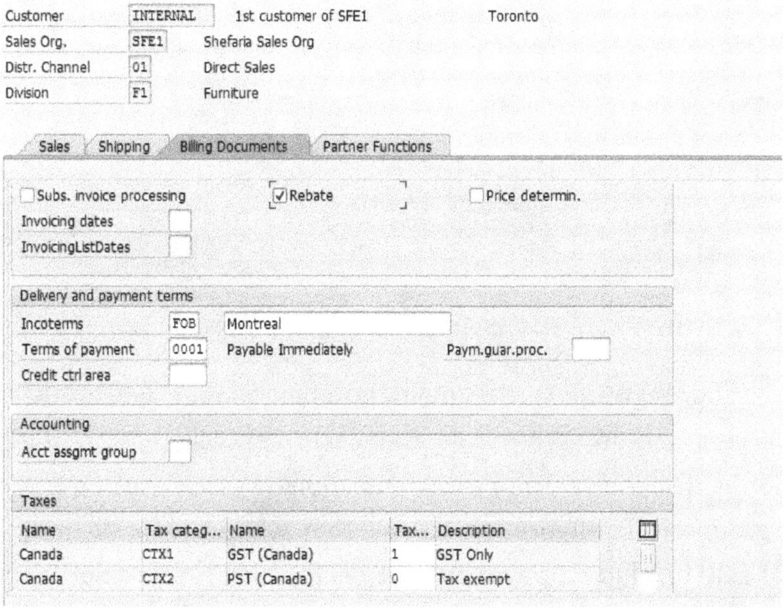

Figure 8: *Customer Create – Sales Area Data, Billing Document Tab*

The rebate button must be checked if you want to give this customer any rebates.

Incoterms are internationally acceptable terms of shipping which essentially, place the responsibility of the shipping costs like insurance, freight etc to the appropriate party

Terms of payment will determine when the customer will pay for the goods or services

Account assignment group is normally used by all companies to drive the G/L account to which this customer's revenue will be posted.

Tax classification will decide if the customer is taxable or not.

On partner function tab:

Customer	INTERNAL	1st customer of SFE1		Toronto
Sales Org.	SFE1	Shefaria Sales Org		
Distr. Channel	01	Direct Sales		
Division	F1	Furniture		

Sales   Shipping   Billing Documents   Partner Functions

Partner Functions

PF	Partner Function	Number	Name	Partner Description
SP	d-to party	INTERNAL	1st customer of SFE1	
BP	Bill-to party	INTERNAL	1st customer of SFE1	
PY	Payer	INTERNAL	1st customer of SFE1	
SH	Ship-to party	INTERNAL	1st customer of SFE1	

Figure 9: *Customer Create – Sales Area Data, Partner function Tab*

The account group is the main grouping under which the customer gets set up. What role the customer will play in the transaction is decided by the partner functions. We can set up the account groups in configuration to say that while a sold to may behave as sold to, ship to, payer and the bill to, a bill to can't behave as a ship to location. Or a ship to can't behave as a payer etc. thereby restricting their behavior in the system in terms of usage.

iv) Company Code Data

Company Code Data

Figure 10: *Customer Create – Company Code Data button*

We covered this in passing earlier under Customer Master – FI perspective. On the Account Management tab the Reconciliation account will be used to post the AR from this customer for current assets in the balance sheet: Figures 11 and 12

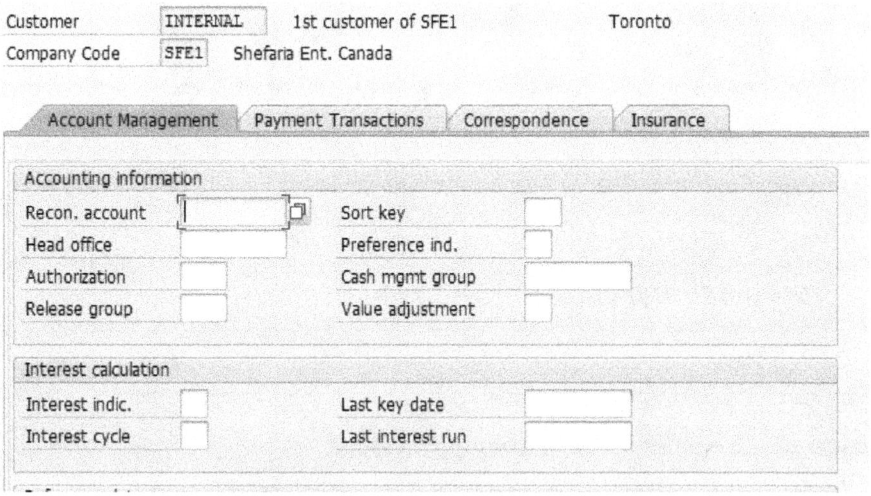

Figure 11: *Customer Create – Company Code Data,*
Account Management Tab

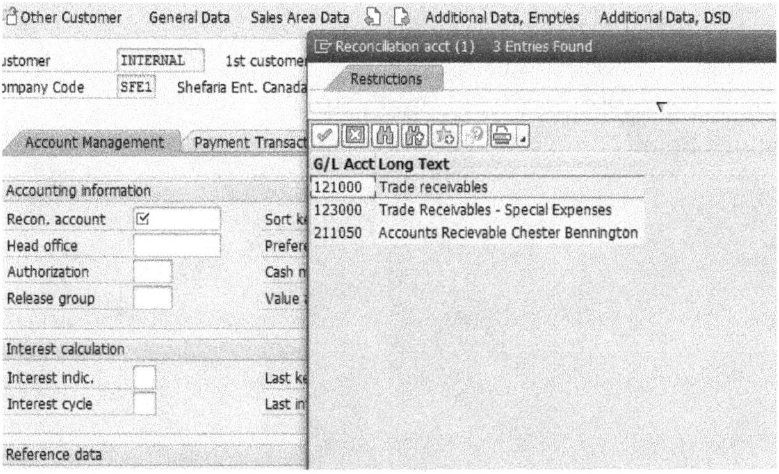

Figure 12: *Customer Create – Company Code Data,*
Reconciliation Account

The rest of the 3 tabs carry data required from the financial and accounting angle and is usually the responsibility of the FI people to maintain. We will skip entering the data in these 3 other tabs – Payment transactions, Correspondence and Insurance.

Figure 13: *Customer Create – Correspondence Tab*

Save the customer.

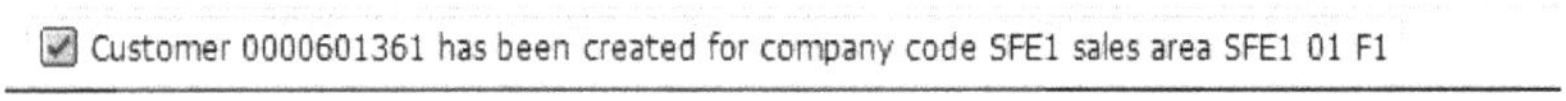

☑ Customer 0000601361 has been created for company code SFE1 sales area SFE1 01 F1

Figure 14: *Customer Create – Creating message*

We can always go back and edit the data in XD02 or view it in XD03 centrally. To change or view only the sales area data, use VD02/VD03 respectively.

We now have our customer ready to use subject to other configurations being complete.

MATERIAL MASTER

We are now ready to create our material and explore the fields and screens in the material master. The transaction to create a material is MM01 or follow the path:

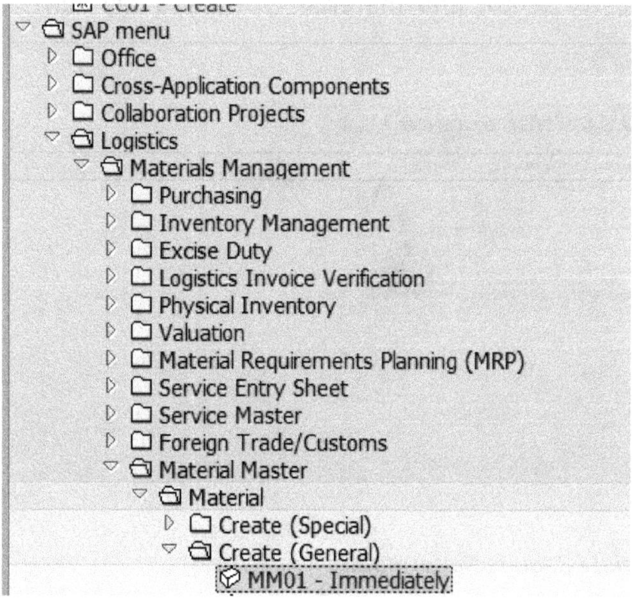

Figure 1: *Create Material*

A typical screen will look like this:

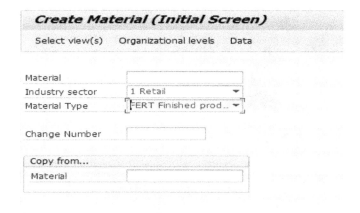

Figure 2: *Create Material*

Choose the industry sector and material type (let's say FERT, finished goods):

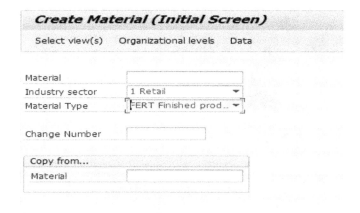

Figure 3: *Create Material - Required information*

Hit Enter:

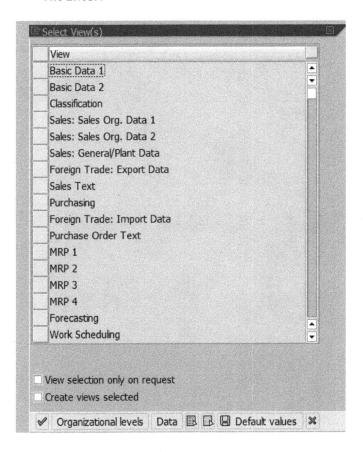

Figure 4: *Create Material - Views*

The above and more (available by scrolling down on the bar at the right) are the different screens available for different areas in a company to maintain data relevant to them.

For the moment, we will maintain only the Basic data and Sales and distribution related views leaving the rest to the other departments to fill.

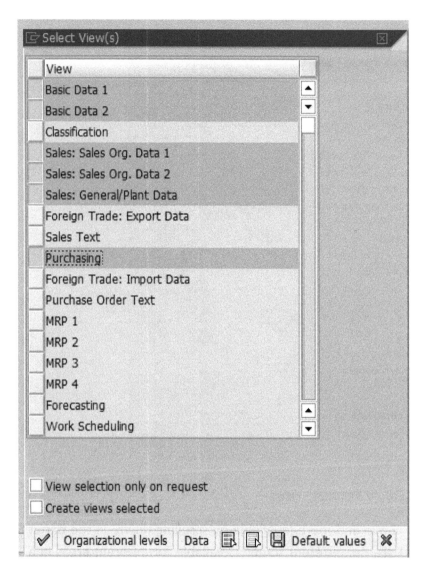

Figure 5: *Create Material – View selection*

On Clicking the green arrow, SAP will also require us to populate the plant and sales org/DC because we chose the relevant views as in Figure 5.

Figure 6: *Create Material – Organizational Levels*

Enter the data as below.

Tip: If you work in a certain sales org and DC most of the time, you can use the button ⟨Default values⟩ to store your values as default values. The, when you come to the material master next time, it will auto-populate it with your default data:

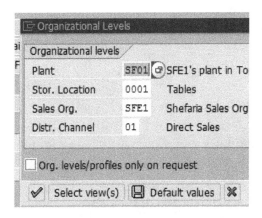

Figure 7: *Create Material – Organizational Levels information*

Click on Enter to get into the first screen:

i) Basic data 1 & 2

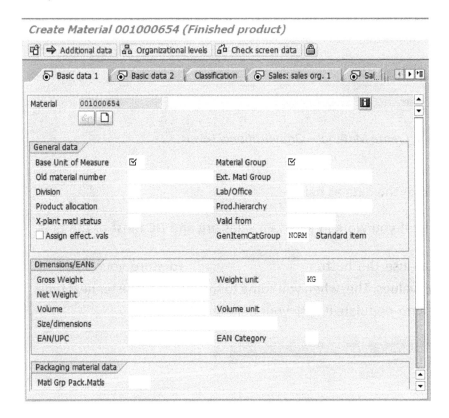

Figure 8: *Create Material – Basic data 1*

As we see, some fields are mandatory, marked with ☑ and some pre-populated which can be changed to other available values.

Basic Data 1 and Basic Data 2 are universal i.e. they always apply. We can't have the weight unit in kg for one sales org and in tons for another. We can define conversion units however and SAP will auto-convert to the appropriate unit in use.

Fill in as much data as you can:

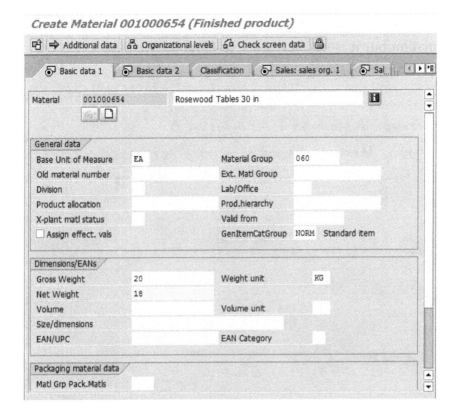

Create Material 001000654 (Finished product)

⇨ Additional data 🔠 Organizational levels 🔒 Check screen data 🔒

| Basic data 1 | Basic data 2 | Classification | Sales: sales org. 1 | Sal | ◀ ▶ |

Material   001000654   Rosewood Tables 30 in

General data

Base Unit of Measure	EA	Material Group	060
Old material number		Ext. Matl Group	
Division		Lab/Office	
Product allocation		Prod.hierarchy	
X-plant matl status		Valid from	
☐ Assign effect. vals		GenItemCatGroup	NORM Standard item

Dimensions/EANs

Gross Weight	20	Weight unit	KG
Net Weight	18		
Volume		Volume unit	
Size/dimensions			
EAN/UPC		EAN Category	

Packaging material data

Matl Grp Pack.Matls	

Figure 9: *Create Material – Basic data 1*

Filling the Division field will restrict this material to be sold only through that Division so best not to populate it.

The material master is very complex and wants a lot of information but it is not necessary to fill in all the data if it is not relevant to your business.

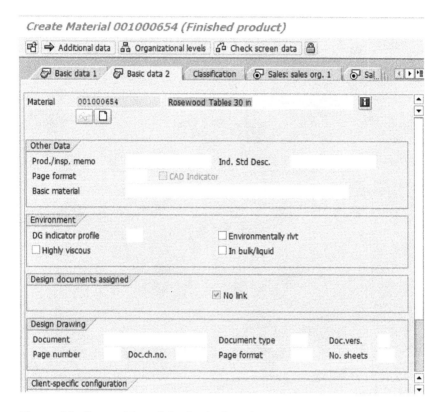

Figure 10: *Create Material – Basic data 2*

The indicator Material is configurable is an important check and used for materials that can be configured e.g. computers, cars etc.

ii) Sales Org 1

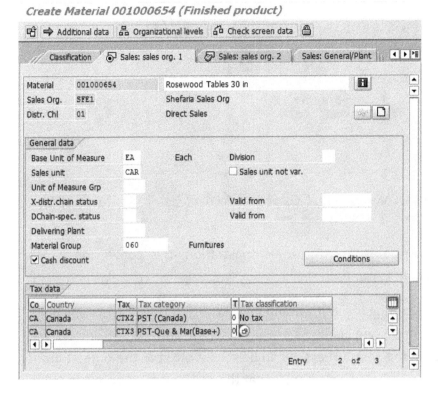

Figure 11: *Create Material – Sales Org 1*

Important fields:

Sales unit – this may differ from the base unit. e.g. a coke can may have a base unit EA, however, if it can be sold only in cartons of 12, then we would define the base unit as EA and the Sales unit as CAR. Then, in the ➡ Additional data (figure 11) we would define the conversion factor/relationship between the two:

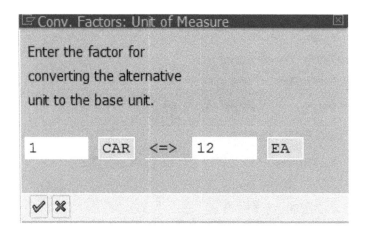

Figure 12: *Create Material -Conversion Factors*

Note: This is only for demonstration, this conversion is not applicable to our material.

Delivering Plant: If we ship this material primarily from one plant or only from one plant, we can set that here and SAP will default that value in the sales orders. It can be over written at the time of order creation. What is necessary is that the material must be *extended* to the plant it is being shipped from.

iii) Sales Org 2 data

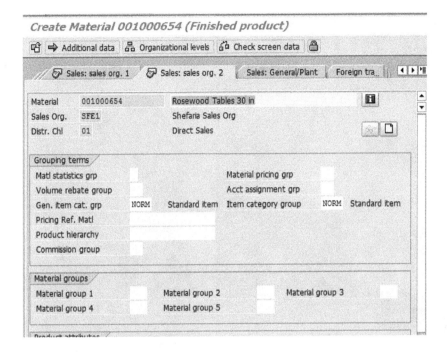

Figure 13: *Create Material – Sales org 2*

The most important field here it the Gen item category grp and Item category group, they are used to determine how the product will, among other things, be shipped, priced, copied from one SD document to another.

Acct assignment grp: Is used to post the revenues of the material/service to the appropriate G/L accounts.

The other fields are informational but can be used to make the system behave in a certain way as required.

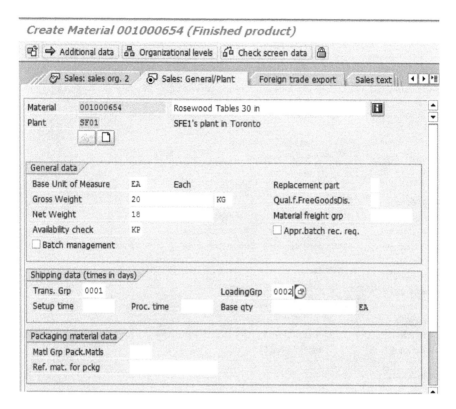

Figure 14: *Create Material – General Plant*

Availability check – with MRP (Materials resource planning) turned on, this is a key indicator to decide how procurement will take place, availability finalized and/or replenishments done. KP means no check required and we work on the premise that stocks will be available for order processing.

Transportation group – how the goods will be transported

Loading group – how they will be loaded onto the truck/ship etc. Both these groups play a pivotal role in the delivery and shipment process in our module.

Other fields as necessary. The serial number profile comes in handy for products that have serial numbering as differentiators e.g. engines, computers, machinery etc.

With the data we now need, we can save the material:

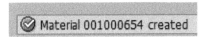

Figure 15: *Create Material message*

iv) Stock overview and posting

Now we have a customer and a finished product ready to be used together to create an order after we complete some other configurations relating to pricing and order management.

To use the material, we need to have sufficient quantity in stock. The stock of material can be checked using transaction MMBE.

In the screen on the next page, Figure 16 enter whatever parameters you need the system to check the stocks with like which plant/s, if you want to see the stock by batches and/or storage locations, special stocks (these can be e.g. consignment stocks lying at customers').

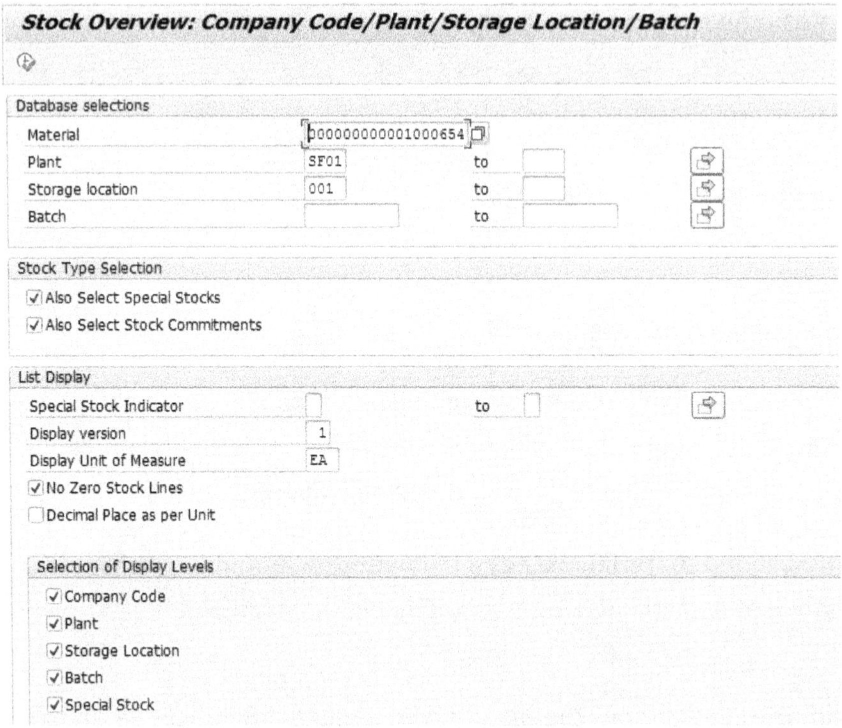

Stock Overview: Company Code/Plant/Storage Location/Batch

Database selections

Material	00000000001000654			
Plant	SF01	to		
Storage location	001	to		
Batch		to		

Stock Type Selection

☑ Also Select Special Stocks
☑ Also Select Stock Commitments

List Display

Special Stock Indicator		to	
Display version	1		
Display Unit of Measure	EA		

☑ No Zero Stock Lines
☐ Decimal Place as per Unit

Selection of Display Levels

☑ Company Code
☑ Plant
☑ Storage Location
☑ Batch
☑ Special Stock

Figure 16: *Stock Overview*

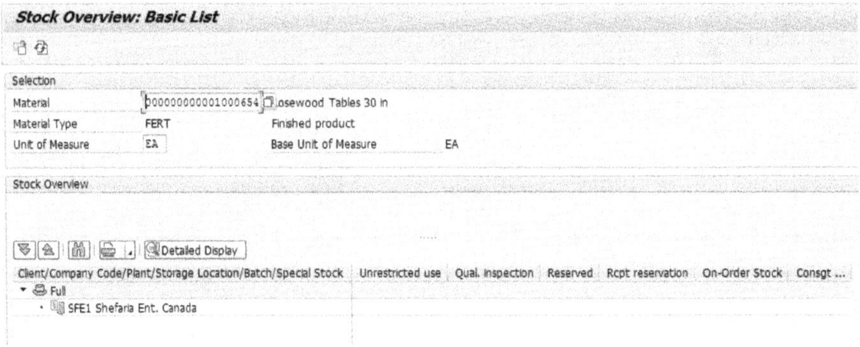

Stock Overview: Basic List

Selection

Material	00000000001000654	osewood Tables 30 in	
Material Type	FERT	Finished product	
Unit of Measure	EA	Base Unit of Measure	EA

Stock Overview

Detailed Display						
Client/Company Code/Plant/Storage Location/Batch/Special Stock	Unrestricted use	Qual. inspection	Reserved	Rcpt reservation	On-Order Stock	Consgt ...
▼ Full						
· SFE1 Shefaria Ent. Canada						

Figure 17: *Stock Overview Basic List*

Execute the input screen and since this is newly created material we do not have any stocks yet as seen above in Fig 17.

While there are many ways of entering stocks – procurement and then a Goods receipt, production and then posting as finished goods via or w/o QM or even returns into stock, we will, in SD, post stocks directly in SAP and use them for our purpose. The transaction to post stocks is MB1C:

Enter Other Goods Receipts: Initial Screen

New Item   To Reservation...   To Order...   WM Parameters...

Document Date	12.05.2017	Posting Date 12.05.2017
Material Slip		
Doc.Header Text		GR/GI Slip No.

Defaults for Document Items

Movement Type	561	Special Stock
Plant	SF01	Reason for Movement
Storage Location	0001	☐ Suggest Zero Lines

GR/GI Slip

☐ Print   ○ Individual Slip
                         ● Indiv.Slip w.Inspect.Text
                         ○ Collective Slip

Figure 18: *Enter Other Goods Receipts*

The movement type 561 is a pre-requisite for this, most other movement types will not work. This movement type is used for initial entries of stock e.g. when a company first goes live with SAP.

Hit Enter to step into the detailed screen:

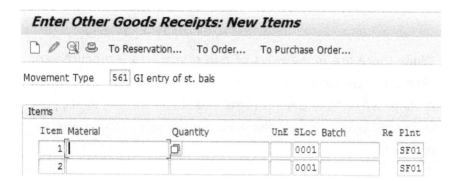

Figure 19: *Goods Receipts required information*

Enter the material and quantity you want to enter:

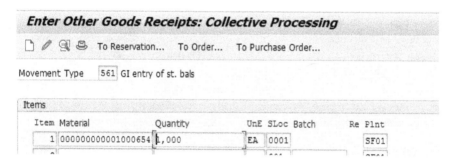

Figure 20: *Goods Receipts required information*

Hit Enter & Save:

Figure 21: *Goods Receipts posting message*

One way to confirm stocks is to look in transaction MMBE. It is very useful for sales people to verify stocks and reservations before committing: See figure 22

Stock Overview: Company Code/Plant/Storage Location/Batch

Database selections				
Material	000000000001000654			
Plant	SF01	to		
Storage location	001	to		
Batch		to		

Figure 22: *Stock Overview*

Execute:

Stock Overview: Basic List

Selection				
Material	000000000001000654 osewood Tables 30 in			
Material Type	FERT	Finished product		
Unit of Measure	EA	Base Unit of Measure	EA	

Stock Overview

Detailed Display

Client/Company Code/Plant/Storage Location/Batch/Special Stock	Unrestricted use	Qual. inspection	Reserved
▾ 🖴 Full	1,000.000		
▾ 🖳 SFE1 Shefaria Ent. Canada	1,000.000		
· 🏭 SF01 SFE1's plant in Toronto	1,000.000		

Figure 23: *Stock Overview - Basic List*

We notice our 1,000 tables stock is in unrestricted use as we entered it as a finished stock available for sale via movement 561. Depending on how it came into the stock, it could be lying in inspection for Quality, reserved for customers etc.

The same stock is also visible in the material master – we can go there in MM03 or via MMBE:

Figure 24: *Display Material view – MM03*

And then to the view:

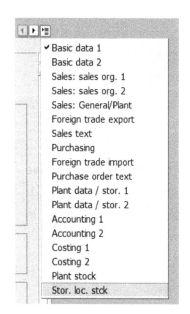

Figure 25: *Material views*

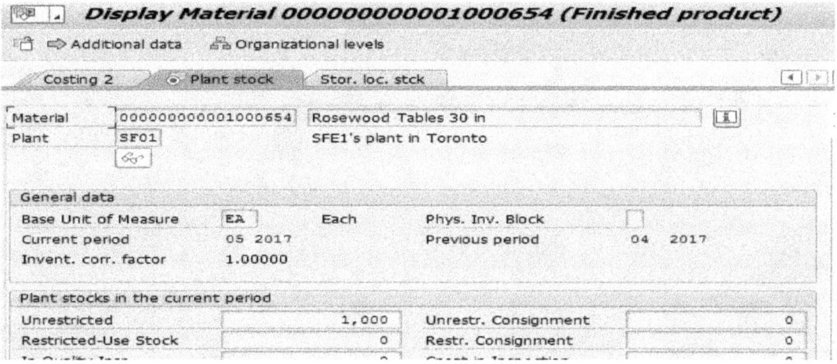

Figure 26: *Display Material – Plant stock screen*

MATERIAL DETERMINATION

On occasions, companies keep variations of essentially the same product but sold or shipped under different names, labels or even brands. SAP has provided for the concept of material determination in such instances when one material can be swapped with some other when certain conditions are met. It can also be used if some material is temporarily or permanently discontinued but there are pending orders that need to be fulfilled and another material can fulfil the required purpose. Using SAP's condition technique that can be found at many places, we define condition records i.e. records that will get fulfilled under certain 'conditions'.

The condition records for material determination are set up in VB11 or follow the path in the screen shot in Figure 1.

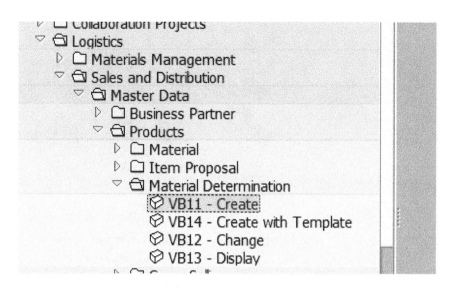

Figure 1: *Create Material Determination*

Create Material Determination: Initial Screen

Condition info. | Key combination

Material determ.type   A001   Material Entered

Key Combination

◉ SOrg/DistrCh/Material Entered
○ Material Entered

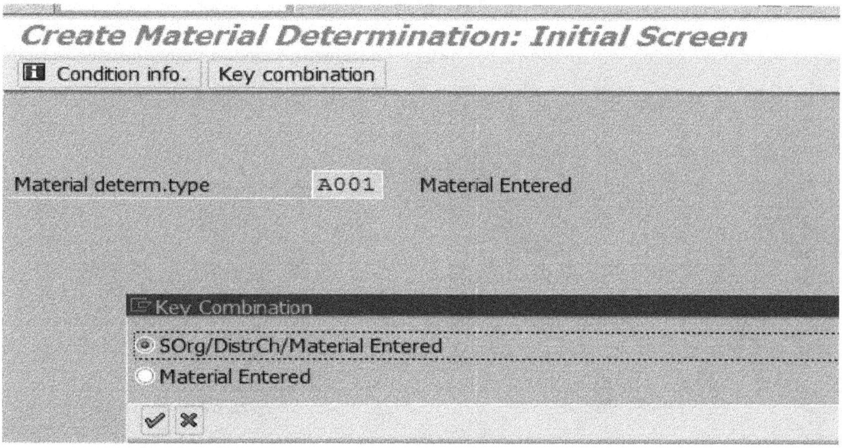

Figure 2: *Material determination type*

Let us say we have replaced material 1000654 with 1000656 as occasion requires, for the sales org SFE1 and DC 01. So, we set up the condition record as with a determination type A001 for SFE1-01 so that 1000654 can be replaced with 1000656 should an order come for 1000654 in SFE1-01 (note that we have kept the DIV out of this, which means, regardless of which DIV will sell 1000654, it will always be replaced with 1000656 if the SO and DC are SFE1-01)

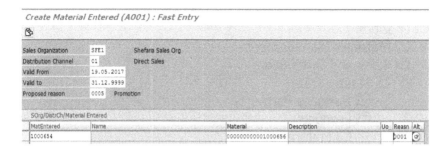

Figure 3: *Create Material Fast Entry*

Now when we try to create the order for 1000654 in transaction VA01 (it is covered in more detail later) let us see what happens:

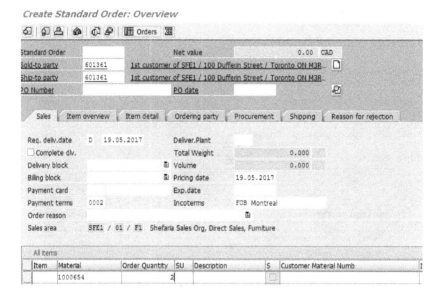

Figure 4: *Create Standard Order*

On Hitting Enter, the material 1000654 gets replaced with 1000656. See figure 5

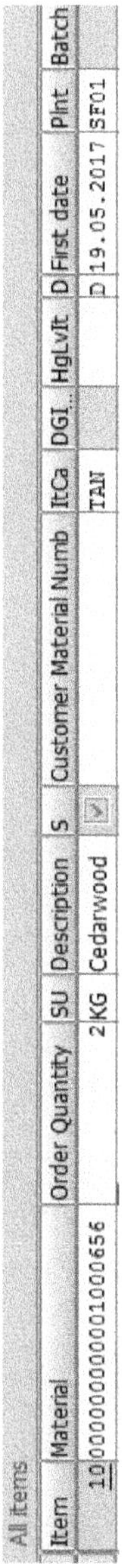

All items

Item	Material	Order Quantity	SU	Description	S	Customer Material Numb	ItCa	DGI..	HgLvIt	D	First date	Plnt	Batch
10	000000000001000656	2	KG	Cedarwood			TAN			D	19.05.2017	SF01	

Figure 5: *Effect of Material determination*

This is the effect of Material determination.

CUSTOMER MASTER INFORMATION RECORD

SAP's entire approach across data search is hierarchical from the most specific to the most generic. When looking for master data to apply in a document, it will search in the order:

1. Customer material master record (CMIR)
2. Customer master data
3. Material master data

A CMIR is a specific record of the *unique* combination of the customer *and* the material. Let us create a CMIR in transaction VD51:

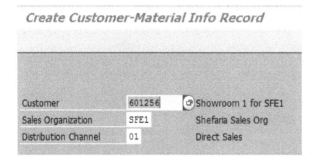

Create Customer-Material Info Record

Customer	601256	Showroom 1 for SFE1
Sales Organization	SFE1	Shefaria Sales Org
Distribution Channel	01	Direct Sales

Figure 1: *Customer information*

Hit Enter and provide the material/s for which you want to create the CMIR:

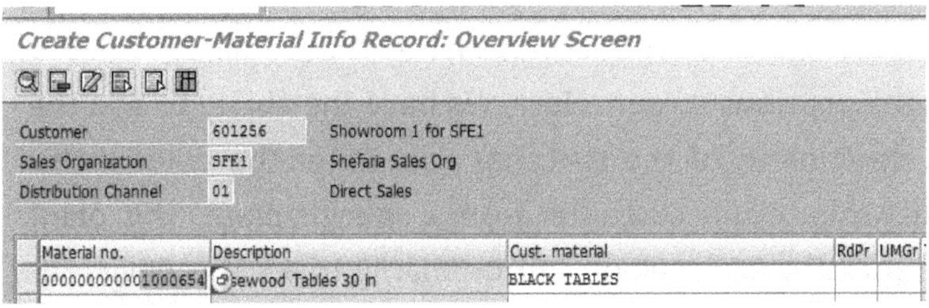

Figure 2: *Create CMIR*

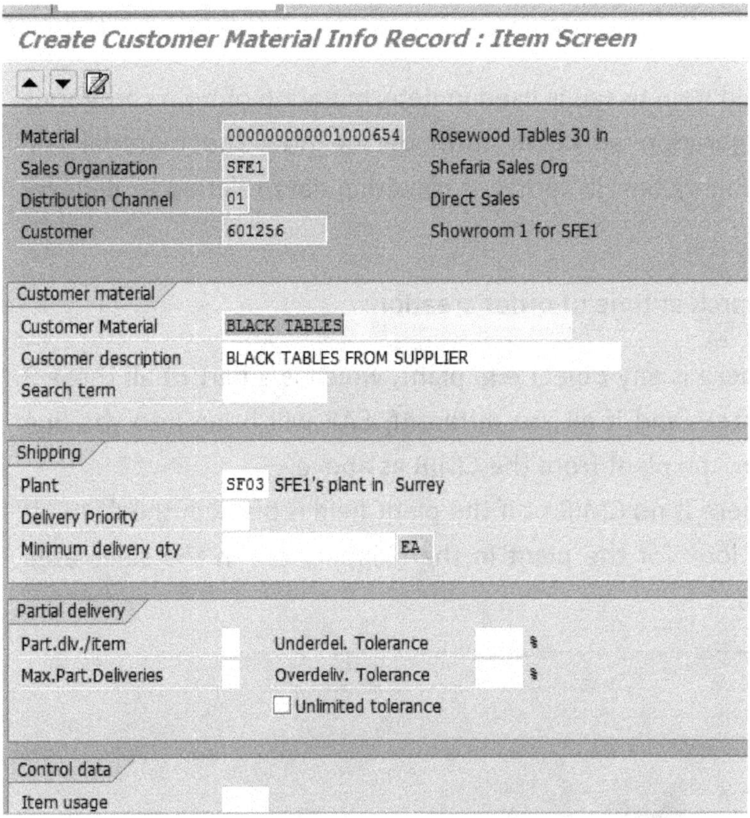

Figure 3: *CMIR – Customer material and description*

Here, you also have the ability to give a Customer material number and/or description. Some customers may want you to print *their* number or code on the delivery and invoice documents also which is where this functionality plays a role.

Double click on the line or select and Click on : See figure 3.

We entered the customer's material # (Black Tables) for our product on the previous screen. Here, we have the ability to add the customer's description of the material also. Enter the plant if this product must ship to this customer from a specific plant. This plant can be different from the plant you ordinarily make the deliveries from to this customer. The rest of the data under delivery will override the proposal from the customer master if it is different specifically for this material.

The field Item usage is used in determination of item categories from configuration which in turn, decide how the material will behave in the system in terms of requiring data relating to delivery and pricing.

Data search at time of order creation:

1. If there is any object e.g. plant, which is a part of all these 3 masters and if all are different, SAP will bring into the line item, the plant from the CMIR as above.
2. If there is no CMIR or if the plant field is blank in the CMIR, it will look for the plant in the shipping tab in the sales area data:

Figure 4: *Display customer – Sales Area Data, Shipping tab*

3. If that is blank too, it will obtain it from the material master:

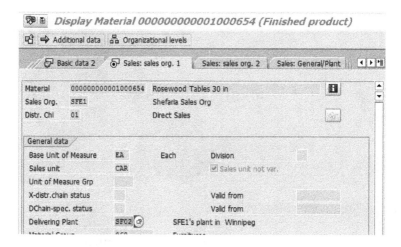

Figure 5: *Display Material*

Thus, in the above scenario, when the sales order for this customer-material combination is created, the plant to be shipped from will be SF03 (from its CMIR).

Saving the CMIR gives a message:

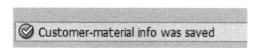

Figure 6: *CMIR creation message*

When we create the sales order, we notice the plant is indeed SF03 from the CMIR (even though the CMR has SF01 and the MMR has SF02):

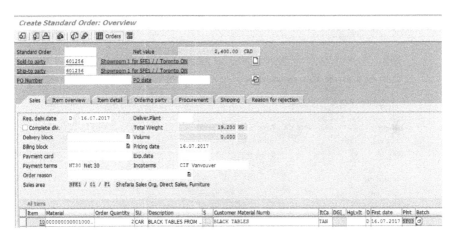

Figure 7: *Create Standard Order*

The only pre-requisite is that the material must exist (extended in) plant SF03 also.

As we also notice above, in the sales order, the material and material descriptions of the customer have also been added from the CMIR.

PRICING

We now have a customer and a material. To sell it, we need pricing. Though pricing can be entered manually in a sales order, volume of transactions usually necessitates setting up of prices as master data also.

Pricing in SAP (as in many other areas also) works on Condition technique. For the moment, we will create a simple price in the system to create a sales order and see how all our data till now comes together.

The transaction code to create pricing is VK11 or follow the path as shown in Figure 1.

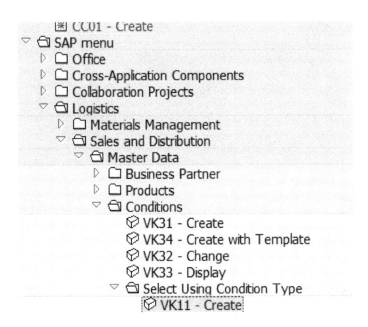

Figure 1: *Create Condition Records*

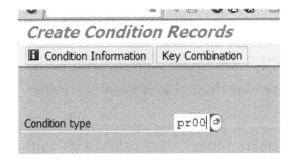

Figure 2: *Condition type*

Hit Enter and choose the 3rd radio button:

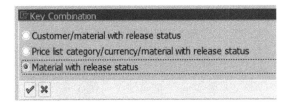

Figure 3: *Pricing – Key Combination*

Enter the data as below:

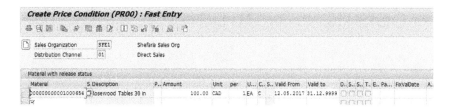

Figure 4 *Pricing Condition*

Just entering the SO, DC, material code (it is not necessary to enter the leading zeros) and the Amount is sufficient. The system determines the rest of the data.

Save this 'condition record':

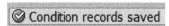

Figure 5: *Pricing condition message*

We now have a customer, material with stocks and the price we will sell at.

LOGISTICS EXECUTION PROCESS

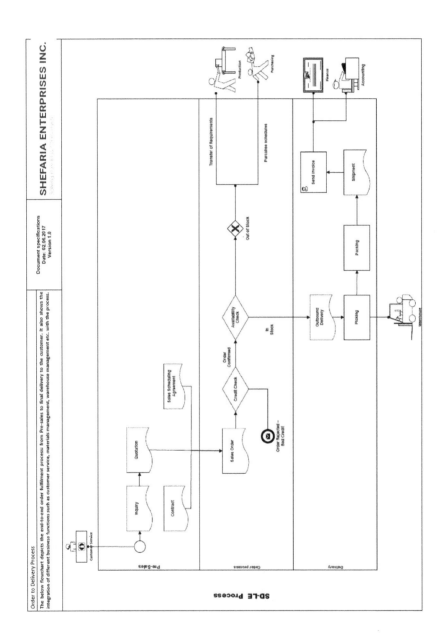

148

SALES ORDER

1. Sales Order Creation

With a customer, material and price, we are now ready to create our first sales order. To do this, use transaction code VA01 or follow the path:

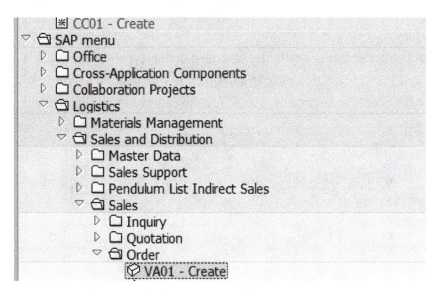

Figure 1: *Path for Create Sales Order*

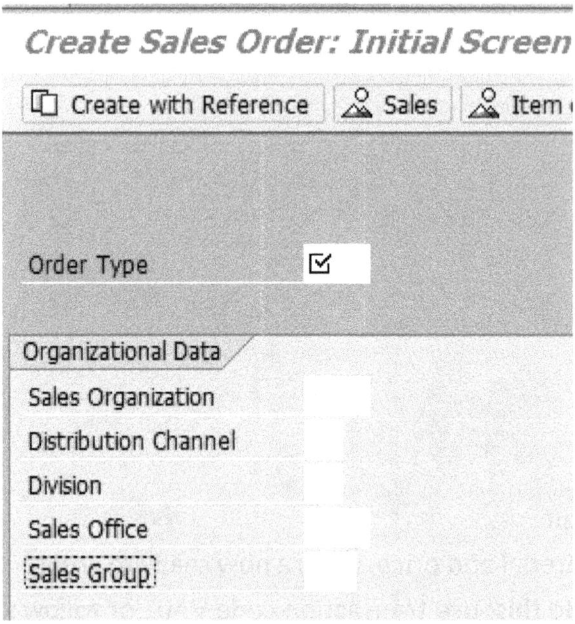

Figure 2: *Create Sales Order – Order Type*

The order type is a mandatory field as we see. Here, we will use one of the order types available, standard order, type OR to create a sales order. You can also pick and choose by pressing F4 in the field Order Type. Enter the order type and/or the sales area on this screen:

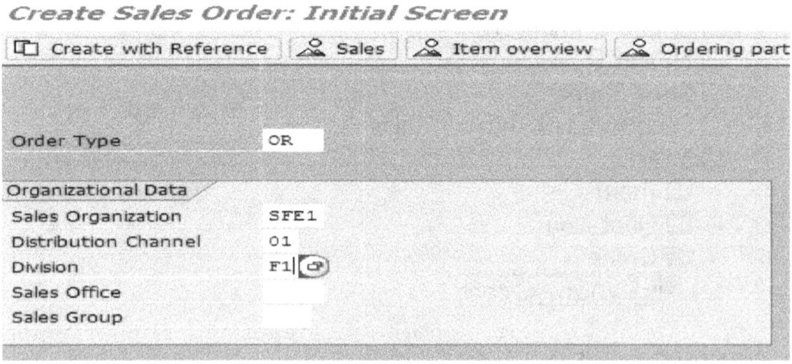

Figure 3: *Create Sales Order – Organizational Data*

Hit Enter.

A blank screen opens:

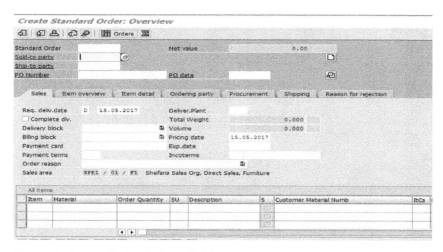

Figure 4: *Create Sales Order – Sold-to-party*

To create an order, SAP needs a lot of data, most of which will default from the customer and material masters, the rest from the configurations. At the minimum, depending on how this data is organized, SAP requires us to enter the sold to party, the material # and quantity as these are the real variables that can change from order to order. All the rest of the data is linked to the sold to and material in some way or the other. Let us then enter our sold to, material # and the order quantity in the respective fields as in Figure 5.

Figure 5: *Create Sales Order – Sales tab*

Hit Enter.

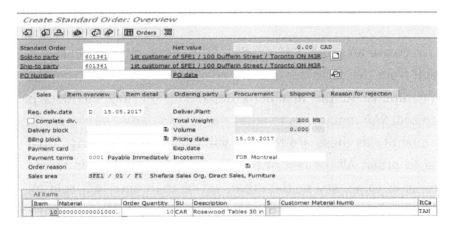

Figure 6: *Create Sales Order – Information*

Notice how SAP got the rest of the information on its own:

a) It defaulted the payment terms 0001 and the Incoterms FOB from the customer master at the header level

b) It got the plant SFE1 at the line item level from the customer master. To default a plant, SAP considers 3 data records – the CMIR, customer material info record (as we saw earlier), the customer master and finally the material master. A Plant is a necessary field to create deliveries so the order will not go beyond if it is missing. Since we have not set up the CMIR, it must have got this from the customer master as we had set it there in the shipping tab area.

c) Price – since we had set the price PR00 @ 100/EA, it also got the CAR from the material master as that is what we said is the sales unit. Using the multiplier 1 CAR (=12 EA), it made the sales order of a value of $3,600 (100*12*3 EA) based on the conversion in the material master:

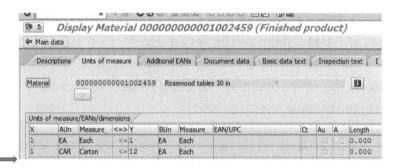

Figure 7: *Material master*

Save the order.

Figure 8: *Create Sales Order – Posting message*

2. Data in a sales document

Since SAP is such an integrated system, on the order to cash cycle, most of the data is determined at the order stage itself and flows from one document to the next. On the SD side, this could mean the sales data transfers the data into the delivery > shipment > cost document > invoice > accounting. Thus, it is imperative we understand where this data originates from and what effects it can have as we process the transaction down the line. There are 3 levels in which the data is stored in a sales order as

1. Header – most of this data originates directly or indirectly from the customer related data and will remain same for the entire document

2. Line item – most of this originates directly or indirectly relating to the material and/or in combination with the customer. It can, for the most part, be different for each line depending on the material number in that line e.g. one material may be a physical material that requires a delivery; another may be services being performed; thus, the way SAP treats them will be very different. Or one may be a free of cost, another may be priced; yet another may be subject to inventory, the other one may not be. If subject to inventory, it will also create schedule lines (see next).

3. Schedule lines – relevant only if goods are being shipped or services being performed in parts. This data is really a part of the line item but important enough to be understood and listed on its own.

Go to Display Sales Order in transaction VA03 to look at all this data in more detail.

i) Header Data

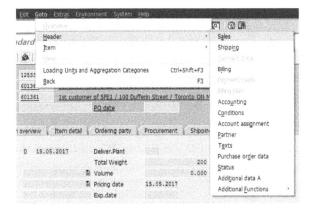

Figure 9: *Display Sales Order – Header Data*

Header data is split into many different screens as above and reached either from the above path, or by clicking on the button

 on the screen which will lead to the same header tabs:

| Sales | Shipping | Billing Document | Accounting | Conditions | Account assignment | Partners | Texts | Order Data | Status | Additional data A | Additional data B | Global Trade |

Figure 10: *Create Sales Order – Header tabs*

One should go through all these tabs individually and verify the data is what is needed. At most places, we can change it to anything else that may be available until the order is executed to the next stage e.g. delivery and/or billing. In all cases, the tabs are self-explanatory as to what kind of data they contain.

As a general rule, 90% of the data in the header of the document comes from the customer master and 90% of the line item data from the material master. The header data applies to the entire document and both data are merely proposals, except for some fundamentally important fields, most other data can be changed at the document level. E.g. even though customer credit terms may be 30 days, you can change them to 60 in one sales order and to 45 in another etc.

ii) Item Data

We can view this data by selecting the relevant line (highlighting) and Goto>Item as below:

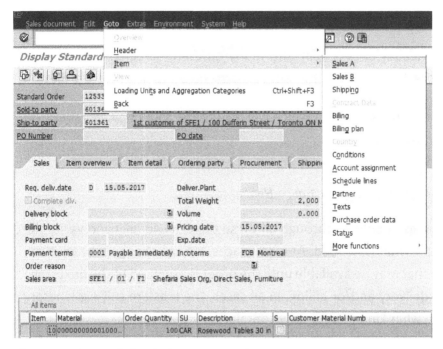

Figure 11: *Create Sales Order – Item options*

Or simply double click the line in the middle and see the same tabs:

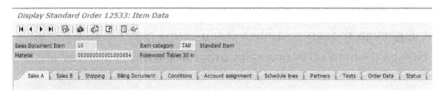

Figure 12: *Create Sales Order – Item Data*

In many cases, they seem same/like the header tabs but they are not and can have their own data different from the header data. For instance, taking the example of the credit terms again, at the header level, we may have a credit terms of 30 days but for a special item, we may decide to extend them to 60. In that case, for that line item, we can change it to 60 if the order has defaulted to 30 (which it will if the customer master has 30 in it).

iii) Schedule Line data

Display Standard Order 12533: Item Data

| Sales Document Item | 10 | Item category | TAN | Standard Item |
| Material | 000000000001000654 | Rosewood Tables 30 in |

Sales A | Sales B | Shipping | Billing Document | Conditions | Account assignment | Schedule lines | Partners | Texts | Order Data | Status

☐ Fixed date and qty   Order Quantity   10 CAR
Delivery time   Delivered qty   0

Quantities/Dates

P	Delivery Date	Order quantity	Rounded qty	Confirmed Qty	Sal	Delivery block	Delivered qty		Sch	Purchase R	Requ
D	15.05.2017	10	10	10	CAR				CP		0

Figure 13: *Create Sales Order – Schedule line*

A schedule line is a *unique* combination of order quantity and delivery date. It is a result of many inputs from the Material master and shipping configurations. The MRP (Materials Resource Planning) and Procurement data of the material master will determine the availability of the material, the shipping points and plants will determine the time it takes to deliver the goods to the customer. Thus, an order of quantity 3 can potentially have up to 3 schedules lines, depending on the product availability.

More individual details about each schedule line are available in the 3 tabs of Sales, Shipping and Procurement under the Schedule Lines tab at the line item level.

Figure 14: *Create Sales Order – Schedule line, individual details tabs*

Each schedule line will become a separate delivery to the customer because the delivery date is at the header level in a delivery. One delivery can't have multiple delivery dates, this, since each schedule line would have its own delivery date, the 2 can't get combined.

We will come to these different screens of a sales order again later when we see the effects of our configurations esp. of pricing, material availability and shipping. At this point, a good understanding of these fields will help so the student is encouraged to read their definitions and usage by clicking on F1 in the important fields.

BILLS OF MATERIALS

Often materials comprise of components, all of which need to be shipped though the order may be created only for the main item. The main item automatically pulls in the sub-items when entered in the sales order. The relationship between the main item and its sub-items is set up in a bill of material. The primary driver of this relationship is a field called item category which we saw in Sales Org 2 view of the material master. In standard SAP, an item category group ERLA has been provided to represent the main item if the main item is an assembly. In this case, the pricing is maintained for the assembled product and it is also the one that is delivered in whole. The sub-items do not get delivered and are not relieved from inventory.

If the material is to be non-assembly type and we need to ship, price and maintain inventory of the individual components and not the main item, then we use the item cat group LUMF instead of ERLA.

It is best understood with an example. A typical BOM could be created for any product that has sub-components e.g. a computer that would have a hard drive, a keyboard and a monitor. The computer then would have ERLA:

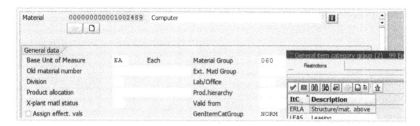

Figure 1: *General Item category group*

Its components are:

1002490 - Hard Drive
1002491 – Keyboard and
1002492 – Monitor

We need to establish a relationship between them so that SAP can understand that 1002489 comprises of 3 components – 1002490 to 1002492. We do this via a BOM – use transaction code CS01 or follow the path:

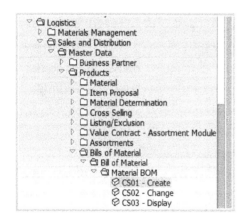

Figure 2: *Create Bills of Materials*

Create a BOM with usage 5 for the computer — Sales & Distribution:

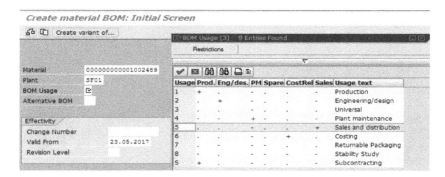

Figure 3: *Bills of Materials - Usage*

Enter how much of each component is needed per one computer:

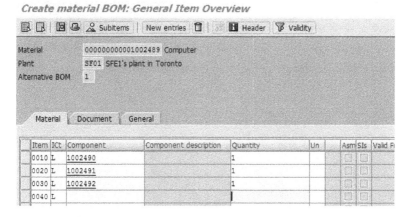

Figure 4: *Bills of Materials – General Item Overview*

Save the BOM.

Figure 5: *Bills of Materials – Create message*

Similarly, another BOM was created for the non-as non-assembled material 1002498 that has item category group LUMF. When we create the sales order, and enter the material # 1002489, the system automatically pulls in the rest. In the order below, we have 2 materials

1002489 which is an assembled computer and 1002498 which is a non-assembled one (sub-components being shipped separately). Note the difference in the pricing of the 2 groups based on different item categories of the sub-items that are determined because of ERLA and LUMF:

Create Standard Order: Overview

Standard Order		Net we	1,500.00 CAD
Sold-to party	100191	1st customer of SFC2100 Dufferin Street / Toronto ON M3R 4W2	
Ship-to party	100191	1st customer of SFC2100 Dufferin Street / Toronto ON M3R 4W2	
PO Number		PO db	

Sales | Item detail | Item overview | Ordering party | ocurement | Shipping | Reason for rejection

Req. delv.date D 14.10.2015   DelverPlant

All items

Item	Material	Order Quantity	SU	Description	S	Customer	ItCa	DGln	HgLvlt	D Frst. date	Pht	Batch	CnTy	Amount	Ccy
10	000000000010002489		1 EA	Computer			TAQ		0 D	14.10.2015	SFC2		ZPR1	850.00	CAD
20	000000000010002490		1 EA	Hard Drive			TAE		10 D	14.10.2015	SFC2		ZPR1		CAD
30	000000000010002491		1 EA	Keyboard			TAE		10 D	14.10.2015	SFC2		ZPR1		CAD
40	000000000010002492		1 EA	Monitor			TAE		10 D	14.10.2015	SFC2		ZPR1		CAD
50	000000000010002498		1 EA	Computer (Non Assembled)			TAP		0 D	14.10.2015	SFC2		ZPR1		CAD
60	000000000010002495		1 EA	Hard Drive (non assembled)			TAN		50 D	14.10.2015	SFC2		ZPR1	250.00	CAD
70	000000000010002496		1 EA	Keyboard (Non Assembled)			TAN		50 D	14.10.2015	SFC2		ZPR1	50.00	CAD
80	000000000010002497		1 EA	Monitor (Non assembled)			TAN		50 D	14.10.2015	SFC2		ZPR1	350.00	CAD

Figure 6: *Create Standard Order – Overview*

LOGISTICS EXECUTION

Logistics Execution (LE) module comprises of 2 primary sub-modules:

A) Delivery

B) Shipment

After an order is created, the first step in executing it is to create a delivery from it if it happens to be a physical product that needs to be shipped. Different order types lead to different kinds of deliveries. Deliveries are also created from Stock transport orders and Purchase orders that originate out of MM hence LE has been made a separate module on its own rather than keeping it confined to SD.

SAP has provided some standard delivery types that can be used for different transactions. The determination of a delivery type for an order or purchase order type is set up in the configuration of the order and Purchase order e.g. for the order type OR that we have been using, SAP has provided delivery type LF to use with it. However new delivery types can be and are often defined for business purposes.

For a delivery, the highest organizational unit is a shipping point.

A shipping point can be used by multiple plants and it must be assigned to at least one plant. A shipment has a physical address e.g. customer location and one of its elements being a transportation zone which will be used to determine the route that the delivery will take. One delivery can have only one shipping point from where it will originate.

A delivery document has a structure very similar to the sales documents type- the delivery document contains header and item data. A delivery document is usually created with reference to the sales document type but it is not always the case. The list of standard delivery document types are as follows:

Delivery with reference to an order - LF
Delivery without reference - LO
Returns delivery - LR
Returns delivery from a purchase order - RL
Replenishment delivery – NL

THE DELIVERY PROCESS

i) Create the sales order

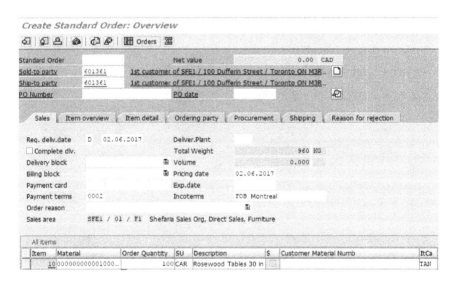

Figure 1: *Create Standard Order*

Check the shipping condition in Header- Sales data

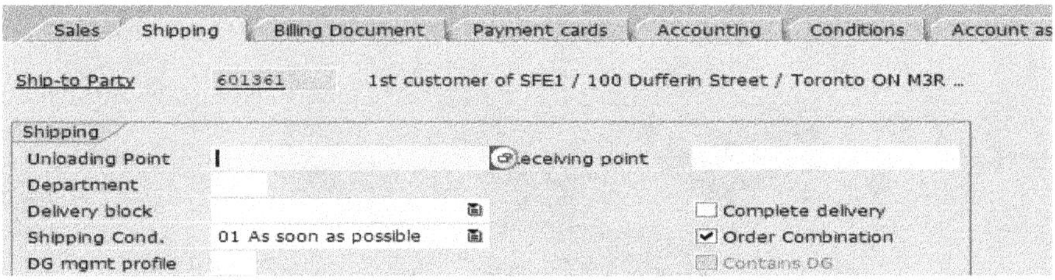

Figure 2: *Create Standard Order – Shipping tab*

In the Item - Shipping tab, the route determined can be checked.

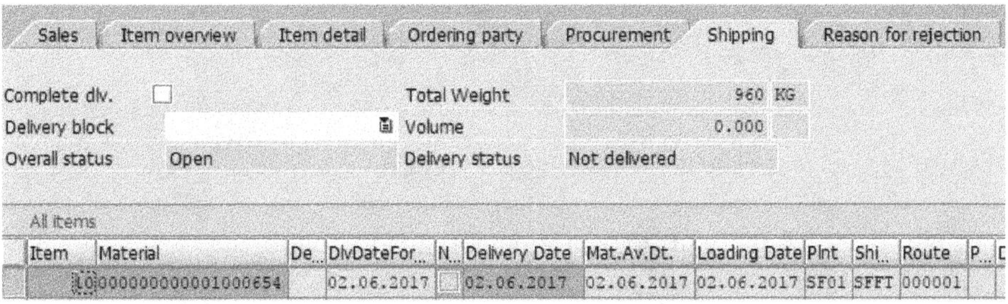

Figure 3: *Create Standard Order –Route determination*

Sales order: 12547

ii) Create delivery

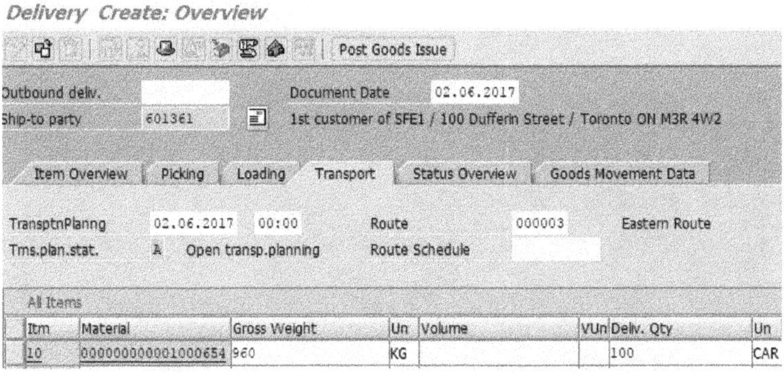

Figure 4: *Create delivery*

The route determined in the delivery is 000003 since Gross weight is above 100kg (this is set up in the configuration to determine the route based on the gross weight). Now let's change deliver quantity from 960 to 9 kg for verifying effect on route determination.

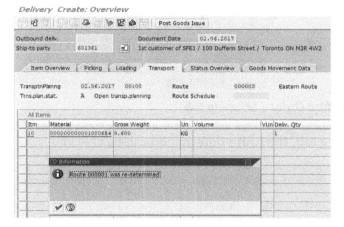

Figure 5: *Create delivery – Route determination*

Route 000001 is determined as weight less than 100 kg.

Further, changing the quantity of delivery items re-determines the weight again leading to a different route:

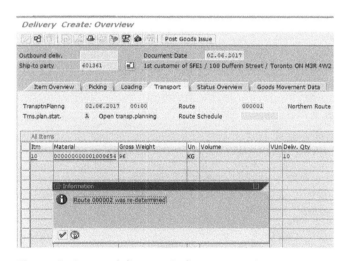

Figure 6: *Create delivery – Delivery quantity*

Change the quantity back to the original and on saving the document, we get the delivery no.: 80015464

Delivery 80015464 has been saved

Figure 7: *Create delivery – Saved message*

iii) Picking and Packing in delivery document

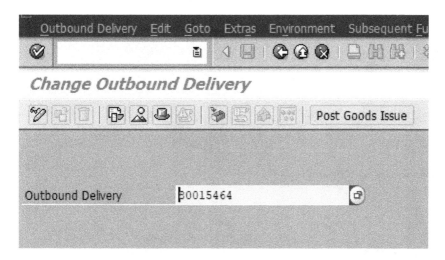

Figure 8: *Change Outbound Delivery*

We picked the entire quantity available for delivery i.e. 100 for this case.

Figure 9: *Outbound Delivery – Picked quantity*

Next, we will do the packing using the packaging material 1000702 (material type: VERP). This can be done through 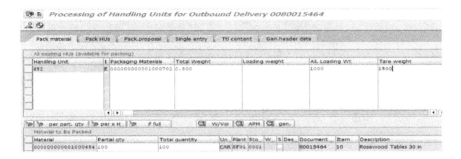 icon on the top of the overview screen.

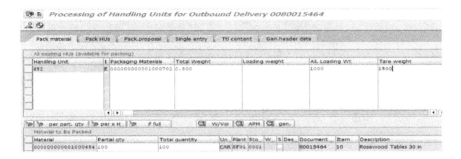

Figure 10: *Outbound Delivery - Packaging*

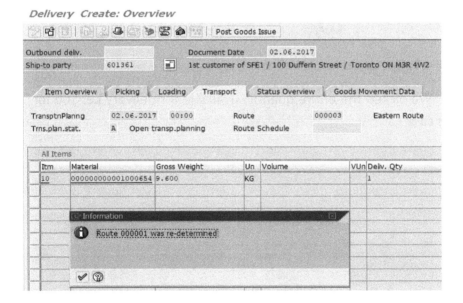

Figure 11: *Create Delivery – Route determination*

Route 000001 is again re-determined as weight less than 10 kg.

Further, changing the quantity of delivery items:

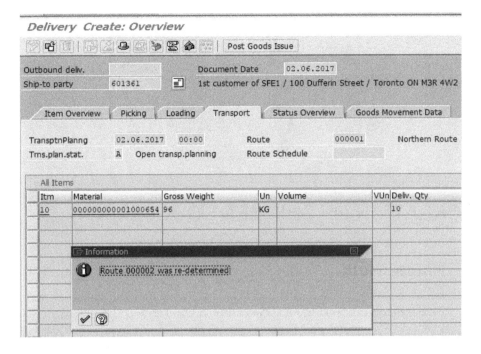

Figure 12: *Create Delivery – Delivery quantity*

Delivery no.: 80015464

⊘ Delivery 80015464 has been saved

Figure 13: *Delivery saved message*

CREATION OF SHIPMENT DOCUMENT

T-code: VT01N

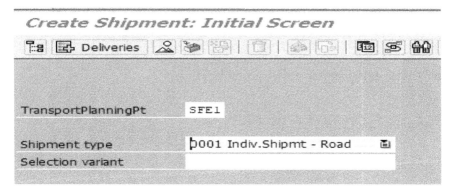

Figure 1: *Create Shipment*

Transportation Planning Point: SFE1

Shipment Type: 0001

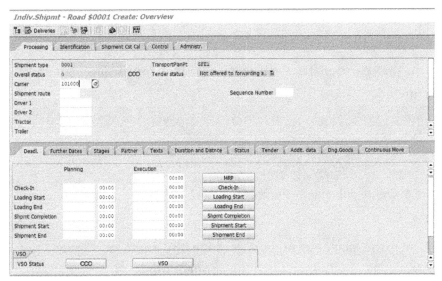

Figure 2: *Create Shipment – Processing tab*

The carrier is the forwarding agent responsible for handling of shipment. See figure 2.

The overall status is indicated by numerical value as well as traffic light code indicator as shown below:

- No traffic light: No planning activities have been performed
- Red light: Transportation planning is complete
- Yellow light: Loading at the plant has either started or is complete
- Green light: Shipment has been processed and is in route or has arrived

Next, we add delivery/deliveries to the document using ![Deliveries] button in top left corner in Fig 2 and using the selection parameters. We used shipping point (SFFT) in our case.

We can see in stages tab that no entries are present since planning activities have not begun.

Figure 3: *Create Shipment – Stages tab*

In the partner tab, we can see the forwarding agent is determined:

Deadl.	Further Dates	Stages	Partner	Texts	Duration and Distnce	Status	Tender	A

Partn.Funct.	Partner	Name	Street	Postal co..	Cty
SP Forwarding age.. 📖 101000		Pronto Logistics Servic..			

Figure 4: *Create Shipment – Partner tab*

Once the planning process is done the route and stages get automatically determined from the configurations:

Indiv.Shipmt - Road $0001 Create: Overview

Processing	Identification	Shipment Cst Cal	Control	Administr.

Shipment type	0001		TransportPlanPt	SFI
Overall status	1	⬛○○	Tender status	Nc
Carrier	101000	Toronto Logistics Services / / CA -		
Shipment route	000003	Eastern Route		
Driver 1				
Driver 2				
Tractor				
Trailer				

Figure 5: *Create Shipment – Processing tab, Carrier*

Deadl.	Further Dates	Stages	Partner	Texts	Duration and Distnce	Status	Tender	Addit. da

St..	Departure point	Destination	FwdAgent	Forw.agent	S..	Shippin..	Distance	Uo..	L	Leg indi..	In
CA/Sh Pt for ..	Terminal Isla..	101000	Toronto Logist..	01	Truck			1	Prelim..		
Terminal Isla..	Elizabeth/072..	SL2468	Rail Trans Inc.	03	Train	3,112	MI	2	Main 1..		
Elizabeth/072..	Toronto/M3R 4..	101000	Toronto Logist..	01	Truck			3	Subseq..		

Figure 6: *Create Shipment – Stages tab*

The packaging can be done through [icon] button (Fig 5) on the top of the overview screen. Note: We can also perform this packing activity in the delivery stage itself.

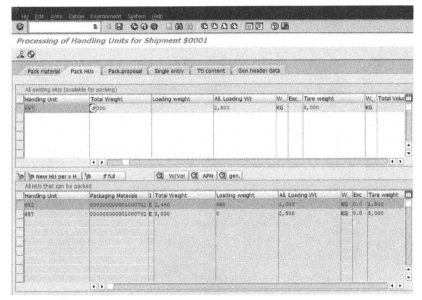

Figure 7: *Packaging – Packaging of Handling Units tab*

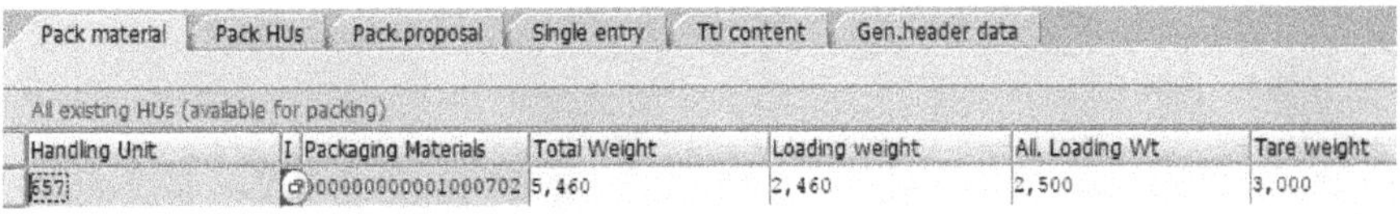

Pack material	I	Packaging Materials	Total Weight	Loading weight	All. Loading Wt	Tare weight
Handling Unit						
657		000000000001000702	5,460	2,460	2,500	3,000

Figure 8: *Packaging – Pack material tab*

You can observe the change in status as the various stages of transportation planning takes place in the processing as well as status tab. See figures 9, 10, 11.

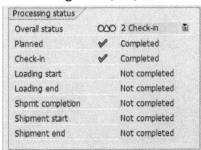

Figure 9: *Processing status - Partial*

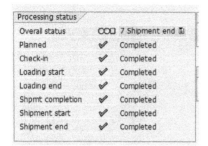

Figure 10: *Processing status - Complete*

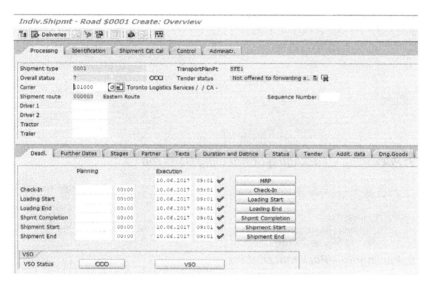

Figure 11: *Individual Shipment – Processing tab*

We can see the output generated via Goto -> Output path or via

button on the top.

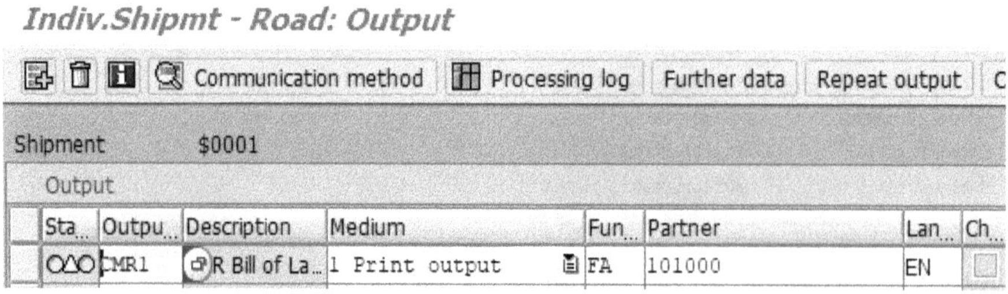

Indiv.Shipmt - Road: Output

Figure 12: *Individual Shipment – generated output*

Finally, the shipment can be saved:

Figure 13: *Shipment saved message*

The output of the shipment document (figure 15) can be viewed through Shipment -> Output path as shown below:

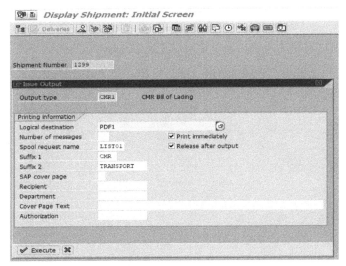

Figure 14: *Display Shipment*

Figure 15: *Shipment Document*

For the most part, a shipment creation is a non value added activity. Though, as users and configurators, you must know the process and various stages, in real life there will likely be background jobs that you should set up to do this activity for you. That will simplify daily life but occasionally, you may be called upon in urgency to create one manually so knowledge of the same is essential.

GOODS ISSUE AND ITS EFFECT ON ACCOUNTING

Goods issue, which is done when finished goods are shipped out to customers has a major effect on inventory and accounting. This effect occurs through the SD module when orders are received and processed by companies. When deliveries are made, they reduce inventory and increase the COGS (Cost of goods sold).

Let us create a sales order (of order type OR) and a delivery, pick and pack it and process it further. The delivery is goods issued in the transaction VL02N by pushing the button Post Goods Issue:

Figure 1: *Change Outbound Delivery*

A message at the bottom says

Figure 2: *Post Goods Issue saved message*

Click on the document flow button in Fig 1

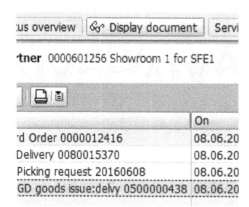

Figure 3: *Document flow – Goods issue*

Check the GD goods issue delivery line and then click on Display Document:

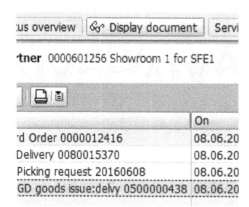

Figure 4: *Document flow – Goods issue delivery line*

Display Material Document 500000438 : Overview
Details from Item
Material
Accounting Documents...
Posting Date
08.06.2016
Mat. Slip
0080015370
Name
IDES0164
Items
Item
Quantity
EUn
Material
Plnt
SLoc
Batch
Re
MvT
S
S
BUn
Material Description
Reserv.No.
Itm
FIs
1
10
CAR
000000000001002459
SF01
0001
601
-
120
EA
Rosewood tables 30 in

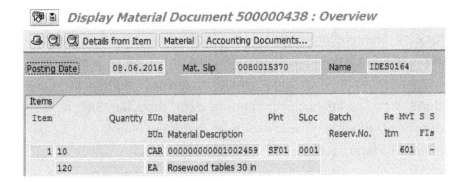

Figure 5: *Display Material Document*

Click on the Accounting Documents tab:

Display Material Document 500000438 : Overview
Details from Item
Material
Accounting Documents...

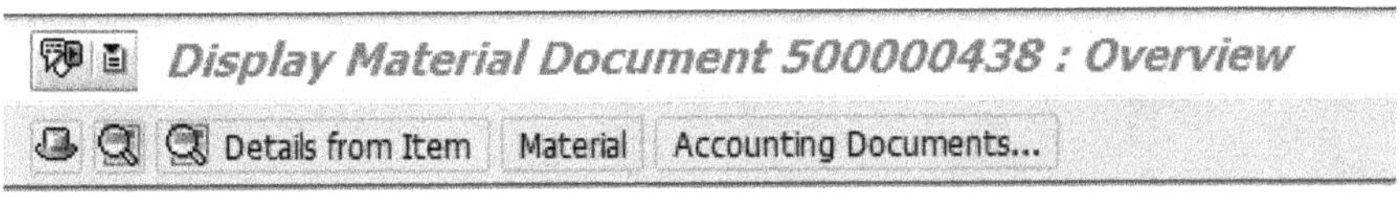

Figure 6: *Display Material Document - Menu*

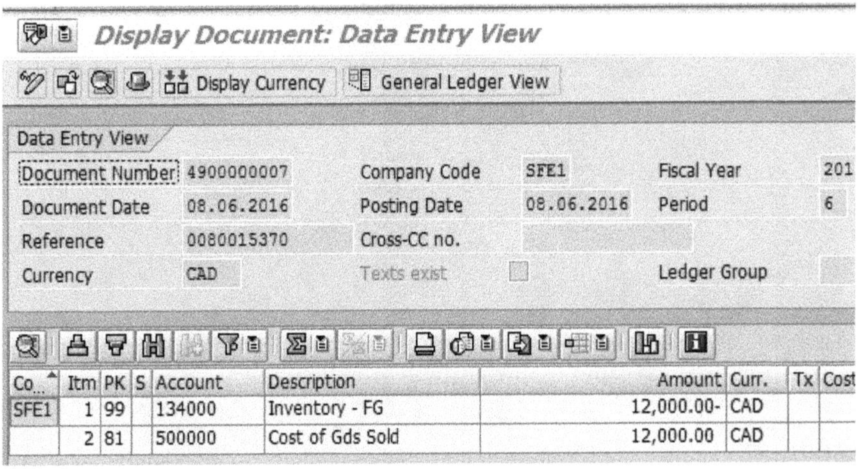

Display Document: Data Entry View
Display Currency
General Ledger View
Data Entry View
Document Number
4900000007
Company Code
SFE1
Fiscal Year
201
Document Date
08.06.2016
Posting Date
08.06.2016
Period
6
Reference
0080015370
Cross-CC no.
Currency
CAD
Texts exist
Ledger Group
Co...
Itm
PK
S
Account
Description
Amount
Curr.
Tx
Cost
SFE1
1
99
134000
Inventory - FG
12,000.00-
CAD
2
81
500000
Cost of Gds Sold
12,000.00
CAD

Figure 7: *Display Material – Accounting Documents*

We notice how SAP credited the inventory and debited the COGS as in figure 7. This COGS will form a part of our P & L statement while calculating the periodic profits.

The goods issue in SAP language means that the goods now belong to the customer under the custody of the shipper or transporter. Once the inventory is relieved, it is time to invoice the customer. Normally, invoicing is a function that has traditionally been performed by the finance or accounting dept. though in SAP, it falls under the SD module. Invoicing will be discussed in detail as a part of Billing in a later section.

REVERSAL OF GOODS ISSUE

Goods issue once done can be reversed with the transaction VL09. The reversal can take place only in the open period i.e. if a goods issue was done in January and you need to fix the document in February, the reversal can happen with a date in February only. The goods issue reversal can be performed only once the subsequent invoice, if created, has been cancelled.

In VL09, enter the delivery # - if it has an invoice subsequent to it, SAP will give a message that it could not find anything to reverse:

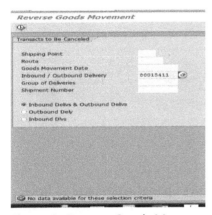

Figure 1: *Reverse Goods Movement*

As noticed below in the document flow, the invoice 90036778 exists which has not (yet) been cancelled:

Business partner 0000601308 ABCD

Document	On
▽ ☐ Standard Order 0000012491	14.0
▽ ☐ ➡ Delivery 0080015411	14.0
☐ Picking request 20170114	14.0
☐ GD goods issue:delvy 0500000003	14.0
▽ ☐ Invoice (F2) 0090036778	14.0
☐ Accounting document 0090036778	14.0
☐ Pro Forma Inv f Dlv 0090036786	14.0

Figure 2: *Document flow*

We will first have to cancel the invoice in VF11 and then reverse the goods from the delivery 80015411. More on invoicing and cancellation in a later section on Billing.

Billing Document Cancel: Billing Document Overview

Log   Split analysis

All bill.docs

Billing Type	Name	Net Value	
Invoice (F2)	ABCD	13,200.00	▲
Invoice Cancellation	ABCD	13,200.00	▼

Figure 3: *Cancel Billing Document*

The cancellation document now shows up in the document flow. See figure 4

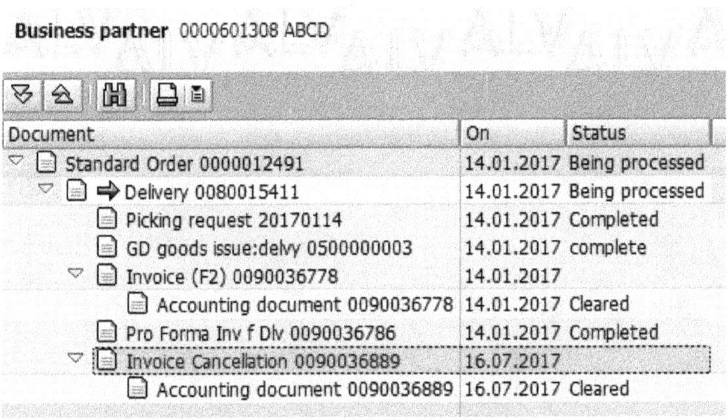

Business partner 0000601308 ABCD

Document	On	Status
▽ 🗎 Standard Order 0000012491	14.01.2017	Being processed
▽ 🗎 ⇒ Delivery 0080015411	14.01.2017	Being processed
🗎 Picking request 20170114	14.01.2017	Completed
🗎 GD goods issue:delvy 0500000003	14.01.2017	complete
▽ 🗎 Invoice (F2) 0090036778	14.01.2017	
🗎 Accounting document 0090036778	14.01.2017	Cleared
🗎 Pro Forma Inv f Dlv 0090036786	14.01.2017	Completed
▽ 🗎 Invoice Cancellation 0090036889	16.07.2017	
🗎 Accounting document 0090036889	16.07.2017	Cleared

Figure 4: *Document flow – Invoice Cancellation*

Let us try VL09 on it again:

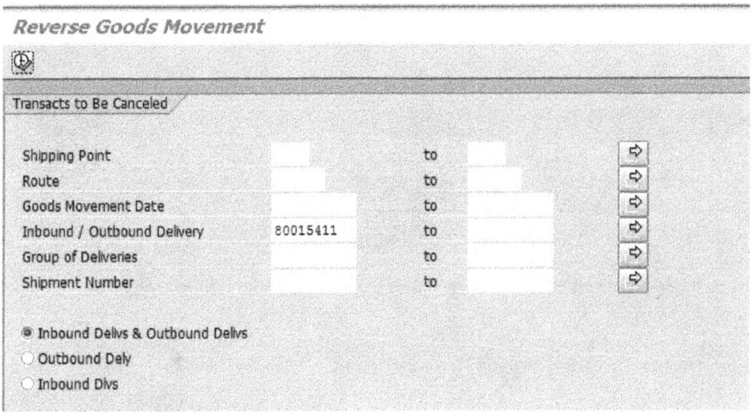

Reverse Goods Movement

Transacts to Be Canceled

Shipping Point		to	⇨
Route		to	⇨
Goods Movement Date		to	⇨
Inbound / Outbound Delivery	80015411	to	⇨
Group of Deliveries		to	⇨
Shipment Number		to	⇨

⦿ Inbound Delivs & Outbound Delivs
○ Outbound Dely
○ Inbound Divs

Figure 5: *Reverse Goods Movement*

Execute the above:

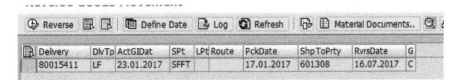

	⊕ Reverse	🗒 🗒	🖼 Define Date	🗒 Log	🔄 Refresh	🗗 🗒 Material Documents..	🔍

🗒 Delivery	DlvTp	ActGIDat	SPt	LPt	Route	PckDate	ShpToPrty	RvrsDate	G
80015411	LF	23.01.2017	SFFT			17.01.2017	601308	16.07.2017	C

Figure 6: *Reverse Goods Movement information*

Check the line and click on ⊕ Reverse in Fig 6 above.

Note that the goods issue was done on 23 January 2017 however the reversal is happening on July 16, 2017 as that is the open period now. Say Yes to the prompt:

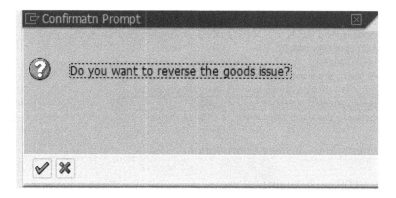

Figure 7: *Reverse Goods Movement - confirmation*

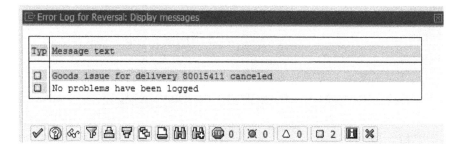

Figure 8: *Reverse Goods Movement – Reversal error message*

If we look at the document flow of the delivery now, we find the reversal line in it: See figure 9

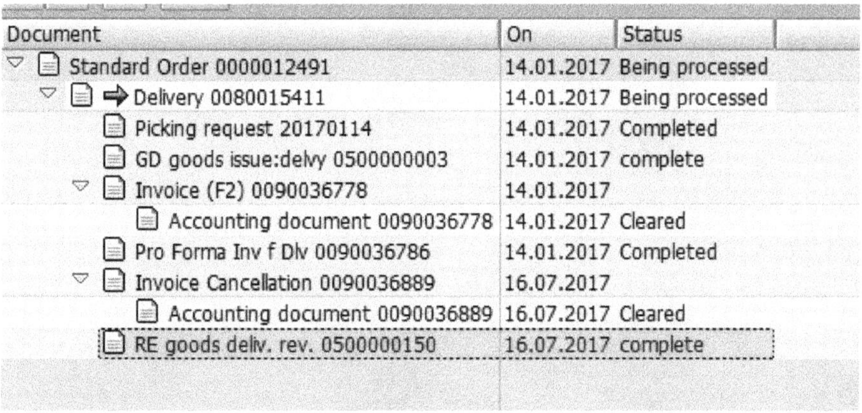

Document	On	Status
▽ 📄 Standard Order 0000012491	14.01.2017	Being processed
▽ 📄 ➡ Delivery 0080015411	14.01.2017	Being processed
📄 Picking request 20170114	14.01.2017	Completed
📄 GD goods issue:delvy 0500000003	14.01.2017	complete
▽ 📄 Invoice (F2) 0090036778	14.01.2017	
📄 Accounting document 0090036778	14.01.2017	Cleared
📄 Pro Forma Inv f Dlv 0090036786	14.01.2017	Completed
▽ 📄 Invoice Cancellation 0090036889	16.07.2017	
📄 Accounting document 0090036889	16.07.2017	Cleared
📄 RE goods deliv. rev. 0500000150	16.07.2017	complete

Figure 9: *Document flow*

Now we can perform whatever changes we need to, on the delivery.

Needless, to say, if we need to fix something in the original order, we will now have to delete the delivery! This underscores how important data, especially master data is, in the world of SAP. Though it validates data for configuration objects at every step, it can be very unforgiving if the master data or transaction data entered by the user is incorrect, inadequate or both.

TAXES IN SAP

Though taxes in SAP are a function of 3 modules - FI, SD and MM, the main structure and configurations are set up in FI and it is worthwhile to look at the user/functional aspect of this set up. The tax procedure in SAP is set up for each country; it is independent of the company code i.e. all company codes in any certain country can have only one tax procedure.

While not going into the details of the configurations as they are not company code specific, it is important to understand what these tax procedures are and how they are implemented in SAP.

Taxes in North America and Europe are calculated in different ways. We will concentrate on the Canadian taxes here which, though calculated the same way as the US ones are, are far less complex than US taxation because of 2 reasons:

1. In Canada, it is a 2-tiered structure of Federal and Provincial taxes only – closer to European where we have only one tax - VAT

2. In the US, it is 4 tiered depending on industry, though generally most will fall under 3 tiers. The 4 tiers are state, city,

county and district. Very few industries will get the district tax applied.

In the case of Europe, there is only VAT, represented by a condition called MWST in SAP. It makes it a 1 tier structure, even simpler than Canada to implement.

For this complex taxation and rates, corporations in the US also depend on external services, the 2 most popular being Vertex (more popular in North America) and Thomson Reuters (called Sabrix, traditionally stronger in Europe). Often these external systems also keep track of the taxes applied and prepare reports for audits and compliance as well as for filing with the appropriate authorities.

There are 2 primary kinds of taxes in SAP:

- Input tax, used for purchases
- Output tax, used for sales

Depending on the complexity of the company's taxation i.e. based on the customer base and product offering, it may decide to:

- Follow a simple tax procedure whereby all calculations in SAP are done in a standard fashion, not dependent on the exact location of the customer. In Canada, this would typically apply to companies which do business only in the same one province.
- May use the location of the customer if the business is done across provincially as the federal tax also will now come into play. This procedure uses Jurisdiction codes (JC) which are provided by the govt. or can be created in SAP and are based on exact locations since taxes are always applied based on the place of consumption. However, the calculation of them still, would take place within SAP.

- If the requirement is complex in terms of product and service offerings which may be subject to different rates of taxation, the company may decide to connect to an external system like Vertex or Sabrix as noted above. The taxes here too, are calculated based on the jurisdiction code however the calculation does not take place within SAP. Instead, the required data is sent out to the external system via a transmission and the taxation numbers are returned by that system and applied in SAP. This is usually real time.

Within SAP, the process is driven by tax procedures, tax codes and tax classifications. The mechanism is as follows:

<u>WHO</u>: Ship to customer in output or purchasing plant in input in SAP. Taxes are generally applied based on the place of consumption/use.

<u>IF</u>: If tax will be applied. Tax classifications are master data and the customers are given the appropriate tax class in their customer master. Alike, vendors in the vendor master. The tax classifications are usually simple – 0 means customer is non-taxable and 1 means taxable. Occasionally we may have something additional also, like partial taxation. A similar indicator exists in the material master which decides if the product or service is taxable or not. Only when both, customer and material are set as taxable, does the tax get applied.

<u>HOW</u>: The tax procedure decides this. How will the tax be applied i.e. directly intra provincial, via jurisdiction codes internally or from an external system? As we know, we can configure only one tax procedure per country so before SAP is implemented this choice is generally made though as business complexities increase through growth or acquisitions, it is easy to add and connect external systems to SAP.

<u>HOW MUCH</u>: This is decided by the tax codes or external systems. In a typical internal taxation setup, the Finance or accounting department sets up these tax codes in a transaction FTXP which replicates the tax procedure being used and sets up the correct tax rates. The same are replicated by SD for sales and MM for purchases in their respective tax pricing conditions.

1. Tax code definition

To set up taxes in a tax code. Go to transaction FTXP, in the pop up window, say CA (for Canada):

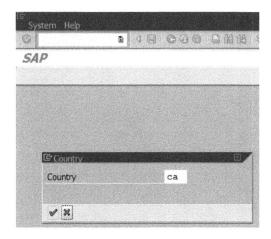

Figure 1: *Maintain Tax Code - Country*

In the window that comes up:

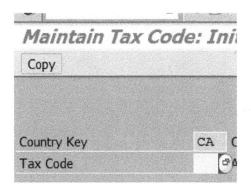

Figure 2: *Maintain Tax Code - Country*

Place the cursor in the Tax code field and hit F4 or ask for the drop down:

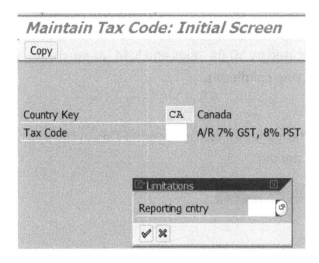

Figure 3: *Maintain Tax Code – Tax code*

Hit Enter again without entering CA and all the tax codes set up for Canada will come up:

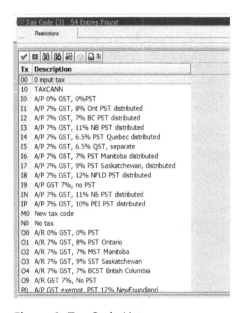

Figure 4: *Tax Code List*

Let us choose O9 as the one we will set up taxation in. Double click on it and Hit Enter:

Maintain Tax Code: Tax Rates

| Properties | Tax accounts | Deactivate line |

Country Key	CA	Canada
Tax Code	O9	A/R GST 7%, No PST
Procedure	TAXCA	
Tax type	A	Output tax

Percentage rates

Tax Type	Acct Key	Tax Percent. Rate	Level	From Lvl	Cond. Type
*			0	0	
Base Amount			100	0	BASB
***********			105	0	
A/P and MM			106	0	
Federal Taxes (US):			107	0	
*	VSC		110	100	GTI1
*	TR1		112	100	TRA1
A/P Sales Tax 1 Inv.	NVV		115	100	AP1I
*	NVV		120	100	GTI2
Subtotal			199	0	
Subtotal			200	0	
Provincial Taxes (Ca			210	0	
*	NVV		220	100	PTI1
*	VST		230	100	PTI2

Figure 5: *Maintain Tax Code*

Percentage rates

Tax Type	Acct Key	Tax Percent. Rate	Level	From Lvl	Cond. Type
*	TR2		232	100	TRA2
*			250	0	
Separate G/L posting			251	0	
*	NVV		260	199	PTI3
*	VST		270	199	PTI4
*	TR3		272	199	TRA3
Subtotal			298	0	
*			299	0	
Self assessed:			300	0	
*	VSC		310	100	GTI3
*	VST		320	100	PTI5
*	VST		330	199	PTI6
*************			399	0	
Self assess Prov.			410	0	

Figure 6: *Maintain Tax Code – Tax Rates*

193

Scroll down to next screen:

Percentage rates					
Tax Type	Acct Key	Tax Percent. Rate	Level	From Lvl	Cond. Type
*	MW1			420	100	PTU1
*	MW2		430	200	PTU2
*			498	0	
**********			499	0	
A/R and SD			600	0	
*	MWS		610	100	GTO0
*			698	0	
Subtotal			700	0	
*	MWS		710	100	GTO1
*	MW1		720	700	GTO2
Subtotal			750	0	
*	MWZ		830	100	PST1
*	MWZ		840	750	PST2

Figure 7: *Maintain Tax Code – Tax Rates*

The above is the tax procedure TAXCA being used in our system in Canada. Thus, all company codes in Canada are using this. The main columns denote:

- Tax type – input, output. Though we have called for tax code 09, the procedure is common to both, input and output.
- Account key. This key is a determining factor of how the tax values are going to post.
- Tax percent rate. This is the field you would be most concerned about. This is where the actual numbers relating to tax percentages will be entered.

Click on the tab Properties (see Fig 5)

Here we can alter/enter the description of what this tax code represents. Let's say we retain this and our customers are charged 7% GST when we sell them the products. Just having 7% in the description does not mean it will get charged. We now need to enter this 7% in the field relating to MWS as the account key.

194

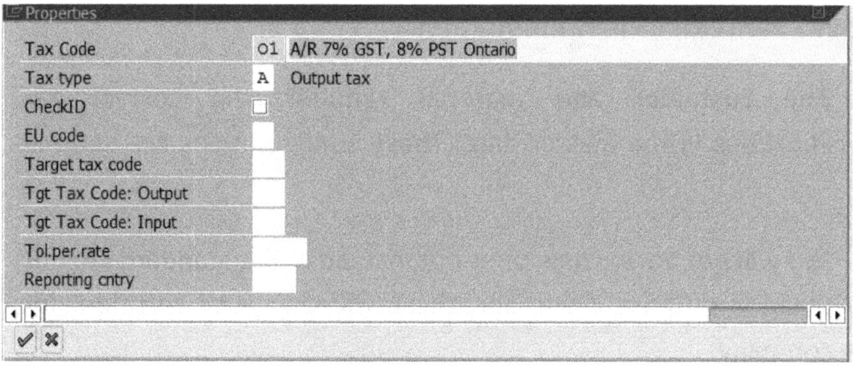
Properties
Tax Code
01 A/R 7% GST, 8% PST Ontario
Tax type
A Output tax
CheckID
EU code
Target tax code
Tgt Tax Code: Output
Tgt Tax Code: Input
Tol.per.rate
Reporting cntry

Figure 8: *Maintain Tax Code – Properties*

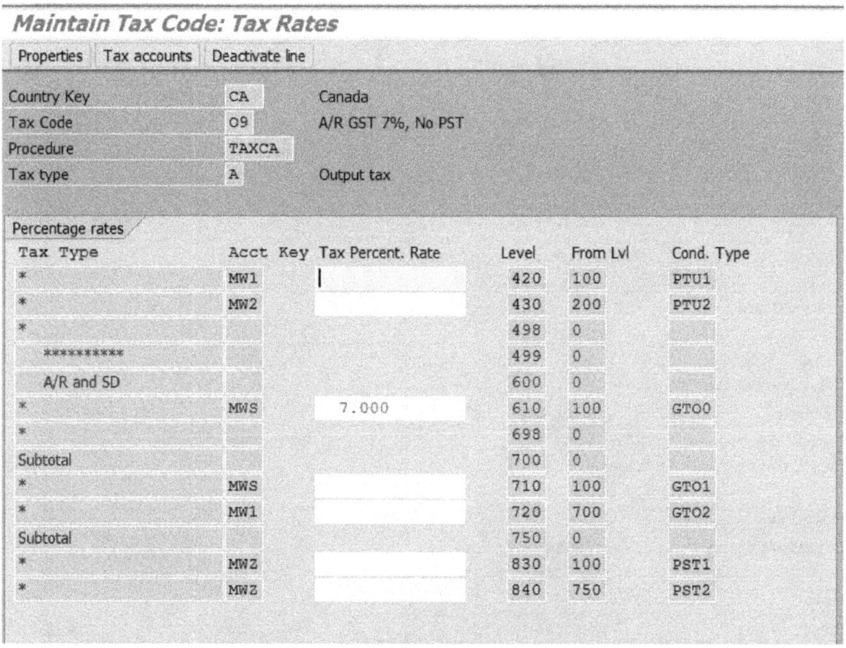
Maintain Tax Code: Tax Rates
Properties
Tax accounts
Deactivate line
Country Key
CA
Canada
Tax Code
O9
A/R GST 7%, No PST
Procedure
TAXCA
Tax type
A
Output tax
Percentage rates
Tax Type
Acct Key
Tax Percent. Rate
Level
From Lvl
Cond. Type
* MW1 420 100 PTU1
* MW2 430 200 PTU2
* 498 0
********** 499 0
A/R and SD 600 0
* MWS 7.000 610 100 GTO0
* 698 0
Subtotal 700 0
* MWS 710 100 GTO1
* MW1 720 700 GTO2
Subtotal 750 0
* MWZ 830 100 PST1
* MWZ 840 750 PST2

Figure 9: *Maintain Tax Code – Tax Rates*

In our case, we are not using the jurisdiction based tax procedure so configurations are missing and we don't want to alter that because it will affect all company codes of others also that have been created in Canada. However, the above must be maintained if we use a JC based procedure. Currently, because the tax procedure being used is not based off the JCs, it will not allow us to save.

2. Tax relevancy of master records

The customer and material requires the correct tax classifications in the master data. These configurations are done in SD.

We will not do any new ones but instead utilize standard SAP for the taxation purpose. Generally, these will always be sufficient for any company.

Our customer must be taxable for GST in the sales area which by having the value 1 in the appropriate field as below under GST:

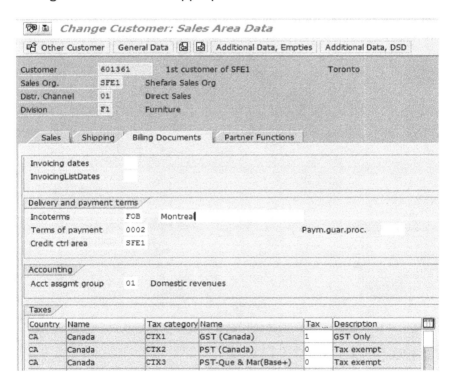

Figure 10: *Change customer – Taxes tab*

Our material must also be taxable as we know taxes get applied only when both are set to taxable on the Sales: Sales Org 1 tab as in Figure 11.

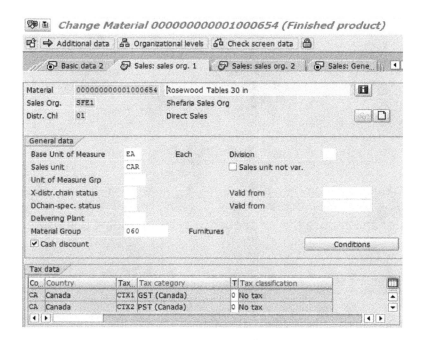

Figure 11: *Change Material – Tax Data tab*

So, we make it taxable for GST and save it:

Co	Country	Tax	Tax category	T	Tax classification
CA	Canada	CTX1	GST (Canada)	1	Full Tax

Figure 12: *Change Material – Tax Data tab*

3. Maintain tax condition record

Next, we set a tax pricing condition only on the SD side. This is done in transaction VK11:

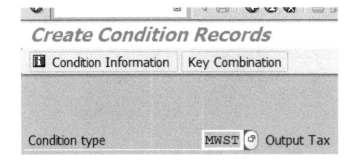

Figure 13: *Create Condition Records*

Hit Enter and choose the 2nd sequence as we are doing domestic sales here:

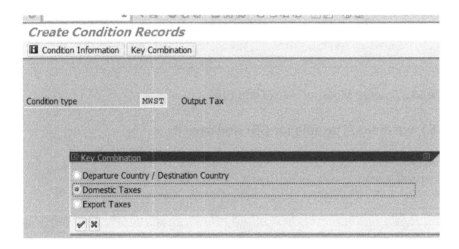

Figure 14: *Create Condition Records – Key Combination option*

Enter data as in figure 15:

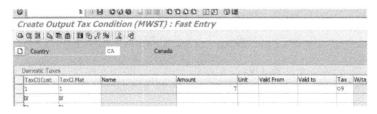

Figure 15 : *Output Tax Condition*

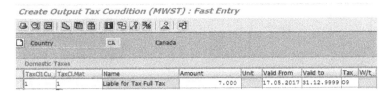

Figure 16: *Output Tax Condition - Information*

Save. We said in the above setup, that when the material and customer, both are taxable i.e. the tax class is 1 for both, then apply a domestic tax of 7% based on the tax code O9 (only GST).

Let us create a sales order and see the effect:

We see on the pricing screen in Fig 17 at the line item level of the order that the system has now applied the 7% tax we set up:

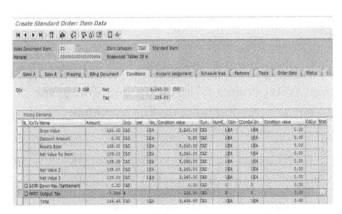

Figure 17: *Create Standard Order – Line item Conditions tab*

BILLING

Billing in SAP is performed in Sales and Distribution. However, in many companies, billing is in reality, done by the Finance or Accounting department.

In SAP, Billing is a very large sub-module and the term is used as a very generic term to encompass all invoicing, credit/debit memos, pro-forma invoices, inter-company invoicing etc. There are many kinds of billing documents that are set up in SAP to represent different requirements. Further, depending on the process, billing may be done with reference to a delivery where actual physical goods are invoiced or done directly referencing the sales order in cases of services or in debit/credit memos for price differences.

We will go through in some detail with 2 kinds of billing:

1. Invoicing wrt deliveries i.e. when tangible, physical goods are sold
2. Invoicing wrt services when services are provided

We will also see how pro-forma invoices are created and debit or credit memos processed in SAP. As also how data is passed from the SD module to the FI module once billing has taken place.

There are many transactions to do billing. Billing for a single or a few transactions can be done by VF01. Large scale billing i.e. for many customer and/or documents is done in VF04. VF06 is utilized for creating background jobs for high volume billing. Depending on needs, invoicing jobs are set up to run in the background or invoicing is done by the users themselves.

In the transaction cycle in the Sales & Distribution module, a transaction typically begins with a sales order or a credit/debit memo request. This sales order may get converted directly into an invoice if it is a services business or via a delivery into invoice if it is shipment of tangible products.

Customer Master Data wrt Billing

Let us understand the sales order and the customer master's invoicing tab under sales area data in more detail.

A customer master has the following fields under the Sales Area data which are significant in accounting.

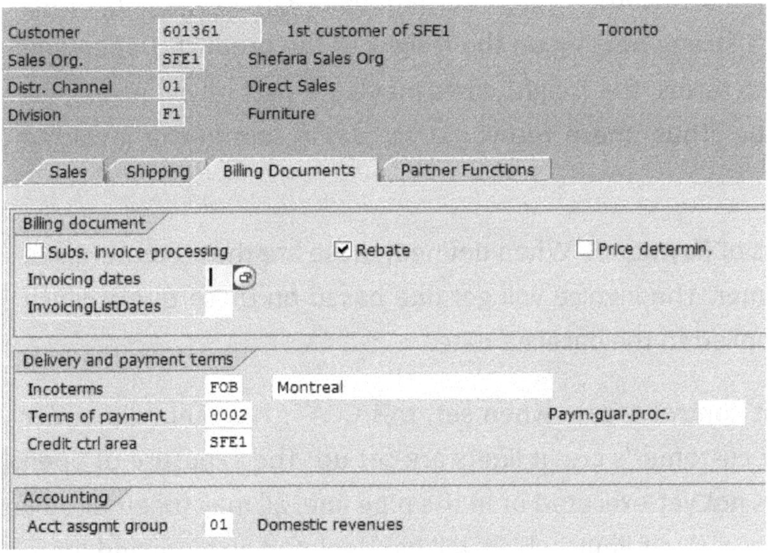

Figure 1: *Customer Master – Sales Area Data*

Invoicing dates – sometimes customers may insist on getting one invoice for the entire period if there are lots of transactions. This field can be populated with a calendar that will define the billing date of the invoices. This date will then default into every sales order and invoicing will take place with that same billing date for all the sales orders. The billing date is a precursor to the Baseline date from where the credit terms of the customer begin. Normally it is kept the same as the billing date though it can be altered. Every invoice in standard SAP leads to an accounting document which is what is reflected in a customer's AR. Usually companies prefer to keep it the same as the invoice number though it can be kept different as per need.

Invoice List Dates – invoices, when in a high number can be combined into an invoice list. An invoice list is merely a 'list' of the invoices. It is not an accounting document. While pricing can be done in an invoice list and it becomes useful in cases of rebate processing, most organizations will prefer not to do it as it is double maintenance. A calendar similar to the one described earlier is maintained in this field to combine the invoices on that date.

Incoterms - Incoterms are internationally agreed shipping terms and have a strong bearing on the freight of the product. Depending on the inco terms, the freight costs may be a part of the invoice or may not be. Thus, these terms get to play a role in the invoicing module.

Terms of Payment – When defined, these are the credit terms of the customer. The invoice will get due based on these terms which will get applied to the baseline date.

Credit control area – when set, this CCA is the umbrella under which the customer's credit limits are set up. The exposure of open AR, orders not yet executed or in the pipe line, all may together be a part of these credit limits which will get depleted as more and more invoicing takes place. Credits will, in the opposite way, release more credit limits of the customers.

Account Assignment group – is often used to define the G/L accounts to which the revenue relating to product sales, freight, surcharges/discounts etc will be directed to.

Taxes						
Country	Name	Tax category	Name	Tax ...	Description	
CA	Canada	CTX1	GST (Canada)	1	GST Only	
CA	Canada	CTX2	PST (Canada)	0	Tax exempt	
CA	Canada	CTX3	PST-Que & Mar(Base+)	0	Tax exempt	

Figure 2 : *Customer – Taxes tab*

The implication of the tax setup was already discussed in the section of Taxes.

Among the check buttons, one is very important:

Figure 3: *Rebate buttons*

If this is not checked the customer will not be entitled to rebates.

i) Different types of Billings and Billing Types

The Billing type defines the purpose and behavior of how the transaction will get billed. Standard SAP has many billing types and they can be made to follow different numbering sequences. Many companies may also prefer this numbering sequence set up by company codes only for the purpose of identification and separation. The more common billing types in SAP are:

F2   Invoice (F2)
F5   Pro Forma for Order
F8   Pro Forma wrf Dlv
G2   Credit Memo

IG   Internal Credit Memo
IV   Intercompany billing
L2   Debit Memo
LG   Credit memo list
LR   Invoice list
LRS Cancel invoice list
S1   Invoice Cancellation

We will look at F2, G2 and F5, the 3 billing types satisfying different purposes.

F2 invoice can be created from a goods issued delivery only or from a sales order only. In the former case, the Actual goods issue date in the delivery serves to become the billing date in the invoice. In the latter case, the billing date flows from the sales order itself.

ii) Billing from a delivery

We have a delivery that has been goods issued. The billing date that that the invoice of this delivery will assume is under the Goods movement tab (Act gds mvmt date as in Fig 4) in the delivery in transaction VL03N:

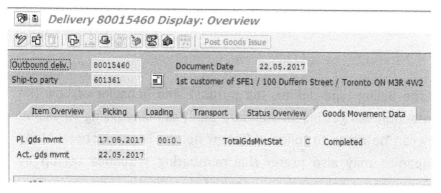

Figure 4: *Delivery Display*

Using the transaction F2 we will create the invoice from this delivery. In the VF01 screen, enter this delivery number:

Create Billing Document

		Billing due list		Billing document overview			Selection list		

Default data
Billing Type   Serv.rendered
Billing Date   Pricing date

Docs to be processed

Document	Item	SD document categ.	Processing status
80015460			

Figure 5: *Create Billing Document*

There is normally no need to enter the Billing type unless a billing type different from the system proposed one is required and in that case, certain configurations must be set up already for the billing to happen.

The open fields are the default criteria that can be changed and/or applied to all the deliveries being invoiced in this transaction.

A drop down of the Billing type will give the choices available:

See figure 6

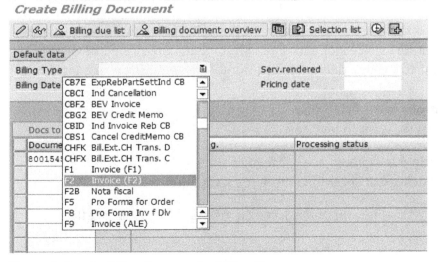

Figure 6: *Create Billing Document – Billing Type*

We can enter any dates in the other fields (SRD will decide applicable taxes on that date and Pricing date will deice the applicable price on that date) - the billing date will decide when the credit terms will begin and it must be in the open period for the document to post to accounting. However, usually there is no need to define any of this data as it comes from the sales order and/or from the delivery into this invoice.

Multiple deliveries can be entered in the screen at the same time and depending on the configuration set up, some of them may combine to create one invoice e.g. if the customers, billing dates, pricing etc are the same, they may be a case to combine on the same invoice if they are of same customer with same dates by entering them in the spaces below

Figure 7 *Create Billing Document – VF01*

If there are multiple lines on the delivery and we need to create separate invoices for each line or a combination of lines, or we simply want to invoice only a limited number now and the rest later, the

button ![Selection list] (see Fig 5) can be used to 'select' the line items we want to invoice now.

In our example, we will invoice the entire delivery of 1 line. With the delivery # entered in the screen, Hit Enter:

At the bottom of the screen a message comes up briefly:

Processing of Document 0080015460

Figure 8: *Processing Document message*

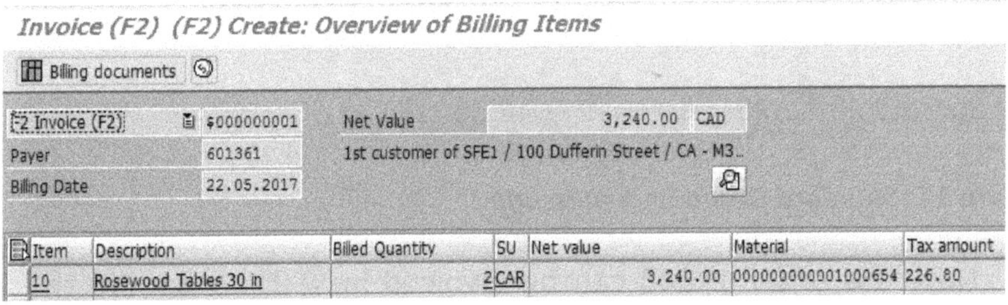

Invoice (F2) (F2) Create: Overview of Billing Items

Item	Description	Billed Quantity	SU	Net value	Material	Tax amount
10	Rosewood Tables 30 in	2	CAR	3,240.00	000000000001000654	226.80

Figure 9: *Create Invoice*

The invoice will get most of the data from the delivery and/or order and may re-determine some depending on how configurations are set up.

iii) Billing from an Order

In businesses that do not sell any tangible goods but provide services, orders are created and invoiced directly when the services are completed or based on any other billing plan/schedule. The order is created in the transaction VA01. We create a sales order for 50 hours of a service which has it's own material number:

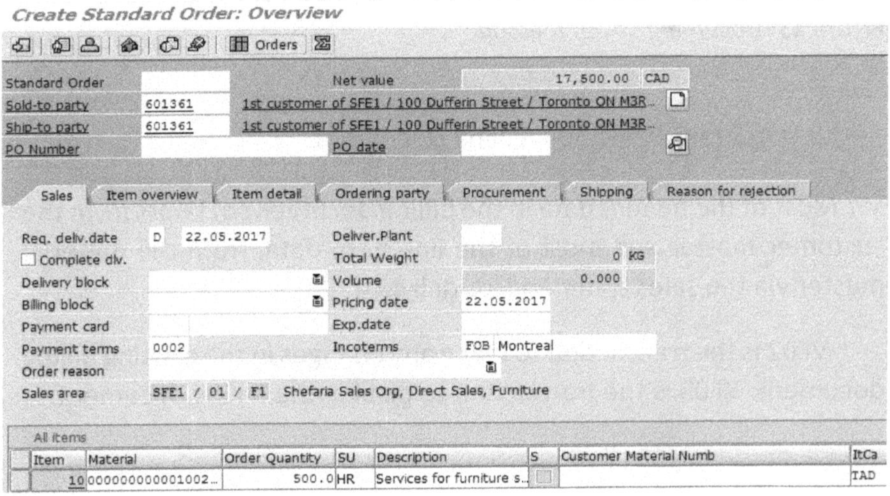

Figure 10: *Create Standard Order*

Save the order:

Figure 11: *Standard Order Save message*

Now this order 12540 can be invoiced in VF01 as we did the delivery earlier:

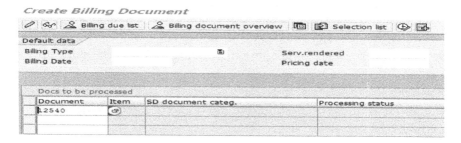

Figure 12: *Create Billing Document*

Save:

⊘ Document 90036870 has been saved

Figure 13: *Document saved message*

iv) Important fields on a Billing Document

Most of the header data in the billing document defaults from the customer master and most of the line item data, from the material master via the sales order and/or delivery.

VF02 is the transaction to make any changes in the existing billing document. VF03 is the transaction to display the billing document.

Payer:

F2 Invoice (F2)	🗎 90036870
Payer	601361

Figure 14: *Invoice and Payer information*

As far as Accounting is concerned, the Payer is the only significant customer. As we saw earlier, a customer master has 4 primary partner functions:

- Sold to party; the party that usually is the main customer that drives the purchases
- Ship to party; the location of the customer where goods are shipped to or services performed at
- Bill to; where the invoice is sent
- Payer; the one who pays and in whose name the AR is created

Billing Date:

Figure 15: *Billing Date*

This is the date when the baseline date usually begins i.e. when the credit terms of the customer begin.

Under the section, Header>Header as in figure 17:

Figure 16: *Header Menu*

Company code:

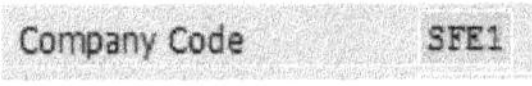

Company Code   SFE1

Figure 17: *Company Code Information*

This is the company code responsible for the sales organization that did the transaction. This company code holds the AR and the receivables will form a part of its current assets.

On the Conditions tab, once can see the value of the document along with the taxes:

Header	Head.prtnrs	Conditions	ForTrade/Customs	Head.text	Global Trade

Net	17,500.00	CAD
Tax	1,225.00	

Figure 18: *Conditions tab*

The accounting document of this invoice can be reached via the accounting tab: 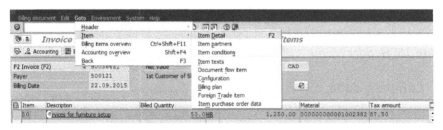 (see Fig 20 below)

Display Document: Data Entry View

Taxes | Display Currency | General Ledger View

Data Entry View

Document Number	90036870	Company Code	SFE1	Fiscal Year	2017
Document Date	22.05.2017	Posting Date	22.05.2017	Period	5
Reference	0090036870	Cross-CC no.			
Currency	CAD	Texts exist		Ledger Group	

Co	Itm	PK	S	Account	Description	Amount	Curr.	Tx	Cost Center	Profit Center	Segment	Billing Doc.
SFE1	1	01		601361	1st customer of SFE1	18,725.00	CAD	O9				90036670
	2	50		451011	Revenue Stream 1	17,500.00-	CAD	O9				
	3	50		216450	VAT A/R (Output)	1,225.00-	CAD	O9				

Figure 19: *Display Document – Data Entry view*

At the line item level, the important fields are (see figure 21):

Billing document Edit Goto Environment System Help

Header

Item
Billing items overview   Ctrl+Shift+F11
Accounting overview   Shift+F4
Back   F3

Item Detail   F2
Item partners
Item conditions
Item texts
Document flow item
Configuration
Billing plan
Foreign Trade item
Item purchase order data

Invoice

Accounting

tems

F2 Invoice (F2)
Payer   500121   1st Customer of SI
Billing Date   22.09.2015

CAD

Item	Description	Billed Quantity	Material	Tax amount
10	rvices for furniture setup	50.0HR	1,250.00	000000000001002382	87.50

Figure 20: *Item – Item Detail*

Service Rendered Date:

AcctSettleStart	
Serv.rendered	22.05.2017
Exchange Rate	1.00000

Figure 21: *Item options, Item Details*

This is the date on which taxes are calculated i.e. the taxes existing on that date in SAP (or external systems) are the valid taxes for this transaction. It is independent of the billing date or date when the order created.

v) Pro-forma invoices

Occasionally the customer may require a pro-forma invoice for purpose of getting prior approvals for imports, or for customs or bank funding in cases of capital goods etc. Two standard pro-forma invoices exist in SAP – the billing type F5 created from a sales order and billing type F8 with reference to a delivery. The delivery does not have to be goods issued for this purpose. Pro-forma invoices do not create accounting entries i.e. they never hit AR. Further, a pro-forma invoice can be created anytime for old, existing sales orders and deliveries also.

From order, type F2:

Create the sales order in VA01, all that is needed to enter are the customer #, material and quantity:

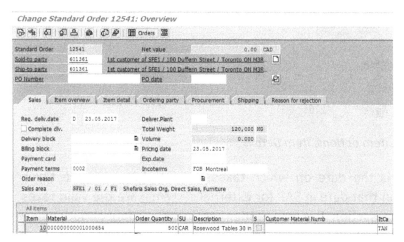

Figure 22: *Change Standard Order – Sales tab*

Save

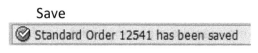

Figure 23: *Standard Order Saved message*

In VF01, enter the order # in the Document field and choose F5 (See figure 25):

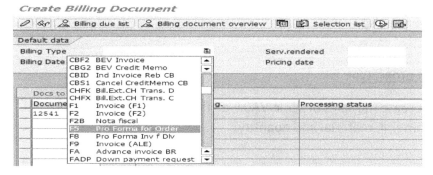

Figure 24: *Billing Type List*

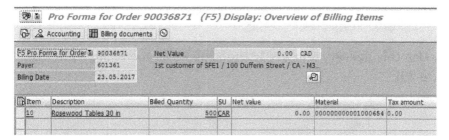

Figure 25: *Pro-forma for Order*

Save

Figure 26: *Document Saved message*

<u>From delivery, F8:</u>

Sometimes information relating to shipping needs to be given on the pro-forma invoice like palletizing, gross weights, net weights, transporter etc and some of it may be available only in the delivery. In those cases, a delivery is created from the sales order and the pro-forma created wrt to that delivery instead of from the order. Unlike the real invoice, for a pro-forma invoice the delivery need not be goods issued for the pro-forma to create.

Create the order in VA01 and then the delivery in VL01N using that sales order.

Delivery Create: Overview

Outbound deliv.				Document Date	23.05.2017		
Ship-to party	601361		1st customer of SFE1 / 100 Dufferin Street / Toronto ON M3R 4W2				

Item Overview	Picking	Loading	Transport	Status Overview	Goods Movement Data

Planned GI	23.05.2017	00:0..	Total Weight	240,000	KG
Actual GI date			No.of packages		

All Items

Itm	Material	Deliv. Qty	Un	Description	B.	ITyp
10	00000000001000654	100	CAR	Rosewood Tables 30 in		TAN

Figure 27: *Delivery Create – Item Overview tab*

> ⊘ Delivery 80015461 has been saved

Use this delivery # in VF01, choosing F8 as the Billing type (See figure 29):

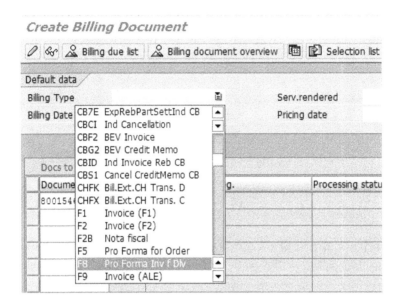

Figure29 : *Choosing the correct billing type F8 from drop down menu*

Press Enter – the following message will appear:

> Processing of Document 0080015461

Figure 30: *Processing Document Saved*

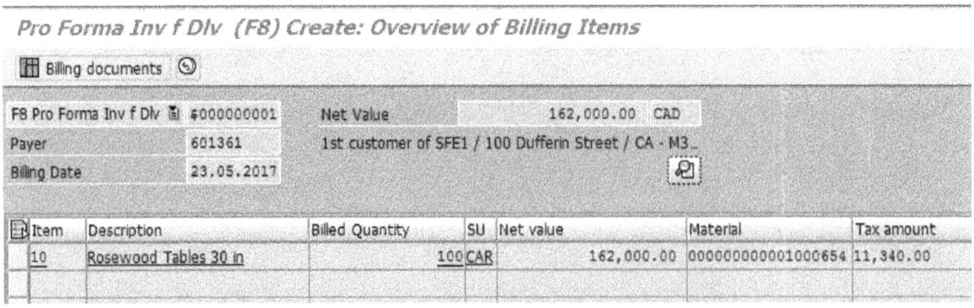

Figure 31: *Pro Forma Invoice*

Save

Document 90036872 has been saved

Figure 32: *Document saved message*

vi) Viewing an Invoice

Although the content of the actual invoice will vary depending on the company's requirements, the process to view them is the same. SAP offers the ability to 'preview' the invoices before the user can decide whether to print or not. Printing can be done in mass scale or individually depending on the volumes.

To look up an individual invoice on the screen go to VF03 (display):

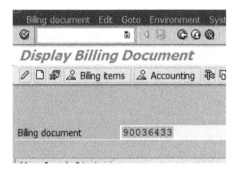

Figure 33: *Display Billing Document*

Figure 34: *Billing Document options*

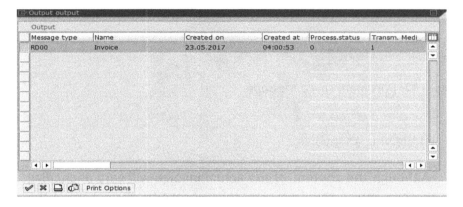

Figure 35: *Billing Document Output*

Every company will have its own Message type (also called Outputs in SAP) and often there will be multiple (usually different formats and reasons thereof). With the appropriate Output highlighted, click on the button ![button] in Fig 35 above

Pro-forma invoice Document in figure 36.

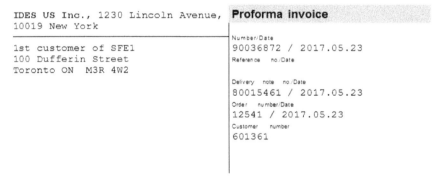

Figure 36: *Pro-forma invoice Document*

Use scrolling keys to see all the pages if there are multiple.

vii) Cancelling a Billing Document

Cancelling a Billing Document is done in transaction VF11 which looks like VF01 except for a different header and that here you have to enter the billing document that needs to be cancelled instead of the order # or delivery #:

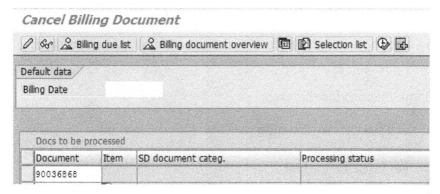

Figure 37: *Cancel Billing Document*

Hit Enter

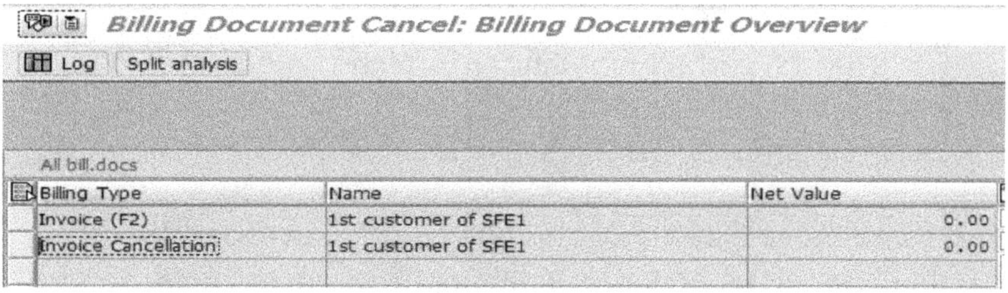

Figure 38: *Cancel Billing Document – Billing Document Overview*

✓ Document 90036873 saved

Once an existing billing document is cancelled, it releases the order or the delivery to get billed again. For the most part, in SAP, it is not possible to cancel a preceding document without first cancelling the subsequent document. Thus, it is very important that the data is good from the origin itself, as SAP can be very unforgiving if the data is wrong.

viii)   Releasing billing documents to Accounting

With Billing over, Sales & Distribution hands off the data to accounting. Once posted to accounting, no changes can be done to it on the SD side. At this cusp of SD and FI is a transaction VFX3 that must be regularly monitored. Most billing documents will lead up to an accounting document unless set up not to (pro-forma invoices being a notable exception). However, due to various reasons these billing documents can get stuck and must be manually fixed by the users so they can make their way to AR.

Some reasons for this are:

1. Old document, billing date is in a closed period – for some reason, a goods issued delivery from the past period did not get invoiced in time
2. Customer was not extended in the company code i.e. does not have company code data
3. Pricing was not correct
4. G/L account determination for revenue/freight etc. does not exist or is incorrect
5. For exports, certain mandatory foreign trade related data is missing
6. Tax calculations are not correct

And some more that may occur due to company specific custom transactions and data. This data will need to be fixed before these documents can be posted and in some cases, documents will need to be cancelled to re-create them with the right data.

CONSIGNMENT PROCESS IN SAP

Many companies keep some stock at their customers' premises for better service, flexibility and saving costs especially on transportation by shipping in bulk. This stock remains at the customer premises and is consumed by the customer as needed and replenished when it reaches re-order levels. Billing for these consignments takes place based on consumption rather than on shipment. SAP has provided 4 standard order types (similar to order type OR we saw earlier) that can be used for this process:

- Consignment fill up: CF
- Consignment Issue: CI
- Consignment Pick-up: CP
- Consignment returns: CONR

To understand the complete Consignment cycle, we will create the 4 types of orders step wise and see the effect.

1. Consignment Fill-up:

Create an order type CF:

Create Sales Order: Initial Screen

☐ Create with Reference	🔏 Sales	🔏 Item overview	🔏 Ordering party

Order Type   CF   Consignment Fill-up

Organizational Data

Sales Organization   SFE1   Shefaria Sales Org

Distribution Channel   01   Direct Sales

Division   F1   Furniture

Sales Office

Sales Group | 🔁

Figure 1: *Create Sales Order and choose order type CF*

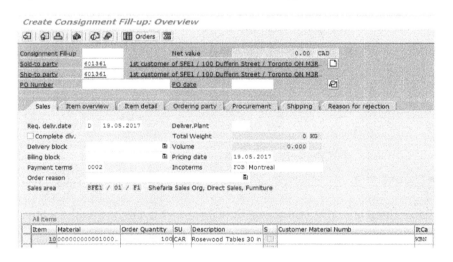

Figure 2: *Create consignment Fill-up order type CF screen*

The main thing to note is that based on the order type CF, SAP auto determined a different item category KBN (instead of the usual TAN) as seen above. Also noteworthy is that the order is of 0 value, again auto determined as a consignment fill up order. Save the order:

Consignment Fill-up 12537 has been saved

Figure 3: *Consignment Fill-up Saved*

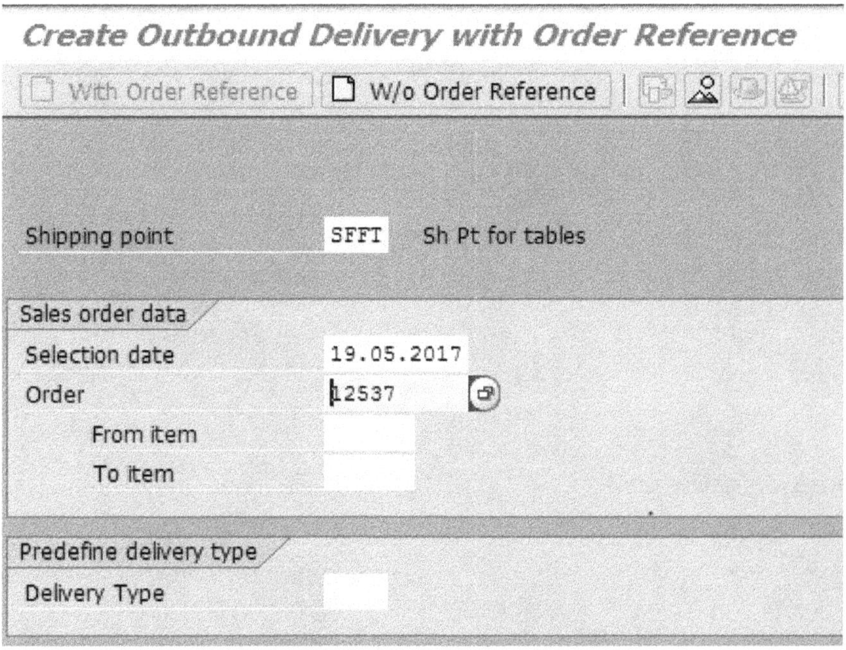

Create Outbound Delivery with Order Reference

With Order Reference | W/o Order Reference |

Shipping point	SFFT Sh Pt for tables

Sales order data
Selection date	19.05.2017
Order	12537
From item	
To item	

Predefine delivery type
Delivery Type	

Figure 4: *Create Outbound Delivery with Order reference*

Let us first see the current stock of this material 1000654 in transaction code MMBE: See figures 5 and 6

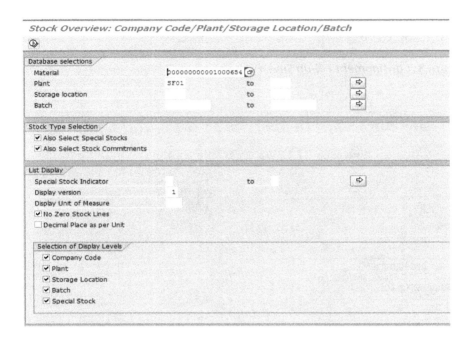

Figure 5: *Stock Overview*

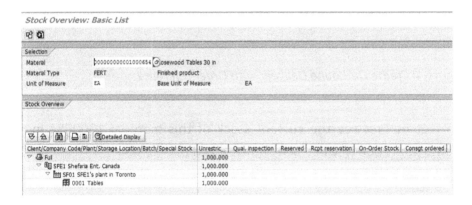

Figure 6: *Stock Overview – Basic List*

We create a delivery, pick and goods issue it in VL01N/VL02N:

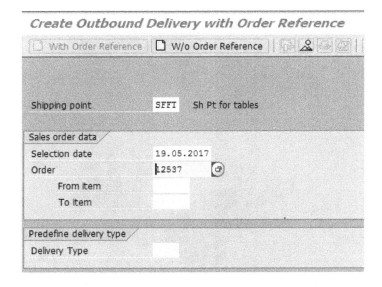

Figure 7: *Create Outbound Delivery with Order reference*

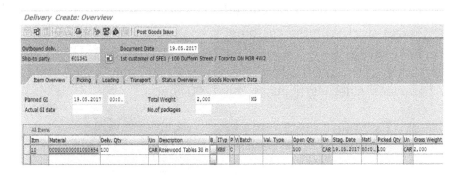

Figure 8: *Delivery Create – Item Overview*

Goods issue the delivery using the [Post Goods Issue] button in Fig 8

✅ Delivery 80015457 has been saved

Figure 9: *Delivery Saved message*

Refreshing the MMBE screen for the new stock we see:

Stock Overview: Basic List

Selection
Material	000000000001000654 ☞osewood Tables 30 in
Material Type	FERT	Finished product
Unit of Measure	EA	Base Unit of Measure	EA

Stock Overview

Client/Company Code/Plant/Storage Location/Batch/Special Stock	Unrestricted use	Qual. inspection	Reserved
▽ 🔩 Full	8,800.000		
▽ 🔳 SFE1 Shefaria Ent. Canada	8,800.000		
▽ 📇 SF01 SFE1's plant in Toronto	8,800.000		
Cust. Consignment	1,200.000		
🔲 0001 Tables	8,800.000		

Figure 10: *Stock Overview – Basic List*

Thus, 1200 EA of this material 1000654 now resides as consignment stock with the customer leaving behind 8800 for other use in our own plant.

To see more details, highlight this 1200 line:

Client/Company Code/Plant/Storage Location/Batch/Special Stock	Unrestricted use	Qual. inspection	Reserved
▽ 🔩 Full	8,800.000		
▽ 🔳 SFE1 Shefaria Ent. Canada	8,800.000		
▽ 📇 SF01 SFE1's plant in Toronto	8,800.000		
Cust. Consignment	1,200.000		
🔲 0001 Tables	8,800.000		

Figure 11: *Customer Consignment*

Click on ☜Detailed Display in Fig 11 above

A new window opens telling us more details about the stock and the customer it is residing with:

Stock Cust. Consignment			
Plnt SF01			
Customer	Name	Stock Type	Stock
0000601361	1st customer of SFE1	Unrestricted use	1,200.000
		Qual. Inspection	0.000
		Restricted-use	0.000

Figure 12: *Customer Consignment*

2. Consignment Issue

The customer may call up the next day advising us they will be consuming 30 CAR of this product. We now need to 'issue' this quantity to the customer. Note that the stock is still regarded as being in our own plant and company code, as seen in the screen shot in MMBE; only the physical location is at the customer.

To create the consignment issue for quantity = 30 CAR, create the order type CI in VA01 for the same customer/material:

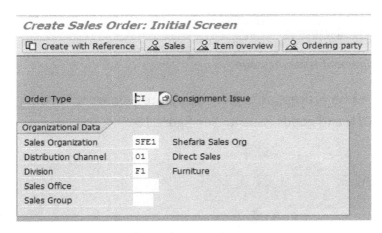

Figure 13: *Create Sales Order type CI*

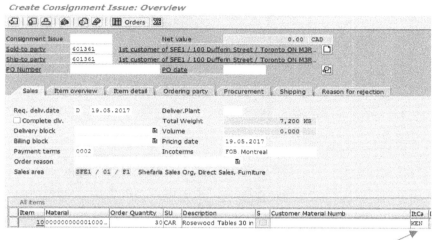

Figure 14: *Create consignment Issue*

Note how the order now gets an item category as KEN and also has a value for the 30 CARs (not for 100 CAR which was sent to the customer).

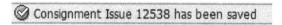

Figure 15: *Consignment Issue message*

Using the same process as earlier, we create a delivery for this quantity in VL01N and goods issue it: See figure 16

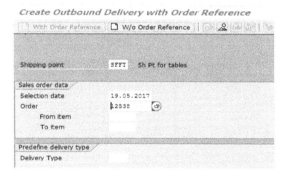

Figure 16: *Create Outbound Delivery with Order reference*

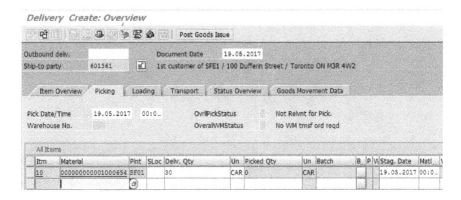

Figure 17: *Delivery Create – Picking tab*

Note that the system is no longer asking us to pick this quantity. This is because the objective of this delivery is to move the stocks to the appropriate place and to invoice the customer for this usage of 30 CAR. The delivery was already picked when the consignment fill up occurred for 100 CAR.

Post the goods:  in Fig 17 above.

Delivery 80015458 has been saved

Figure 18: *Post Goods Issue has been done*

Let us now look at the stock situation again in MMBE to confirm if anything happened to the stock. See Fig 19.

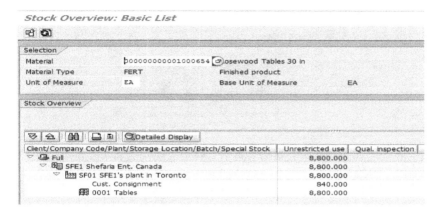

Stock Overview: Basic List

Selection

Material	000000000001000654	osewood Tables 30 in	
Material Type	FERT	Finished product	
Unit of Measure	EA	Base Unit of Measure	EA

Stock Overview

Detailed Display

Client/Company Code/Plant/Storage Location/Batch/Special Stock	Unrestricted use	Qual. inspection
Full	8,800.000	
SFE1 Shefaria Ent. Canada	8,800.000	
SF01 SFE1's plant in Toronto	8,800.000	
Cust. Consignment	840.000	
0001 Tables	8,800.000	

Figure 19: *Stock Overview – Basic List*

We notice the stock has reduced from 1,200 to 840, the different of 360 = 30 CAR * 12 EA = 360 EA.

This delivery will now get invoiced to the customer for payment since the customer has consumed the stocks. In the now familiar transaction, VF01, invoice the customer using the delivery:

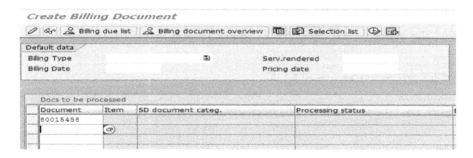

Create Billing Document

Billing due list | Billing document overview | Selection list

Default data

Billing Type		Serv.rendered	
Billing Date		Pricing date	

Docs to be processed

Document	Item	SD document categ.	Processing status	
80015458				

Figure 20: *Create Billing Document*

Hit Enter & Save.

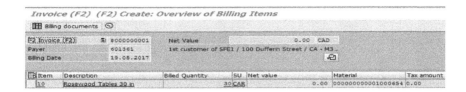

Figure 21: *Billing Items Overview*

3. Consignment Pickup

A consignment pick up is used when there is left over material and needs to be brought back as the customer will not be using it. This may be due to over stock or pre-agreed terms or due to possibility of expiration of the product etc.

In the same way, in VA01, create the order type CP for 45 CAR of this product as that is what will be brought back. See figure 22

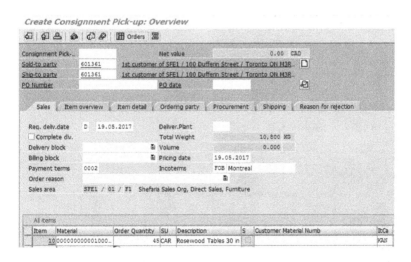

Figure 22: *Create Consignment Pick-up*

Once again SAP has determined a new item category KAN and not assigned any value to this order because it was never invoiced. This is a part of the quantity still lying unused with the customer.

Save the order.

Figure 23: *Consignment Pick-up saved message*

Note that the numbering sequence has changed. Though it is possible to assign the same numbering sequence, a different one is a better choice as the consignment pick up is in reality a return order.

As before, we will create a new delivery for this consignment pick up in t code VLO1N:

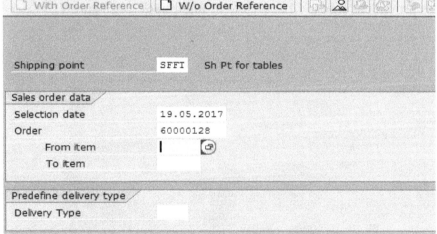

Figure24: *Create Outbound Delivery with Order reference*

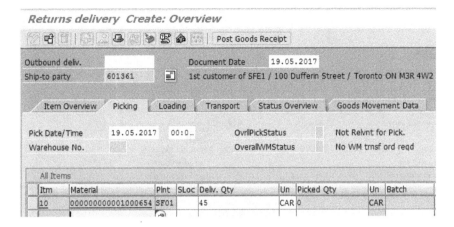

Figure25: *Return Delivery Create - Picking*

SAP automatically creates a returns delivery as above and this time, after defining the storage location where we want to receive these goods, instead of a goods issue, we do a goods receipt by

clicking on  in Fig 25

> ⊘ Returns delivery 84000041 has been saved

Figure 26 : *Returns delivery saved message*

Note the delivery # also follows a different series as it is a returns delivery, not an outbound delivery. Usually companies will keep different numbering sequences depending on what kind of delivery they are – customer outbound, vendor inbound, returns, stock replenishment, inter company etc. for easier identification.

Let us look at the stocks again in MMBE:

BEFORE:

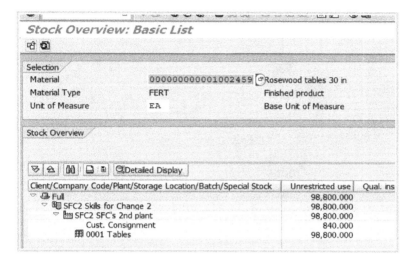

Figure 27: *Stock Overview – Basic List*

AFTER:

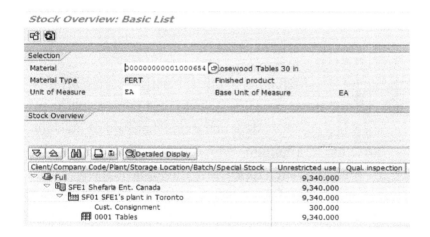

Figure 28: *Stock Overview – Basic List*

We see that because of this return of 45 CAR (= 45*12 = 540 EA) the consignment stock at the customer has depleted to 300 and the stock in the storage location has increased by the same amount to 9,340 EA.

4. Consignment return

This is the last type of the consignment order in the consignment landscape. A consignment return occurs when a customer returns goods already bought (for which he was invoiced already) back to us. In out example, we had invoiced the customer 30 CAR earlier. If the customer were to return 10 CAR of these back to us, a consignment return would be created in VA01 using the order type CONR: See figure 29:

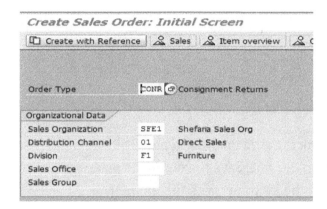

Figure 29: *Create Sales Order*

As a standard SAP process, all credits are given a billing block automatically and all returns require a return reason:

Complete dlv.		Total Weight	0.000
Delivery block		Volume	0.000
Billing block	08 Check credit memo	Pricing date	19.05.2017
Payment terms	0002	Incoterms	FOB Montreal
Order reason			
Sales area	SFE1 / 01 / F1 Shefaria Sales Org, Direct Sales, Furniture		

Figure 30: *Consignment Return – Required information*

These can be de-activated but for prudence's sake, all companies prefer to let them remain for reasons of accountability. Give an appropriate reason and provide the material and quantity details:

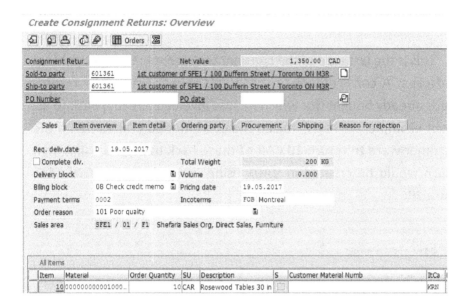

Figure 31: *Create Consignment Returns – Sales tab*

Yet again, as we notice, based on order type CONR, SAP applied the item category KRN to this line. Save the order and gave it a value as we will need to credit the customer with this amount.

Figure 32: *Consignment Returns Saved message*

Since this too is a physical return of goods, we need to create another delivery and receive the stock into 0001 storage location. We do it in VL01N again using this consignment return order:

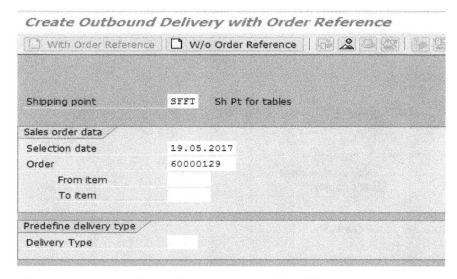

Figure 33: *Create Outbound Delivery with Order reference*

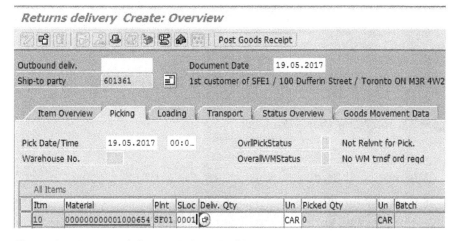

Figure 34: *Returns delivery create - Picking*

Post goods receipt.

⊘ Returns delivery 84000042 has been saved

Figure 35: *Returns delivery Saved message*

View the stock again:

BEFORE:

Client/Company Code/Plant/Storage Location/Batch/Special Stock	Unrestricted use
▽ 🗄 Full	9,340.000
▽ 📱 SFE1 Shefaria Ent. Canada	9,340.000
▽ 🏭 SF01 SFE1's plant in Toronto	9,340.000
Cust. Consignment	300.000
🏢 0001 Tables	9,340.000

Figure 36: *Stock Overview – Basic List*

AFTER:

Client/Company Code/Plant/Storage Location/Batch/Special Stock	Unrestricted use	Qual.
▽ 🗄 Full	9,340.000	
▽ 📱 SFE1 Shefaria Ent. Canada	9,340.000	
▽ 🏭 SF01 SFE1's plant in Toronto	9,340.000	
Cust. Consignment	420.000	
🏢 0001 Tables	9,340.000	

Figure 37: *Stock Overview – Basic List*

We notice that due to the return the customer consignment stock quantity has increased by 10 CAR (120 EA – from 300 to 420) while the storage location stock remains unaffected. Once the QC department has passed its judgement on this stock, it will get moved out of the customer consignment.

MATERIAL MASTER FROM PURCHASING PERSPECTIVE

i) Purchasing Data

Figure 1: *Create Material – Purchasing Tab*

In this screen we are entering the plant specific data for purchasing. Thus, it can be different for different plants.

Purchasing group – we configured one Purchasing group, it can be used here to default it if one group is responsible for purchasing this material all the time. It can be changed in the Purchase order. A purchasing group can be an entity representing a particular area, geographic or product line/functional in the Purchasing department.

Var OUn – Variable ordering unit. Only if this is set to 1 can we use a different unit to order in the PO else SAP forces us to order in the base unit only. Thus, it is always advisable to set it as 1. Of course, conversion units have to be defined between the ordering unit and the base unit.

GR Processing time (in days) – is the time we set aside to receive, inspect and put the stock into the system. This time is used to calculate the delivery times in SD for deriving the delivery dates.

Purchasing value key – for the moment, enter 1, this key is useful to order/procure on behalf of other plants and its effect is primarily for transactions where one plant can substitute for another at times of product scarcity or unavailability.

ii) PO Text

This can come in very handy when creating POs on foreign vendors or to print material related text in different languages due to legal reasons like in Quebec. We can set up the material description

in multiple languages. Click on the icon to get the window in the frame and choose your language: See figure 2 below.

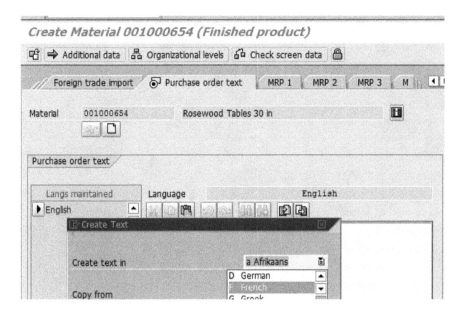

Figure 2: *Create Material – Purchase Order Text Tab*

Say OK:

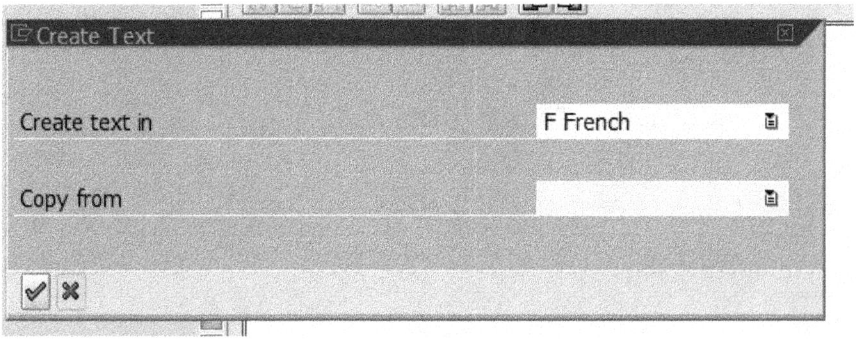

Figure 3: *Create Material – Create text window*

Figure 4: *Create Material – Purchase Order Text Tab*

This way we can set up the material names/descriptions in different languages.

iii) Plant/Storage Location Data

Create Material 001000654 (Finished product)

[icons] ⇒ Additional data | Organizational levels | Check screen data

| Prod.resources/tools | Plant data / stor. 1 | Plant data / stor. 2 | Wareho... |

Material   001000654   Rosewood Tables 30 in

Plant   SF01   SFE1's plant in Toronto

Stor. Loc.   0001   Tables

General data

Base Unit of Measure	EA	Each	Unit of issue
Storage Bin			Picking area
Temp. conditions			Storage conditions
Container reqmts			Haz. material number
CC phys. inv. ind.		☐ CC fixed	Number of GR slips
Label type		Lab.form	☐ Appr.batch rec. req.
		OBManagmnt	OB Ref. Material
☐ Batch management			

Shelf life data

Max. storage period		Time unit
Min. Rem. Shelf Life		Total shelf life
Period Ind. for SLED	D	Rounding rule SLED
Storage percentage		

Figure 5: *Create Material – Plant Data / Stor. 1 Tab*

This data is useful to store in the material master as it relates to shelf lives, storage conditions etc. Apart from being a direct input for transactions, it is also helpful in identifying products close to their SLED (Shelf life) so they can be disposed of at discounts before they expire.

iv) Accounting Data 1 and 2

Figure 6: *Create Material – Accounting 1 Tab*

This screen captures the price of the product – we can either give it a standard price of our choosing or a moving average price based on procurement over a defined term from different vendors. For our learning, we will keep it as S and the pricing unit at 1. The valuation class is necessary to drive the accounting entries.

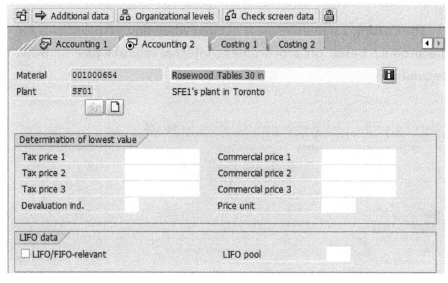

Figure 7: *Create Material – Accounting 2 Tab*

The above Accounting 2 screen is not very important except in inventorying the products based on Last in, First out or First in, First out method.

v) Costing Data 1 and 2

The Costing 1 screen below is needed when doing costing runs for the product based on procurement/internal manufacture or BOM calculations.

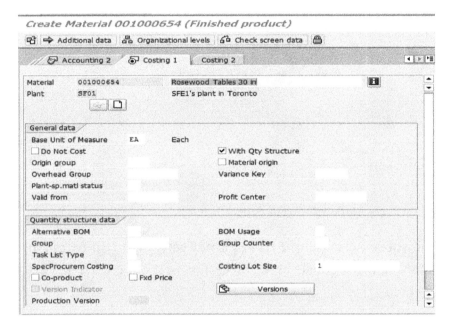

Figure 8: *Create Material – Costing 1 Tab*

The Costing 2 screen below keeps historical costs of the material and is also used for planning the future planned costs.

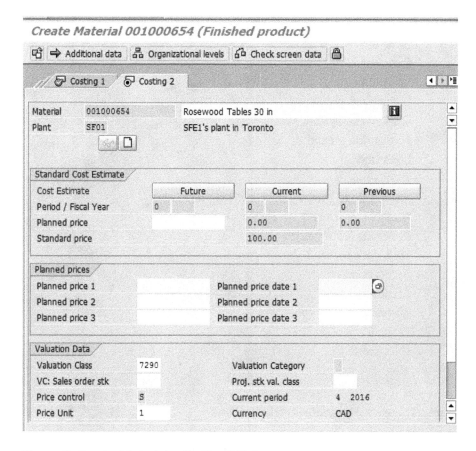

Figure 9: *Create Material – Costing 2 Tab*

We now have most of the data we will need to work with Accounting and SD Module. We can now save this material.

Figure 10: *Material created message*

The data can always be changed in MM02 or viewed in MM03. To see the views available for the material, we can use the key:

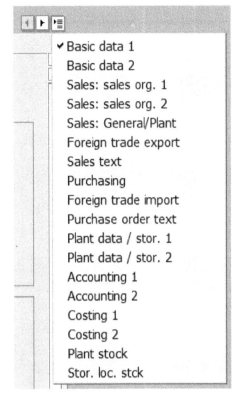

Figure 11: *Create Material – Available views*

Which views will be available will depend on the material type of the material.

VENDOR MASTER FROM PURCHASING PERSPECTIVE

i) Purchasing data

From the MM point of view, this is the most important screen in vendor master data. The ordering currency is a mandatory field and can be changed in the PO or Purchase requisitions – the system will simply use the exchange rates set up by Finance to calculate the values in the desired currency.

The transaction code to create a vendor for purchasing data is MK01. A Purchasing Organization is the highest object in Purchasing and mirrors the Sales Organization on the SD side. To enable buying from a vendor, the vendor must be created in the P. Org as Purchase Orders are created in the name of the P.Org.

Create Vendor: Initial Screen

Vendor	
PurchasingOrganization	SFE1
Account group	0001

Create Vendor: Purchasing data

Vendor	INTERNAL	1st vendor of SFE1		Toronto
Purchasing Org.	SFE1	P. Org of SFE1		

Conditions

Order currency	CAD
Terms of paymnt	0005
Incoterms	EXW Calgary
Minimum order value	1,000.00
Schema Group, Vendor	Standard procedure vendor
Pricing Date Control	No Control
Order optim.rest.	

Sales data

Salesperson
Telephone
Acc. with vendor

Control data

☑ GR-Based Inv. Verif.	ABC indicator	
☑ AutoEvalGRSetmt Del.	ModeOfTrnsprt-Border	
☑ AutoEvalGRSetmt Ret.	Office of entry	
☐ Acknowledgment Reqd	Sort criterion	By VSR sequence number
☐ Automatic purchase order	PROACT control prof.	
☐ Subsequent settlement	☐ Revaluation allowed	
☐ Subseq. sett. index	☐ Grant discount in kind	
☐ B.vol.comp./ag.nec.	☐ Relevant for price determ. (del.hierarchy)	
☐ Doc. index active	☐ Relevant for agency business	
☐ Returns vendor		
☐ Srv.-Based Inv. Ver.	Shipping Conditions	

Default data material

Purchasing group
Planned deliv. time   Day(s)
Confirmation Control
Unit of measure grp
Rounding Profile

Service data

Price marking agreed
Rack-jobbing service agreed   ☐
Order entry by vendor   ☐
Serv. level

Figure 1: *Create Vendor – Purchasing data*

Terms of payment: if entered, will override the terms of payment in the payment transactions accounting view. These terms will take precedence in the PO since they have been negotiated by the purchasing dept with the vendor.

Incoterms: are internationally accepted terms of shipment which decide who will pay the freight. They default into the PO and can be changed. These affect the shipping costs same way as they do in sales orders.

Min Order value: if so set based on the vendor's terms of business.

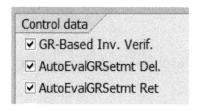

Figure 2: *Create Vendor – Control data*

GR based Inv Verif means the vendor can't get paid till the Purchasing department has vetted the inbound receipt of goods.

The other 2 fields are required if the vendor is on ERS. ERS (evaluated receipt settlement) in which accruals can be automatically converted to payables for deliveries and returns.

☑ Automatic purchase order   Automatic PO whereby POs can be generated automatically from Purchase requisitions.

Purchasing Group: If any particular PG is responsible for purchases from this vendor, it can be entered here and made to default in the PO to the vendor.

ii) Partner functions

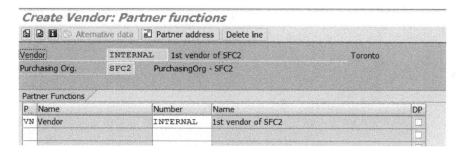

Figure 3: *Create Vendor – Partner functions*

If the vendor has different places for shipping goods from or a different entity that needs to be paid instead of itself, then we need to create those as separate vendors and can link them to the main vendor in this screen.

We now have all the data we need to use this vendor so we can now save it:

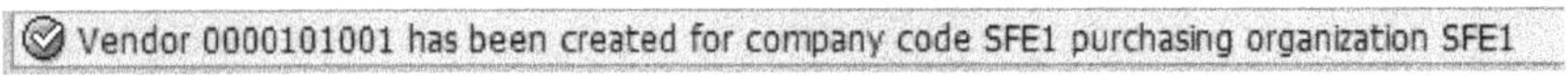

Vendor 0000101001 has been created for company code SFE1 purchasing organization SFE1

Figure 4: *Vendor created message*

PURCHASING INFO RECORDS

A PIR serves as a source of information for Purchasing. The purchasing info record (also referred to in abbreviated form as the "info record") contains information on a specific material and a vendor supplying the material. For example, the vendor's current pricing is stored in the info record.

It can be defined via t-code ME11 or via the following menu path: Logistics -> Material Management -> Purchasing -> Master Data -> Info Record -> Create

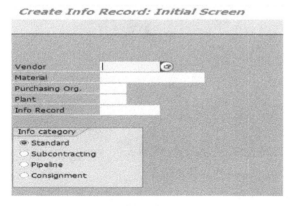

Figure 1: *Create Info Record*

Procurement Types in Info Records

- Standard: A standard info record contains information for standard purchase orders. The info records can be created for materials and services with and without master records.
- Subcontracting: A subcontractor info record contains ordering information for subcontract orders.
- Pipeline: A pipeline info record contains information on a vendor's commodity that is supplied through a pipeline or pipes (for example, oil or water) or by similar means (for example, electricity through the mains).
- Consignment: A consignment info record contains information on a material that vendors keep available at their own cost on the customer's premises. The info record contains the vendor's price for withdrawals by the customer from consignment stock.

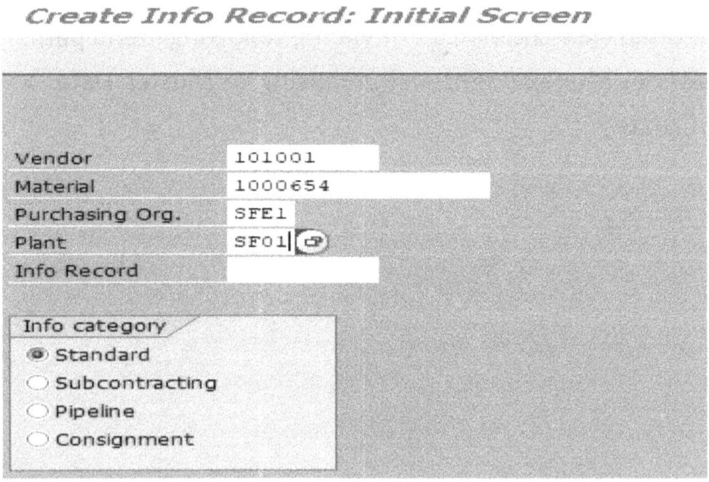

Create Info Record: Initial Screen

Figure 2: *Create Info Record – Required Information*

In the initial screen, we enter the required fields such as vendor and purchasing type for the creation of the info record. It is to be noted here that purchasing info record can be created without specifying the material number. In this case, material group and material description. That will mean that this PIR will apply to all materials having that particular product group in their material master, provided they don't have a PIR based on the material code also as that will take precedence (being more specific). This reduces the need to maintain multiple PIRs based on material codes.

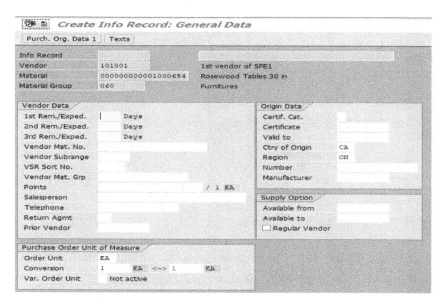

Figure 3: *Create Info Record – General Data*

We can also maintain data at the purchasing org. as shown below. This makes the PIR specific to that Purchasing Org. (P Org)

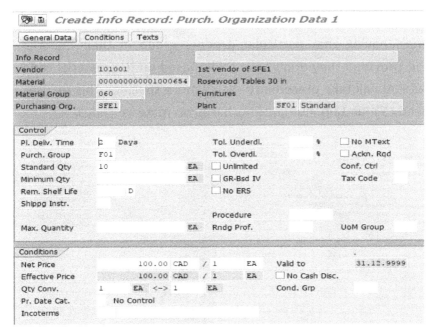

Figure 4: *Create Info Record – Organization Data 1*

In the conditions tab, the pricing conditions can be maintained. We will use SAP standard PB00 pricing condition for our purpose.

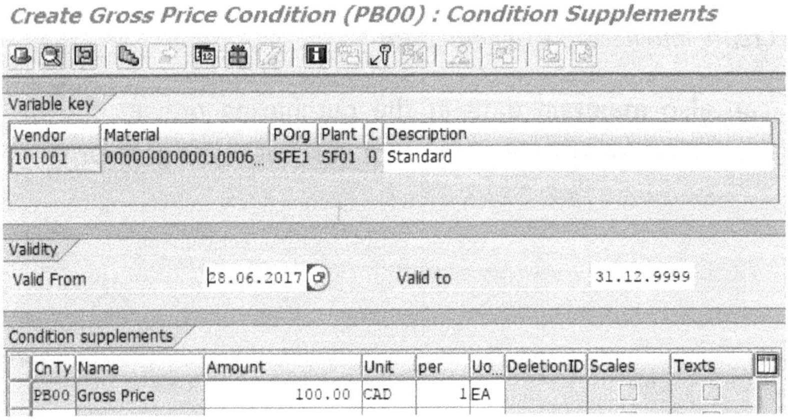

Figure 5: *Create Info Record - Condition*

Next, we maintain any special instructions for a vendor or for internal purposes in the material master record.

Info record note: An internal note or comment that is adopted in the PO item. The info record memo is not printed out.

Purchase order text: This text serves to describe the order item and corresponds to the PO text in the material master record. It is adopted in the PO item and included in the printout.

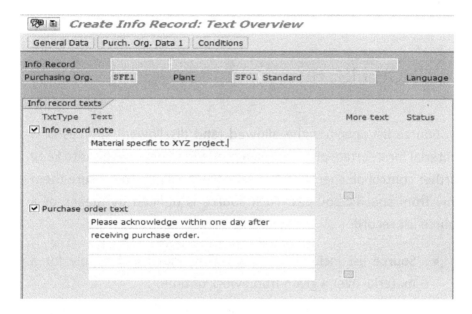

Figure 6: *Create Info Record – Info Record Text*

⊘ Purchasing info record 2000000390 SFE1 SF01 created

Figure 7: *Create Info Record created message*

SOURCE LISTS

Source list specifies the allowed (and disallowed) sources of a material for a certain plant within a predefined period. This is to keep further control on specialized or sensitive products to procure them only from specific sources. Each source is defined by means of a source list record.

- Source list include list of possible sources of supply for a material over a given framework of time.
- Source list specifies the time period of ordering of a particular material from a given vendor.
- Source list can be copied from one plant to another plant.

In the purchasing view, tick the source list option for automatic creation of source list.

Change Material 000000000001000654 (Finished product)

⟲ ⇨ Additional data | Organizational levels | Check screen data | 🔒

Sales text | Purchasing | Foreign trade import | Purchase order text | P | ◀

Base Unit of Measure	EA	Each	Order Unit		Var. OUn
Purchasing Group			Material Group	060	
Plant-sp.matl status			Valid from		
Tax ind. f. material			Qual.f.FreeGoodsDis.		
Material freight grp	01		☐ Autom. PO		
			OB Management		
☐ Batch management			OB ref. matrial		

Purchasing values

Purchasing value key			Shipping Instr.		
1st Rem./Exped.	0	days	Underdel. Tolerance	0.0	percent
2nd Reminder/Exped.	0	days	Overdeliv. Tolerance	0.0	percent
3rd Reminder/Exped.	0	days	Min. Del. Qty in %	0.0	percent
StdValueDelivDateVar	0	days	☐ Unltd Overdelivery		☐ Acknowledgment Reqd

Other data / manufacturer data

GR Processing Time		days	☐ Post to insp. stock		☐ Critical Part
Quota arr. usage			☑ Source list		JIT Sched. Indicator
					Mfr Part Profile

Figure 1: *Change Material – Purchasing Tab*

If this option is checked, then one can't place a PO for this material without it's having a source list in the system. If an attempt is made to do so, an error will flag at the time of PO creation:

⊗ Source not included in list despite source list requirement

Figure 2: *Source list error message*

This is not to be confused with the vendor though in terms of entity they are the same. The vendor is necessary for a PO of course but here, it also needs to be backed up with a source list that has that particular vendor as a 'source' of procurement.

Creation of source list

Source list can be created manually via t-code ME01 or via following menu path:

Logistics -> Material Management -> Purchasing -> Master Data -> Source List -> Maintain

Maintain Source List: Initial Screen

Material	000000000001000654
Plant	SF01

Figure 3: *Maintain Source List*

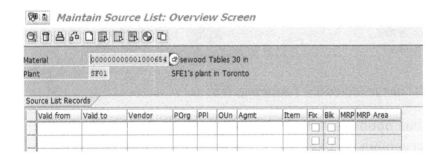

Figure 4: *Maintain Source List – Overview screen*

Here the records can be generated by clicking on ⊕ button or can be manually filled.

Material	000000000001000654	sewood Tables 30 in									
Plant	SF01	SFE1's plant in Toronto									

Source List Records

Valid from	Valid to	Vendor	POrg	PPl	OUn	Agmt	Item	Fix	Blk	MRP
28.06.2017	31.12.2999	101001	SFE1					☐	☐	
								☐	☐	

Figure 5: *Maintain Source List – Source List Records*

Multiple vendors can be entered in the same source list and the lines further made more specifically restricted to particular plants. Save the source list.

PHYSICAL INVENTORY

Physical inventory in SAP covers all aspects of counting material at the plant. This includes yearly inventory, cycle counting, continuous inventory and inventory sampling. It can be performed on stock that is held in unrestricted, quality inspection or on blocked status.

1. Types of Physical Inventory

- **Periodic Inventory**: Most of the companies follow this method of physical inventory. In most of the cases, it is done once a year or quarter or after the season ends (in seasonal industries).

- **Continuous Inventory**: In this method, stocks are counted continuously throughout the entire fiscal year. In this case, it is important to ensure that every material is physically counted at least once during the fiscal year. This type of inventory is mainly utilized in warehouse management based warehouses, but it can be done in inventory management too. It can also be used in continuous manufacturing like in pipe lines.

- **Cycle Counting**: This type of inventory allows us to set a period for regular intervals for physical inventory on the material level. So, a fast moving and high value material can be counted four times a year while slow moving and low value material can be counted once a year. The indicator for this is set in material master in the Plant/Storage Location 1 View, in the field.
- **Inventory Sampling**: Only a number of randomly selected materials are counted on the balance sheet key date, and if those materials show small enough differences, the other materials can also be considered to have a correct stock levels. Not really used that often, as it is essentially an approximation, but in some cases, it can be used if material and warehouse structure imply that.

2. Physical Inventory Preparation

Before the physical inventory count can begin, a series of operations needs to be done to prepare for this count. This includes deciding upon counting procedures on different materials/material types based on their relative importance, most of which are operational in nature.

i) Preparing for a Physical Inventory Count

The following steps are prerequisites for physical inventory process:

- Process and post all transaction that will effect inventory counts such as Goods receipts, transfer postings, inventory adjustments, sales orders that have been filled and shipped.
- Put away all the materials that are being counted in the warehouse.

- Segregate from the rest of the warehouse material stock that has been used to fill sales orders but physically not left the warehouse.
- Stop all stock movements within the warehouse.
- Stop all transactions in the warehouse.
- Run a stock-on hand report for the item s to be counted. This report can be fetched via t-code MB52. This shows the material in unrestricted, quality inspection and blocked stock for each storage location. It is record of inventory status before we start the physical inventory count.

Display Warehouse Stocks of Material

Material	Material Description		Plnt Name 1					
SLoc S V Special stock number	SL	Unrestricted Unit Total Value Crcy	Stock in transfer Total Value	In Quality Insp. Total Value	Restricted-Use Total Value	Blocked Total Value	Returns Total Value
000000000001000654 Rosewood Tables 30 in			SF01 SFE1's plant in Toronto					
W E013E1		420 EA	0	0	0	0	0
		42,000.00 CAD	0.00	0.00	0.00	0.00	0.00
0001		16,985 EA	0	0	0	0	0
		1,698,500.00 CAD	0.00	0.00	0.00	0.00	0.00
0002		35 EA	0	0	0	0	0
		3,500.00 CAD	0.00	0.00	0.00	0.00	0.00
* Total							
		1,744,000.00 CAD	0.00	0.00	0.00	0.00	0.00

Figure 1: *Display Warehouse Stocks of Material*

ii) Creating the physical inventory count document

The physical inventory count document can be created via t-code MI01 or the following menu path:

Logistics -> Materials Management -> Physical Inventory -> Physical Inventory Document -> Create

Document date	14.07.2017
Planned count date	14.07.2017

Loc.of phys.inv.

Plant	SF01
Storage Location	0001
Special Stock	

Other information

- ☑ Posting Block
- ☐ Freeze book invntory
- ☑ Batches w. del. flag

Phys. inventory no.	
Phys. Inventory Ref.	
Grouping type	

Figure 2: *Create Physical Inventory Document*

Posting Block: This indicator is used to ensure that there is no discrepancy between physical warehouse stock and the book inventory due to a delay between the material movement and actual posting of the movement. The posting block is automatically removed when the counting results are posted for the physical inventory document.

Freeze Book Inventory: This prevents the book inventory balance from being updated by any goods movements which could lead to inventory differences and mismatches.

Include Deleted Batches: This option allows the count document to include batches of material that has been flagged for deletion.

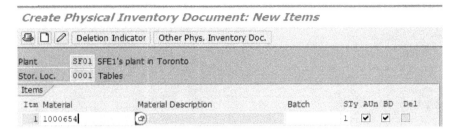

Create Physical Inventory Document: New Items

Figure 3: *Create Physical Inventory Document - Items*

Save the document.

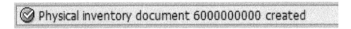

Physical inventory document 6000000000 created

Figure 4: *Create Physical Inventory Document – created message*

iii) Printing Physical Inventory Count documents

Once the physical inventory documents have been entered, the count documents can be printed out for actual physical count using MI21.

Figure 5: *Print Physical Inventory Document*

3. Counting and Recounts

Once the physical inventory sheets are printed, they are distributed to the personnel allocated for the counting process and the count starts.

i) Entering counts

Once the count has been completed, the physical count needs to be entered into the system. This is accessed by the inventory user using the transaction MI04 or the navigation path:

Logistics -> materials management -> Physical inventory -> Inventory Count -> Enter

Figure 6: *Enter Inventory Count*

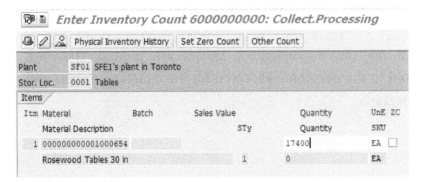

Figure 7: *Enter Inventory Count – Collect Processing*

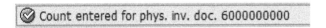

Figure 8: *Count entered message*

If the user makes an error while entering count document, it can be changed via MI05.

ii) Difference list

The count can be compared against the book inventory using transaction MI20 or via the following menu path:

Logistics -> Materials Management -> Physical inventory -> Difference -> Difference list

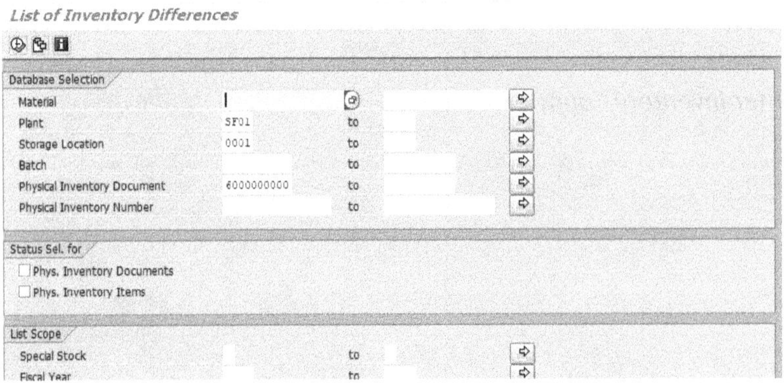

Figure 9: *List of Inventory Differences - Required Information*

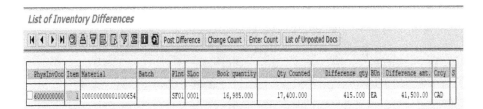

PhysInvDoc	Item	Material	Batch	Plnt	SLoc	Book quantity	Qty Counted	Difference qty	BUn	Difference amt.	Crcy	S
6000000000	1	000000000001000654		SF01	0001	16,985.000	17,400.000	415.000	EA	41,500.00	CAD	

Figure 10: *List of Inventory Differences - Report*

In case of differences, recount is carried out or the difference is posted if it is within allowable limits. It is management decision how to find the missing material. Many companies have incorporated auditing procedures to adjust physical inventory process in investigating discrepancies.

iii) Recounts

If the management does not accept the discrepancy or it is above tolerance limit, then those materials needs to be recounted.

The recount can be entered through transaction MI11 or the following path:

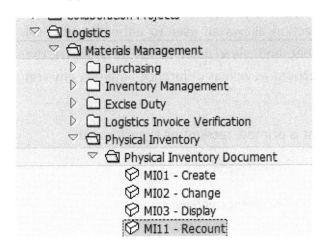

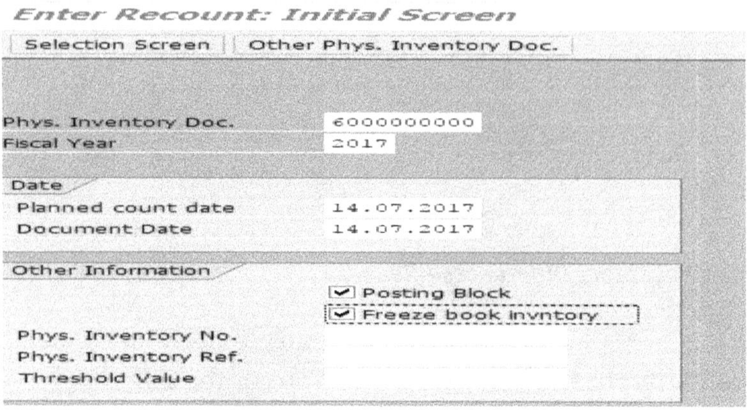

Enter Recount: Initial Screen

Selection Screen	Other Phys. Inventory Doc.

Phys. Inventory Doc.	6000000000
Fiscal Year	2017

Date	
Planned count date	14.07.2017
Document Date	14.07.2017

Other Information	
	☑ Posting Block
	☑ Freeze book invntory
Phys. Inventory No.	
Phys. Inventory Ref.	
Threshold Value	

Figure 11: *Enter Recount Screen*

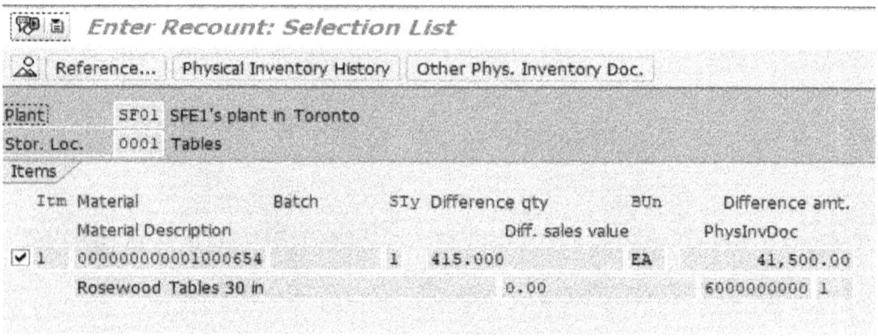

Enter Recount: Selection List

☐ Reference...	Physical Inventory History	Other Phys. Inventory Doc.

Plant	SF01	SFE1's plant in Toronto
Stor. Loc.	0001	Tables

Items

Itm	Material	Batch	STy	Difference qty	BUn	Difference amt.
	Material Description			Diff. sales value		PhysInvDoc
☑ 1	000000000001000654		1	415.000	EA	41,500.00
	Rosewood Tables 30 in			0.00		6000000000 1

Figure 12: *Enter Recount – Selection List*

The recount transaction allows an user to enter the physical count document number and view detail lines. This shows the material relevant for recount as well as difference between physical and booked quantity.

Once this document is printed, recounting is performed.

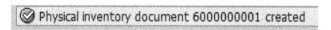
⊘ Physical inventory document 6000000001 created

Figure 13: *Physical Inventory Document created message*

Once the recounting is complete, material count can be entered through MI04.

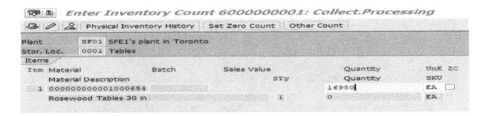

```
   ▽ 🗁 Logistics
      ▽ 🗁 Materials Management
         ▷ 🗀 Purchasing
         ▷ 🗀 Inventory Management
         ▷ 🗀 Excise Duty
         ▷ 🗀 Logistics Invoice Verification
         ▽ 🗁 Physical Inventory
            ▷ 🗀 Physical Inventory Document
            ▽ 🗁 Inventory Count
                  📦 MI04 - Enter
```

Enter Inventory Count 6000000001: Collect.Processing

| Physical Inventory History | Set Zero Count | Other Count |

Plant   SF01 SFE1's plant in Toronto
Stor. Loc. 0001 Tables

Items						
Itm	Material	Batch	Sales Value		Quantity	UnE ZC
	Material Description			STy	Quantity	SKU
1	00000000001000654				16980	EA ☐
	Rosewood Tables 30 in			I	0	EA

Figure 14: *Enter Recount – Collect Processing*

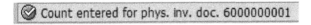

📀 Count entered for phys. inv. doc. 6000000001

Figure 15: *Count entered message*

4. Physical Inventory Posting

i) Posting the Count Document

Once the count is entered, the document is posted using t-code MI07 or the following menu path:

```
▽ 🗀 Logistics
   ▽ 🗀 Materials Management
      ▷ 🗀 Purchasing
      ▷ 🗀 Inventory Management
      ▷ 🗀 Excise Duty
      ▷ 🗀 Logistics Invoice Verification
      ▽ 🗀 Physical Inventory
         ▷ 🗀 Physical Inventory Document
         ▷ 🗀 Inventory Count
         ▽ 🗀 Difference
            🎲 MI07 - Post
```

Post Inventory Difference: Initial Screen

| 🖨 | Selection Screen | Other Difference |

Phys. Inventory Doc.	6000000001
Fiscal Year	2017

Date

Posting Date	14.07.2017

Other Information

Threshold Value	20

Figure 1: *Post Physical Inventory Difference*

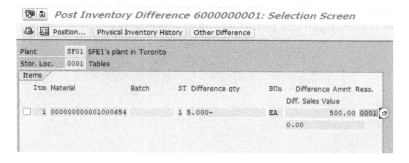

Figure 2: *Post Physical Inventory Difference – Selection Screen*

The difference can be posted as long as it is within the threshold value(absolute) entered. The inventory user can enter the reason for posting the difference.

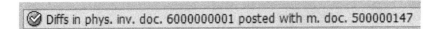

Figure 3: *Physical Inventory Difference posted message*

ii) Posting a document without a count document

In case the count is made without a physical count document, the inventory user can enter the count directly via transaction code MI10 which can be posted immediately if it is within allowed variance limits.

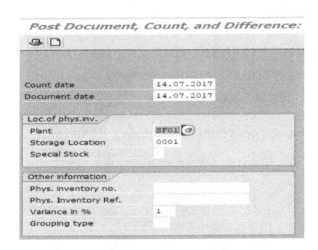

Figure 4: *Posting a Document – Required Information*

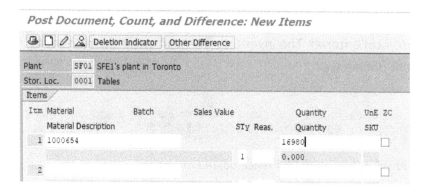

Post Document, Count, and Difference: New Items

| | | | | Deletion Indicator | Other Difference |

| Plant | SF01 SFE1's plant in Toronto |
| Stor. Loc. | 0001 Tables |

Items						
Itm Material		Batch	Sales Value		Quantity	UnE ZC
Material Description			STy Reas.	Quantity	SKU	
1 1000654					16980	☐
				1	0.000	
2						☐

Figure 5: *Posting a Document – Items*

Phys. inventory document 6000000002 posted without differences

5. Cycle Counting

Cycle counting is a method of physical inventory whereby inventory is counted at regular intervals within a fiscal year. Physical inventory may be required by financial accounting rules or tax regulations. Cycle counting process is less disruptive to operations. This process can be integrated in daily operations.

Cycle Counting allows us to count fast-moving items more frequently than slow-moving items.

i) Cycle Counting – Material Master indicator

The CC physical inventory indicator is set in the Plant data/storage 1 data of the material master.

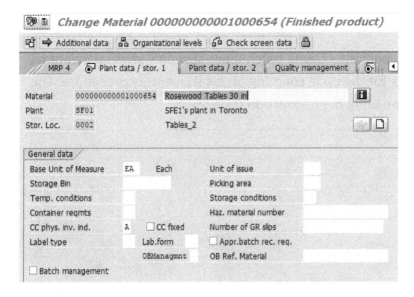

Figure 1: *Create Material – Plant data stor. 1*

ii) Execution/ process flow chart

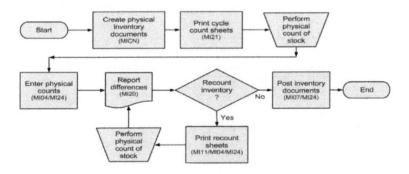

Figure 2: *Process chart flow*

The above chart shows the process flow of cycle counting. The various steps in the process flow are as described below.

iii) Create Physical Inventory Documents to Cycle Count

This report is to create batch input session's physical inventory documents for the cycle counting physical inventory procedure. This can be done using the transaction code MICN.

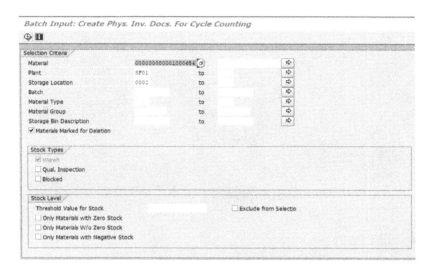

Figure 3: *Batch Input – Documents for Cycle counting*

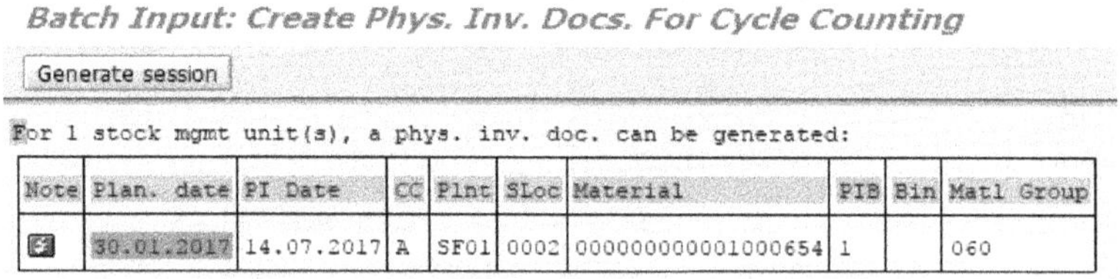

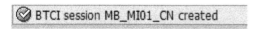

Figure 4: *Documents for Cycle counting*

BTCI session MB_MI01_CN created

Figure 5: *BTCI session Created message*

iv) Print Physical Inventory List

This can be done using the transaction code MI21.

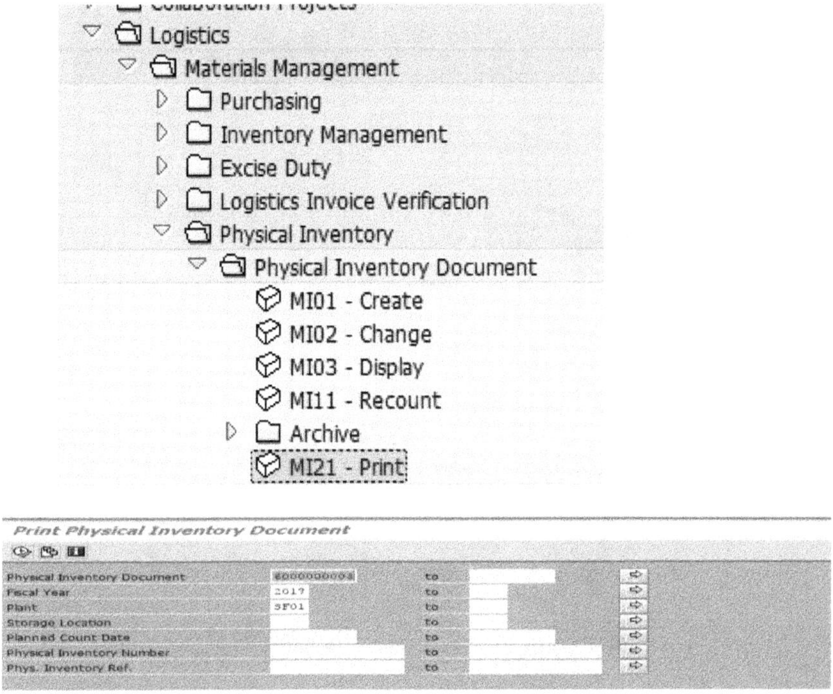

Figure 6: *Print Physical Inventory Document*

v) Physical inventory list

This transaction can be used as a working transaction for inventory administrators. User can use inventory reference number to group cycle counting document. This can be executed via t-code MI24.

In this transaction a user can enter count, monitor progress, run analysis and post counts.

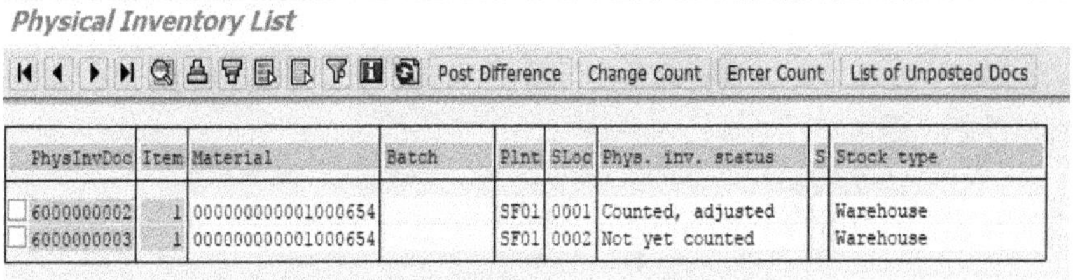

Figure 7: *Physical Inventory List*

For storage location 0002, we select it and press on `Enter Count` to enter inventory count for cycle counting (see Fig 7)

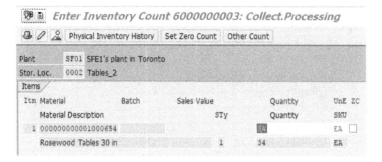

Figure 8: *Enter Inventory count – Collect Processing*

A warning message pops for difference in inventory.

> ① Qty counted for mat. 000000000001000654 differs from book inv. bal. by 1.000- EA

Figure 9: *Difference in inventory message*

The count can be accepted if inventory user believes it to be under tolerance limits.

> ⊘ Count entered for phys. inv. doc. 6000000003

Figure 10: *Count entered message*

Physical Inventory List

Post Difference | Change Count | Enter Count | List of Unposted Docs

PhysInvDoc	Item	Material	Batch	Plnt	SLoc	Phys. inv. status	S	Stock type
6000000002	1	000000000001000654		SF01	0001	Counted, adjusted		Warehouse
6000000003	1	000000000001000654		SF01	0002	Counted		Warehouse

Figure 11: *Physical Inventory List*

See the change in the status against storage location 0002. Now, we can post the document, using `Post Difference` button in Fig 11.

Post Inventory Difference: Initial Screen

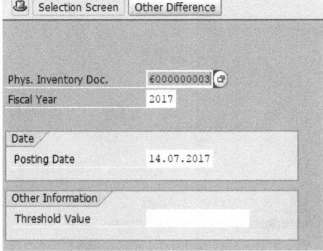

| Selection Screen | Other Difference |

Phys. Inventory Doc. 6000000003

Fiscal Year 2017

Date

Posting Date 14.07.2017

Other Information

Threshold Value

Figure 12: *Post Inventory Difference*

⊘ Diffs in phys. inv. doc. 6000000003 posted with m. doc. 500000148

PhysInvDoc	Item	Material	Batch	Plnt	SLoc	Phys. inv. status	S	Stock type
6000000002	1	000000000001000654		SF01	0001	Counted, adjusted		Warehouse
6000000003	1	000000000001000654		SF01	0002	Counted, adjusted		Warehouse

Figure 13: *Inventory Difference Document*

Notice the change in status of the document. This completes the cycle counting process.

ENTERING INITIAL STOCKS

The first step of materials management is to make initial stock available. We touched upon this section briefly in Material Master; here we will expand our knowledge of stocks. Most of the stock will ordinarily come from purchases or production with or without Quality Management; however at times of new system installation or inventory mismatches, sometimes direct stock entries are made. This initial stock can be made available through MB1C using movement type 561 as below. Different movement types have different roles to play, so all of them are not inter changeable. 561 is reserved for initial stocks w/o any reference of where they came from. As we will see in transaction MIGO later, another primary mvt type is 101 which posts stocks from procurement.

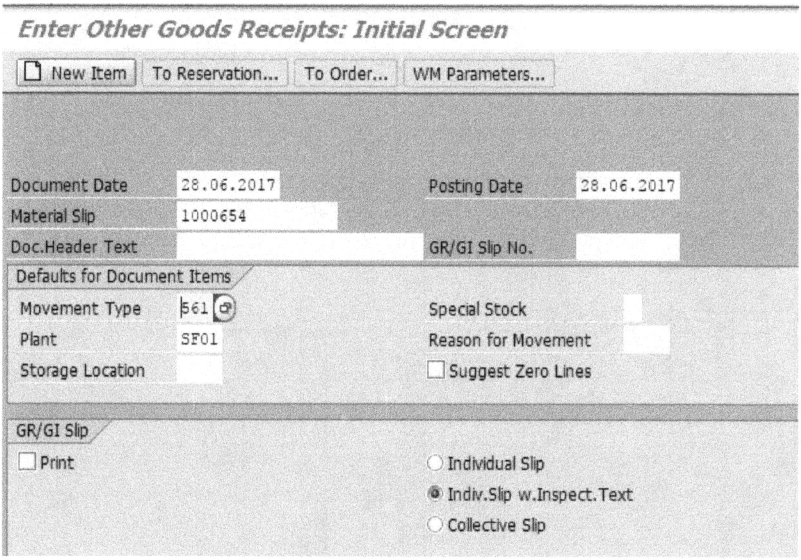

Enter Other Goods Receipts: Initial Screen

| New Item | To Reservation... | To Order... | WM Parameters... |

Document Date	28.06.2017	Posting Date	28.06.2017
Material Slip	1000654		
Doc.Header Text		GR/GI Slip No.	

Defaults for Document Items

Movement Type	561	Special Stock	
Plant	SF01	Reason for Movement	
Storage Location		☐ Suggest Zero Lines	

GR/GI Slip

☐ Print

○ Individual Slip
◉ Indiv.Slip w.Inspect.Text
○ Collective Slip

Figure 1: *Enter Other Goods Receipts*

Enter Other Goods Receipts: Collective Processing

| 🗋 ✏ 🔍 🖨 | To Reservation... | To Order... | To Purchase Order... |

Movement Type   561 GI entry of st. bals

Items

Item	Material	Quantity	UnE	SLoc	Batch	Re	Plnt
1	000000000001000654	10,000	EA	0001			SF01
2							SF01

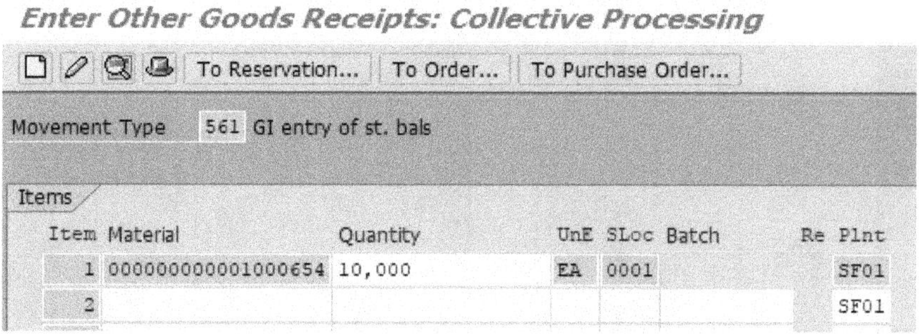

Figure 2: *Enter Other Goods Receipts – Collective Processing*

 Document 500000122 posted

Figure 3: *Document was posted message*

PROCURE TO PAY PROCESS CHART

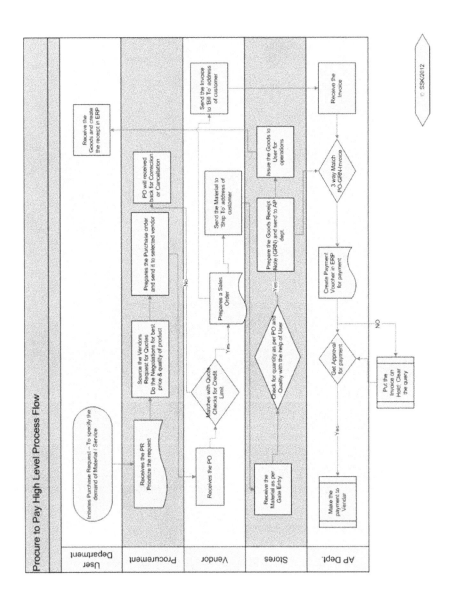

PROCUREMENT PROCESS

i) Purchase Requisition

Logistics -> Materials Management -> Purchasing -> Purchasing Requisition -> Create

Purchase requisition is the document which triggers the procurement cycle. It is the request that is made to the purchasing department to procure a certain list of materials. It may or may not be a requirement for creating POs depending on the kinds of products, company policies, complexity of business etc.

T- Code: ME51N

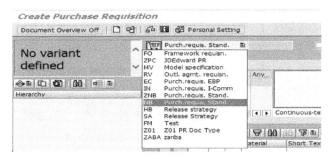

Figure 1: *Create Purchase Requisition*

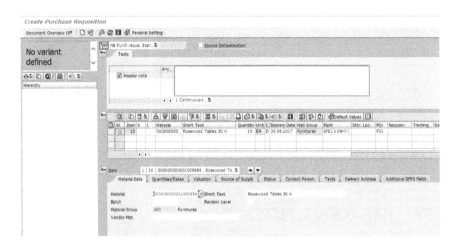

Figure 2: *Create Purchase Requisition*

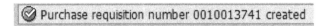

Figure 3: *Purchase Requisition created message*

ii) Request for Quotation

After, the list of requirements is made available to the purchasing department, the requirement is passed on to the vendors in the form of a purchase order or purchase schedules. However, if there is no identified vendor for a given material, the process of onboarding the vendor is initiated.

In this process, a list of vendors who supply the product with required specification at the best price is identified and screened. Then, a request is made to the vendors to submit their quotations indicating the price of the material along with their terms and conditions. This request is known as the request for quotation (RFQ).

A RFQ can be created manually or with reference to a purchase requisition. It can be created via t-code ME41 or via the following path: See figure 4

Logistics -> Materials Management -> Purchasing -> RFQ/Quotation -> Request for Quotation -> Create

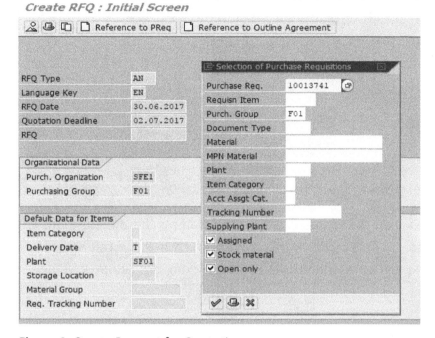

Figure 4: *Create Request for Quotation*

Enter the mandatory fields as mentioned above in the screenshot. Use the selection "Reference to PReq" to create the RFQ with reference to purchase requisition.

In the header data, the fields like quotation deadline date (date by which vendors must submit the quotation to be considered for bidding process) and Coll. No. (number which is used to group together and search the purchase requisition belonging to the same project) are specified.

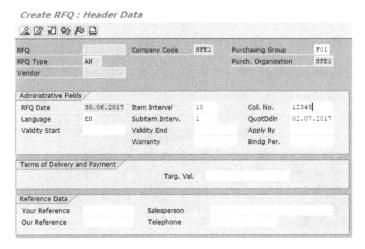

Create RFQ : Header Data

Figure 5: *Create Request for Quotation – Header Data*

Based on the values entered, the list of purchase requisitions is populated. The purchased requisition which is to be referenced is selected and entered into the RFQ by clicking on "Adopt + Details" button.

Create RFQ : Selection List: Purchase Requisitions

Pur. Req.	Item	Material	Short Text	Plnt	SLoc	I	A	Cls	Qty		Un	C	Delv. Date	Rel. Date	Fixed V.	S	Batch
10013741		000000000001000654	Rosewood Tables 30 in	SF01	0001				10.000	EA	D	30.06.2017	30.06.2017		K	

Figure 6: *Create Request for Quotation – Selection List*

Create RFQ : Item 00010

Item	10	ItCat.		Plant	SF01
Material	000000000001000654	Mat. Grp	060	Stor. Loc.	0001
Short Text	Rosewood Tables 30 in				

Quantity and Date

RFQ Quantity	10	EA	SubmDdln	02.07.2017
Delivery Date	D 03.07.2017			

Deadline Monitoring

1st Rem./Exped.		Reqt No.	
2nd Rem./Exped.		V. Mat.	
3rd Rem./Exped.			
No. Exped.	0		

Figure 7: *Create Request for Quotation – Item*

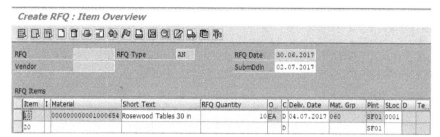

Create RFQ : Item Overview

Item	I	Material	Short Text	RFQ Quantity	O	C	Deliv. Date	Mat. Grp	Plnt	SLoc	D	Te
10		00000000001000654	Rosewood Tables 30 in	10	EA	D	04.07.2017	060	SF01	0001		
20						D			SF01			

Figure 8: *Create Request for Quotation – Item overview*

Once all the details have been entered, the purchase requisition is assigned the vendors whom it is intended to be sent to for the bidding process and saved.

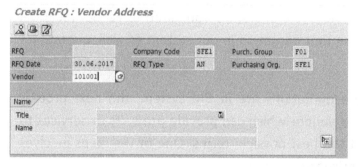

Create RFQ : Vendor Address

Figure 9: *Create Request for Quotation – Vendor Address*

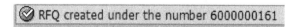

RFQ created under the number 6000000161

iii) Maintain and Compare Quotation

After the organization receives the quotation from the vendors before the deadline date, these quotations are entered in to the SAP system. This can be done using the transaction code ME47.

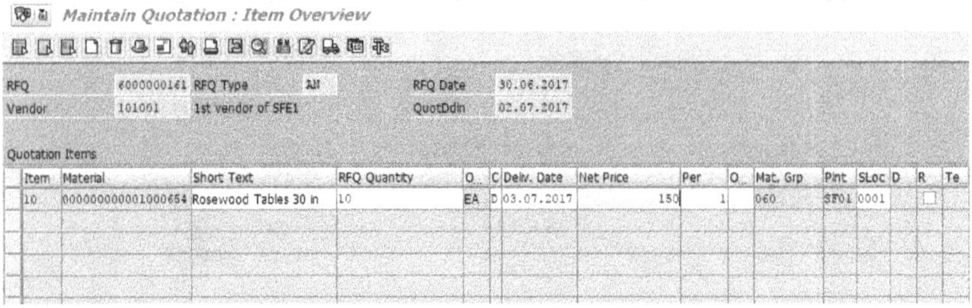

Item	Material	Short Text	RFQ Quantity	O.	C	Delv. Date	Net Price	Per	O.	Mat. Grp	Pint	SLoc	D	R	Te
10	00000000001000654	Rosewood Tables 30 in	10	EA	D	03.07.2017	150	1		060	SF01	0001	☐		

Figure 10*: Maintain Quotation*

⊘ Quotation for RFQ 6000000161 maintained

Figure 11: *Quotation Maintained created message*

Suppose, we receive a quotation from another vendor (101000) also. We maintain that quotation in our system as well, quotation - 6000000162.

Once all the quotations are in the system, the next process involves choosing vendor which can provide products or services to the company at the best possible terms. One of the steps involves comparing the prices of the quotations using transaction ME49.

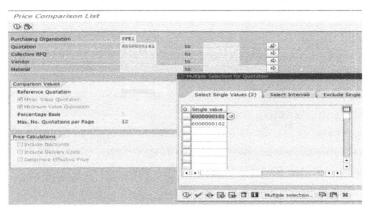

Figure 12: *Price Comparison List*

Price Comparison List in Currency CAD

Quotation | Material | Vendor | Additional Info

Material Sh. Text Qty. in Base Unit	Quot.: Bidder: Name:	6000000161 101001 1st vendor of SFE	6000000162 101000 Toronto Logistics	MEAN	MINIMUM
000000000001000654 Rosewood Tables 30 in 10 EA	Val.: Price: Rank:	1,500.00 150.00 1 92 %	1,750.00 175.00 2 108 %	1,625.00 162.50	1,500.00 150.00
Total Quot.	Val.: Rank:	1,500.00 1 92 %	1,750.00 2 108 %	1,625.00	1,500.00

Figure 13: *Price Comparison List Report*

As we can see above, the vendor 101001 is offering better prices for the product, after due assessment of other governing factors, they can be selected to supply the material.

PURCHASE ORDER

It is the commercial document provided by the purchasing department to the buyer specifying the material, their quantity and the negotiated prices for the materials and services which would be supplied by the vendor. A purchase order includes important information such as name of the material with its corresponding plant, details of purchasing organization with its company code, name of vendor, and date of delivery. In most legal systems, the Purchase order is the primary legal document in a business transaction.

It can be created via the t-code ME21N or via the following menu path:

Logistics -> Materials Management -> Purchasing -> Purchase Order -> Create

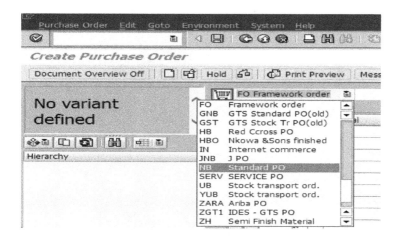

Figure 1: *Create Purchase Order*

A purchase order can be created manually or with reference to the preceding documents such as purchase requisition, request for quotation, scheduling agreement etc.

Here, we will create purchase order with reference to the request for quotation. For selecting, the option, click on ![icon] icon on left hand side of the screen and select the desired option.

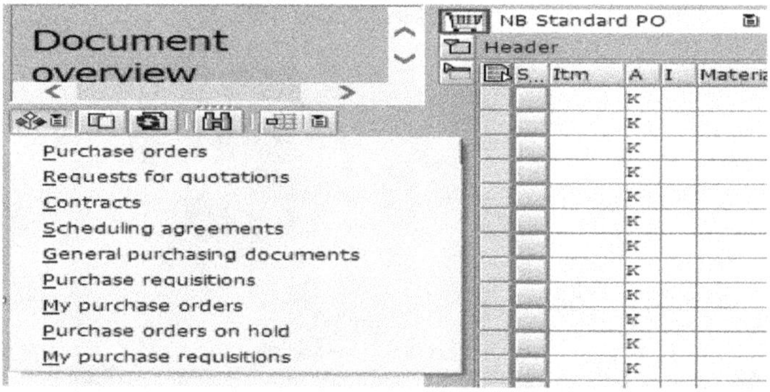

Figure 2: *Create Purchase Order options*

Once the option is selected from drop down, it direct to a screen where parameters for selecting the purchasing document is specified.

Purchasing Documents

General selections

Max. no. of hits	5000

Program selections

Material Number		to		⇨
Selection Parameters		to		⇨
Plant		to		⇨
Material Short Text		to		⇨
Supplying Plant		to		⇨
Storage Location		to		⇨

Figure 3: *Create Purchase Order – General Selections*

The value populated on the left side of the screen (as shown below) is populated based on our selection criteria. This document can be used by dragging and dropping it in the basket icon .

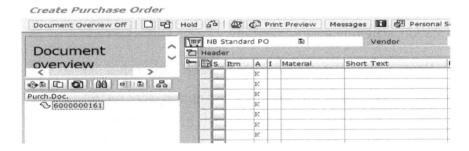

Figure 4: *Create Purchase Order – Document overview*

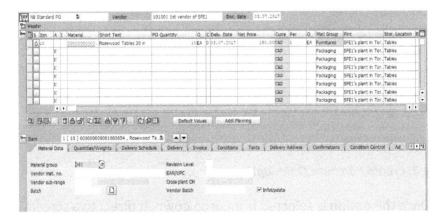

Figure 5: *Create Purchase Order*

Next, we need to maintain the account assignment data based on the value of the account assignment category. In our case, the account assignment category is standard, so we do not need to specify the cost center/GL account.

Thereafter, we should check the delivery tab to remove any discrepancies:

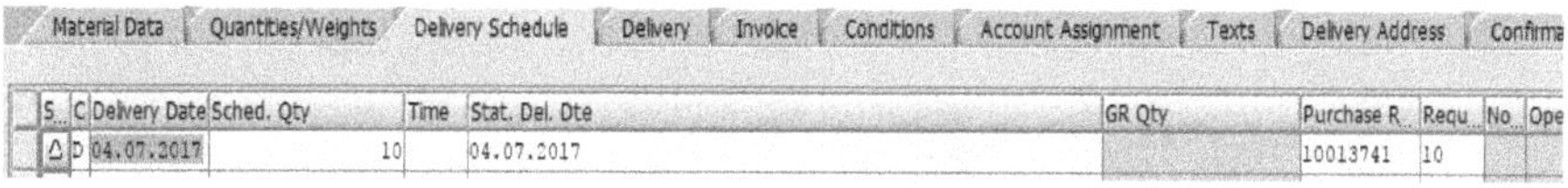

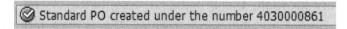

		Material Data	Quantities/Weights	Delivery Schedule	Delivery	Invoice	Conditions	Account Assignment	Texts	Delivery Address	Confirma
S.	C	Delivery Date	Sched. Qty		Time	Stat. Del. Dte		GR Qty		Purchase R	Requ	No	Ope
△	D	04.07.2017		10		04.07.2017				10013741	10		

Figure 6: *Create Purchase Order – Delivery Schedule Tab*

⊘ Standard PO created under the number 4030000861

Figure 7: *PO Created message*

POST GOODS RECEIPT

Once the goods have been dispatched by the vendor and they arrive at the delivery location, the process of acceptance of the materials by the customer is called goods receipt. This is reflected into SAP system by creating and posting a goods receipt document. This process can be executed via t-code MIGO or via the following menu path:

Logistics -> Materials Management -> Inventory management -> Goods movement -> Goods movement

Figure 1: *Goods Receipt Purchase Order*

Here, the option purchase order is selected from the drop-down menu. We need to specify the purchase order number and movement type based on our requirement. Movement type 101 is used for goods receipt into unrestricted stock.

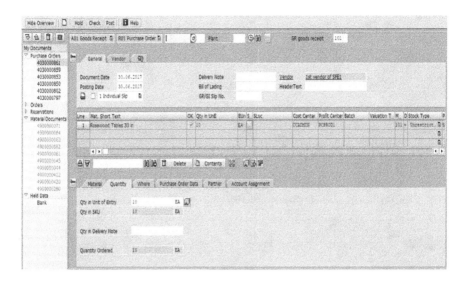

Figure 2: *Goods Receipt Purchase Order*

At the bottom of the screen, check Item OK:

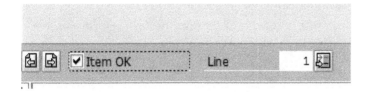

Figure 3: *Goods Receipt Purchase Order – Item OK checkbox*

After this, click on Check (top row in Fig 2) button confirm that the document is complete and can be posted. The message ✅ Document is O.K. pops up if there are no issues. Then, click on Post (top row in Fig 2) button to post the document.

Once the goods receipt is done, we can see the material document through transaction MB03.

Display Material Document: Initial Screen

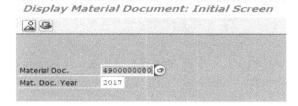

Material Doc.	4900000080
Mat. Doc. Year	2017

Figure 4: *Display Material Document*

Display Material Document 4900000080 : Overview

Details from Item | Material | Accounting Documents...

Posting Date	30.06.2017	Name	IDES018

Items

Item	Quantity	EUn	Material	Plnt	SLoc	PO	Item	S	DCI
		BUn	Material Description		Batch		R	MvI	S S
1	10	EA	000000000001000654	SF01	0001	4030000861	10		☑
			Rosewood Tables 30 in				101	+	

Figure 5: *Display Material Document - Overview*

By clicking on the Accounting Documents... (Fig 5) option on the top, we can view the associated accounting documents and G/L accounts to which the posting are made.

Display Document: Data Entry View

Display Currency | General Ledger View

Data Entry View

Document Number	5000000112	Company Code	SFE1	Fiscal Year	2017
Document Date	30.06.2017	Posting Date	30.06.2017	Period	6
Reference		Cross-CC no.			
Currency	CAD	Texts exist	☐	Ledger Group	

Co	Itm	PK	S	Account	Description	Amount	Curr.	Tx	Cost Center	Profit Center	Segment
SFE1	1	89		134000	Inventory - FG	1,000.00	CAD				
	2	96		211200	Gds Rcvd / Inv Rcvd	1,500.00-	CAD				
	3	86		530000	G/L Price Var	500.00	CAD				

Figure 6: *Display Material Document – Data Entry View*

As noticed above, SAP has calculated a price variant of CAD 500. This variance (+ or -) is the different of the cost of this product from this vendor and the actual cost of this material as maintained in the material master. The latter can be maintained based on standard cost (one determined cost entered by the user in the material master) or a variable cost (which is calculated based on weighted averages of that product bought from various vendors over a certain pre-determined period, to be calculated by costing runs, something out of scope of this book). Thus, if we dive into the accounting 1 screen, we notice the cost of this material to be 100 per 1 unit:

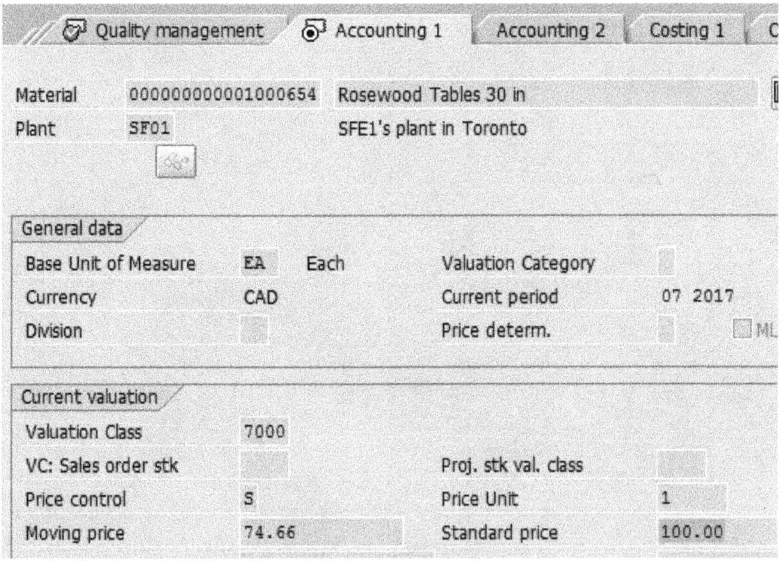

Figure 7: *Display Material – Accounting view*

Since the quantity is 10, the Inventory – FG is valued @ 100*10 = CAD 1,000

The goods received based on the PO are valued @ 1,500 based on the price in the PO:

Figure 8: *Purchase Order – Conditions Tab*

Thus, the variance of 500 (1,500-1,000). Since, in this case, we bought @ 1,500 while the standard price was 1,000, we actually made a 'loss' of 500 by buying form this vendor. As a user we must have a good handle on these price variances to enable better decision making.

INVOICE RECEIPT

Unlike Goods receipt MIGO which is primarily performed by the purchasing dept., Invoice receipt, t-code MIRO is done by Finance/Accounting as this is SAP's equivalent of booking of vendor invoices for AP based on how the vendor master data is set up.

To explain this process, we will continue working with the same PO. Since MIGO had already occurred, Purchasing has freed up this transaction for FI to take over to book the vendor invoice when it is available against the same PO we did MIGO against – we will use the highlighted line below:

Item		1 [10] 001000656 , Cedarwood							

Sh.	MvT	Material Doc	Item	Posting Date Σ	Quantity	Delivery cost quantity	OUn Σ	Amount in LC	L.cur Σ
WE	101	4900000375	1	07.06.2016	150	0	KG	1,500.00	CAD
WE	102	4900000374	1	04.06.2016	100-	0	KG	1,000.00-	CAD
WE	101	4900000373	1	04.06.2016	200	0	KG	2,000.00	CAD
WE	101	4900000372	1	04.06.2016	100	0	KG	1,000.00	CAD
Tr./Ev. Goods receipt			■		350		KG ■	3,500.00	CAD ■
RE-L		5105608953	2	05.06.2016	200	0	KG	2,000.00	CAD
Tr./Ev. Invoice receipt			■		200		KG ■	2,000.00	CAD ■

Figure 1: *Purchase Order History*

For the purpose of this demo we will assume the vendor submits the invoice equal to the PO we created which is more than the actual Goods received. Go to screen for t-code MIRO or follow the path below and enter the Invoice date, amount of the vendor invoice and the PO number as below and Hit Enter:

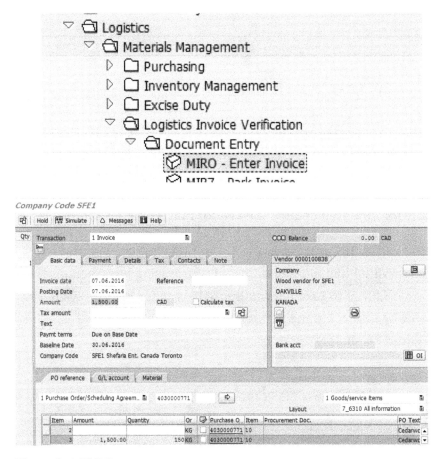

Figure 2: *MIRO Screen*

Select the line as above against which this payment has been made and post it by clicking Save. We can choose multiple lines also to post against the same vendor invoice if the invoice is for multiple deliveries.

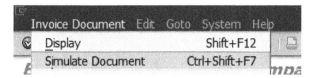

Figure 3: *Invoice Document options*

Figure 4: *Document Simulation*

It tells us that the vendor will be credited and the GR/IR account debited for the same amounts.

Since it looks good, we can go back to the previous screen and save the document or post it directly from the simulation screen via the Post button at the bottom left:

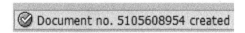

Figure 5: *Post button*

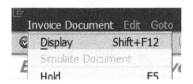

Figure 6: *Document created message*

We can view this document by:

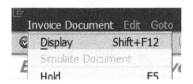

Figure 7: *Invoice Document options*

Or in transaction MIR4: See figure 8

Figure 8: *MIR4 - View*

Click on the tab

to see the details of the actual accounting document:

Data Entry View									
Document Number	5100000001		Company Code	SFE1		Fiscal Year	2016		
Document Date	07.06.2016		Posting Date	07.06.2016		Period	6		
Reference			Cross-CC no.						
Currency	CAD		Texts exist			Ledger Group			

Co.	Itm	PK	S	Account	Description	Amount	Curr.	Tx	Cost Cent
SFE1	1	31		100838	Wood vendor for SFE1	1,500.00-	CAD	00	
	2	86		211200	Gds Rcvd / Inv Rcvd	1,500.00	CAD	00	

Figure 9: *Accounting Document*

Note that it credited the vendor and cleared the amount in 211200 with a debit which had earlier been credited when we did the MIGO (goods receipt).

This amount should now show up in the accounts payable to this vendor which we can look up via t-code FBL1N:

	S	Document	Doc. Type	Doc. Date	ᵗ	DD	Σ	Amount in doc. curr.	Curr.	Clng doc.	PayT	Curr. cash disc. amt	Disc.1	Day1	Day2	Net	DD
	☼	1900000002	KR	10.05.2016		⎙		1,100.00-	CAD		0003	22.00-	2.000	14	30	45	⎙
	☼	1900000004	KR	28.05.2016		⎙		1,450.00-	CAD		0003	30.81-	2.125	14	30	45	⎙
	☼	1900000011	KR	28.05.2016		⎙		1,230.00-	CAD		0003	26.14-	2.125	14	30	45	⎙
	☼	1900000017	KR	20.01.2016		⎙		12,800.00-	CAD		0001	0.00	0.000	0	0	0	⎙
	☼	1900000019	KR	20.01.2016		⎙		1,400.00-	CAD		0001	0.00	0.000	0	0	0	⎙
	☼	1900000020	KR	25.01.2016		⎙		2,300.00-	CAD		0001	0.00	0.000	0	0	0	⎙
	☼	1900000029	KR	10.05.2016		⎙		2,000.00-	CAD		0003	40.00-	2.000	14	30	45	⎙
	☼	5100000000	RE	04.06.2016		⎙		2,000.00-	CAD		0008	0.00	0.000	0	0	0	⎙
	☼	5100000001	RE	07.06.2016		⎙		1,500.00-	CAD		0008	0.00	0.000	0	0	0	⎙
	☼	5100000002	RE	07.06.2016		⎙		100.00-	CAD		0008	0.00	0.000	0	0	0	⎙
						*		25,880.00-	CAD								
	Account 100838					**		25,880.00-	CAD								
						***		25,880.00-	CAD								

Figure 10: *Vendor Line Item Display*

EVALUATED INVOICE RECEIPT (ERS)

Often there can be vendors whose payments are required to be sent directly from accruals or after goods have been received i.e. the company does not wait for the vendor to submit the actual invoices for the goods or services. SAP has a concept of Evaluated Invoice Receipt (ERS) to enable this. The pre-requisite for this is the check on 2 fields in the vendor master in Purchasing data:

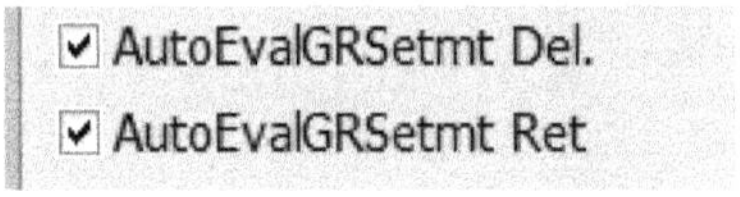

- ☑ AutoEvalGRSetmt Del.
- ☑ AutoEvalGRSetmt Ret

Figure 1: *pre-requisite Checked field*

Alternatively, this check can be put in the PO on the line item invoice tab at time of creation or modification. In MM there are purchase info records that are material specific settings, and they over ride what is in the vendor master – in the PIR, we must also ensure that the indicator – No ERS – is NOT set else that will over ride this setting.

The Goods receipt must exist before this GR can be converted into a payable. Let us do a GR (MIGO) against an existing PO: See figure 2

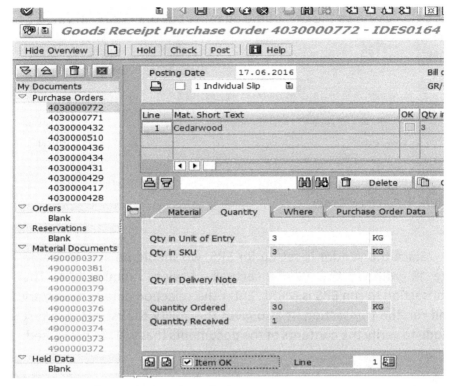

Figure 2: *Goods Receipt Purchase Order*

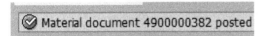

Figure 3: *Material Posted message*

The PO shows the GRs of the quantity but there is no IR yet.

Sh..	MvT	Material Doc	Item	Posting Date	Σ	Quantity	Delivery cost quantity	OUn	Σ	Amount in LC	L.cur	
WE	101	4900000382	1	17.06.2016		3	0	KG		30.00	CAD	
WE	101	4900000378	1	07.06.2016		1	0	KG		10.00	CAD	
Tr./Ev. Goods receipt						4		KG		40.00	CAD	

Figure 4: *Purchase Order*

Since the vendor is set up for ERS, we should be able to create the IR without the vendor actually having submitted it. The transaction to run ERS is MRRL. Enter the selection data as necessary and run the transaction. It also gives the ability to first run it in test mode to verify the contents of the documents that will get processed:

Evaluated Receipt Settlement (ERS) with Logistics Invoice Verification

Document Selection

Company Code	SFE1	to	
Plant		to	
Posting Date of Goods Receip		to	
Goods Receipt Document		to	
Fiscal Year of Goods Receipt		to	
Vendor	100838	to	
Purchasing Document		to	
Item		to	

Processing Options

Doc. selection	3	Document selection per order item
Test Run	☑	
☐ Settle Goods Items + Planned Delivery Costs		

Figure 5: *Evaluated Receipt Settlement*

Execute to view in this test mode and we find the lines of our PO along with some others are ready to create IRs:

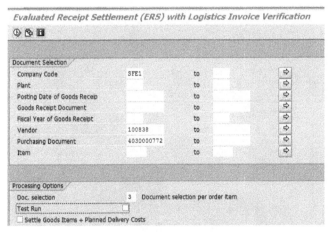

	Pstable	Vendor	Ref. Doc.	FYrRef	Rflt	Purch.Doc.	Item	Reference	Doc. N	Ye	InfoTe	FI Doc.	DC	B/Lac
	X	100838	4900000372	2016	1	4030000771	10							
	X	100838	4900000373	2016	1		10							
	X	100838	4900000375	2016	1		10							
	X	100838	4900000376	2016	1		10							
	X	100838	4900000377	2016	1		10							
	X	100838	4900000381	2016	1		10							
	X	100838	4900000378	2016	1	4030000772	10							
	X	100838	4900000382	2016	1		10							

Figure 6: *Evaluated Receipt Settlement*

The X indicator in the Postable field means this line item will get posted when not run in test mode. The field Info text blank is an indicator that all is well with this line. Any error would have got reflected in this field.

Now we can go back and remove the test flag and post it by executing again. If we want to restrict only to one PO, we can enter that in the selection criteria also and post only for that:

Document Selection

Company Code	SFE1	to
Plant		to
Posting Date of Goods Receip		to
Goods Receipt Document		to
Fiscal Year of Goods Receipt		to
Vendor	100838	to
Purchasing Document	4030000772	to
Item		to

Processing Options

Doc. selection	3	Document selection per order item
Test Run		
Settle Goods Items + Planned Delivery Costs		

Figure 7: *Evaluated Receipt Settlement*

This time, it gives the actual Invoice doc # and the FI document #:

Pstable	Vendor	Ref. Doc.	FYrRef	RfIt	Purch.Doc.	Item	Reference	Inv. Doc. No.	Year	InfoText	FI Doc.	D
X	100838	4900000378	2016	1	4030000772	10		5105608960	2016		5100000006	
	100838	4900000382	2016	1	4030000772	10		5105608960	2016		5100000006	

Figure 8: *Evaluated Receipt Settlement*

The PO history will now reflect this number:

Item 1 [10] 000000000001000656 , Cedarwood

Material Data | Quantities/Weights | Delivery Schedule | Delivery | Invoice | Conditions | Purchase Order History | Te

Sh..	MvT	Material Doc.	Item	Posting Date	Σ	Quantity	Delivery cost quantity	OUn	Σ	Amount in LC	L.cur	Σ	Qty i
WE	101	4900000382	1	17.06.2016		3	0	KG		30.00	CAD		
WE	101	4900000378	1	07.06.2016		1	0	KG		10.00	CAD		
Tr./Ev. Goods receipt					▪	**4**		**KG**	▪	**40.00**	**CAD**	▪	
RE-L		5105608960	1	17.06.2016		1	0	KG		10.00	CAD		
RE-L		5105608960	2	17.06.2016		3	0	KG		30.00	CAD		
Tr./Ev. Invoice receipt					▪	**4**		**KG**	▪	**40.00**	**CAD**	▪	

Figure 9: *Purchase Order History*

As will the AP of the vendor in FBL1N:

Vendor 100838
Company Code SFE1
Name Wood vendor for SFE1
City Oakville

Document	Doc. Type	Doc. Date	Amount in doc. curr.	Curr.	Clrng doc.	PayT	Curr. cash disc. amt	Disc.1	Day1	Day2	Net
1900000002	KR	10.05.2016	1,100.00-	CAD		0003	16.50-	2.000	14	30	45
1900000004	KR	28.05.2016	1,450.00-	CAD		0003	30.81-	2.125	14	30	45
1900000011	KR	28.05.2016	1,230.00-	CAD		0003	26.14-	2.125	14	30	45
1900000017	KR	20.01.2016	12,800.00-	CAD		0001	0.00	0.000	0	0	0
1900000019	KR	20.01.2016	1,400.00-	CAD		0001	0.00	0.000	0	0	0
1900000020	KR	25.01.2016	2,300.00-	CAD		0001	0.00	0.000	0	0	0
1900000029	KR	10.05.2016	2,000.00-	CAD		0003	30.00-	2.000	14	30	45
5100000000	RE	04.06.2016	2,000.00-	CAD		0008	0.00	0.000	0	0	0
5100000001	RE	07.06.2016	1,500.00-	CAD		0008	0.00	0.000	0	0	0
5100000002	RE	07.06.2016	100.00-	CAD		0008	0.00	0.000	0	0	0
5100000003	RE	11.06.2016	120.00-	CAD		0008	0.00	0.000	0	0	0
5100000004	RE	11.06.2016	6,280.00-	CAD		0008	0.00	0.000	0	0	0
5100000005	RE	11.06.2016	6,280.00	CAD		0008	0.00	0.000	0	0	0
5100000006	RE	17.06.2016	40.00-	CAD		0008	0.00	0.000	0	0	0
			26,040.00-	**CAD**							
Account 100838			**26,040.00-**	**CAD**							
			26,040.00-	**CAD**							

Figure 10: *Vendor Line Item Display*

Reversing an ERS is done by creating a credit memo via MIRO. The GR can also be reversed after that if necessary.

For example, if we now want to reverse this ERS, in MIRO, we choose:

Figure 11: *Enter Incoming Invoice – Transaction option*

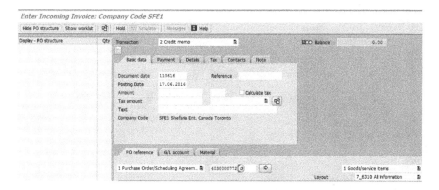

Figure 12: *Enter Incoming Invoice – Reverse IR with Credit Memo*

Enter the amount in the Amount column that is being reversed, Hit Enter and the 2 lines against which we have the IR will come up. Choose one for partial or both for total reversal.

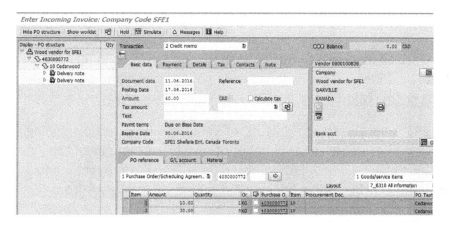

Figure 13: *Enter Incoming Invoice – Choose lines to be reversed for IR*

We have the option to select only one and reverse only that amount or if we just save this, it will reverse both:

✅ Document no. 5105608961 created

Figure 14: *Document created*

If we go back to the PO, we find that the IR has been reversed: See figure 15:

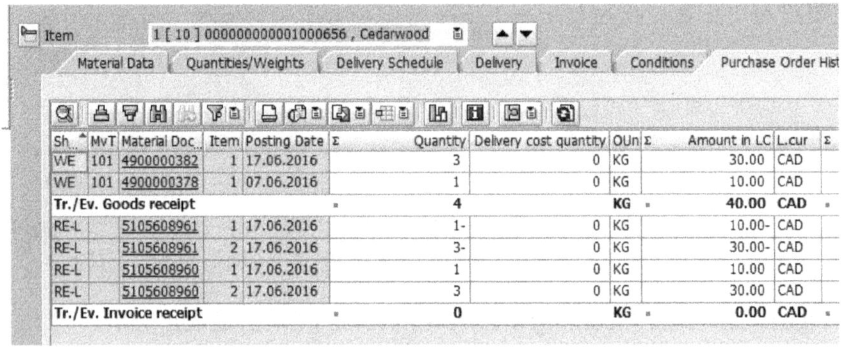

| Item | 1 [10] 000000000001000656 , Cedarwood |

| Material Data | Quantities/Weights | Delivery Schedule | Delivery | Invoice | Conditions | Purchase Order Hist |

Sh	MvT	Material Doc	Item	Posting Date Σ	Quantity	Delivery cost quantity	OUn Σ	Amount in LC	L.cur	Σ
WE	101	4900000382	1	17.06.2016	3	0	KG	30.00	CAD	
WE	101	4900000378	1	07.06.2016	1	0	KG	10.00	CAD	
Tr./Ev. Goods receipt				■	4		KG ■	40.00	CAD	■
RE-L		5105608961	1	17.06.2016	1-	0	KG	10.00-	CAD	
RE-L		5105608961	2	17.06.2016	3-	0	KG	30.00-	CAD	
RE-L		5105608960	1	17.06.2016	1	0	KG	10.00	CAD	
RE-L		5105608960	2	17.06.2016	3	0	KG	30.00	CAD	
Tr./Ev. Invoice receipt				■	0		KG ■	0.00	CAD	■

Figure 15: *Purchase Order*

As has the AP in FBL1N: See figure 16

	5100000006	RE	17.06.2016		40.00-	CAD	0008	0.00	0.000	0	0	0		0.00	0.000
	5100000007	RE	11.06.2016		40.00	CAD	0008	0.00	0.000	0	0	0		0.00	0.000
					26,000.00-	CAD									

Figure 16: *Reversal in FBL1N*

Once an IR done via ERS has been reversed, SAP no longer allows ERS to be done on it again. It has to be now posted manually only via MIRO not via MRRL.

ERS is very useful to post AP of vendors who provide shipping services; in most cases the number of invoices is large even though amounts may be small. ERS comes in very handy to prevent manual work and can be run as background jobs to post the AP from the accruals of shipment costs and other service costs.

OTHER TYPES OF PURCHASE ORDERS

Procurement can be done for various types of goods and services. Procurement starts with creating a purchase order that is a formal document given to vendors and it includes the list of goods and materials that are to be procured. So, accordingly a purchase order can be created for different types of procurement. The type of procurement can be maintained in a field that is known as item category as shown below.

Figure 1: *Create Purchase Order*

For different procurement types, there are four types of purchase orders listed below:

- Subcontracting Purchase Order
- Consignment Purchase Order
- Stock Transfer Purchase Order
- Service Purchase Order

i) Subcontracting Purchase Order

In this process, the vendor (subcontractor) receives the components for producing the product from the ordering party. The components required for producing the ordered product are listed in the purchase order and provided to the subcontractor.

The item category for creating subcontracting purchase order is L.

Figure 2: *Create Purchase Order*

Then we can enter the components required for the product by clicking on ![Components] button (Material data tab in figure 2).

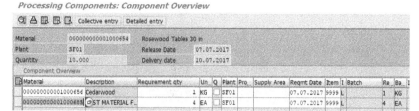

Figure 3: *Processing Components*

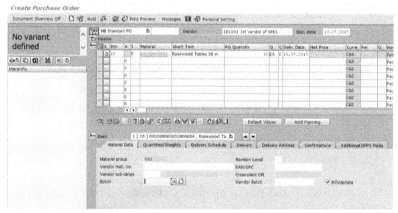

Figure 4: *Purchase Order created message*

> Standard PO created under the number 4030000871

Figure 4: *Purchase Order created message*

ii) Consignment Purchase Order

In consignment process, the material is available at the customer premises but the ownership is with the vendor. To consume materials from the consignment stock, purchase order must be raised. The item category used for consignment purchase order is K.

Figure 5: *Create Purchase Order*

> Standard PO created under the number 4030000872

Figure 6: *Purchase Order created message*

iii) Stock Transfer order

In stock transfer, goods are procured and supplied within the same company code. One plant orders the goods internally from another plant. The goods are procured with a special type of purchase order known as the stock transport order. The item category used for stock transfer order is U and PO type to be used is UB.

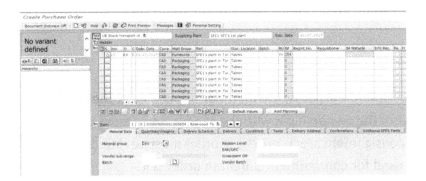

Figure 7: *Create Purchase Order*

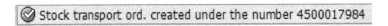

Figure 8: Stock Transport Order created message

iv) Service Purchase Order

Under this process, third party provides service to the company. The PO usually used for this is also called a Framework PO or a standing PO or an Open PO. The PO type is FO. These services can be like electricity, water, maintenance, oiling of machines etc. These services are availed through a service purchase order. The item category used for service purchase order is D. The PO is usually given a validity period normally the financial year but can be anything.

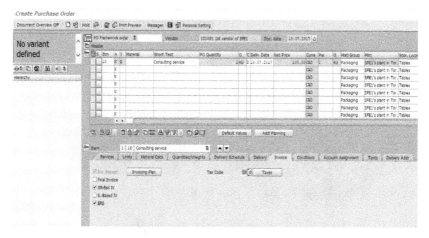

Figure 9: *Create Purchase Order*

In this case, we need to specify the service name (short text), material number is not required.

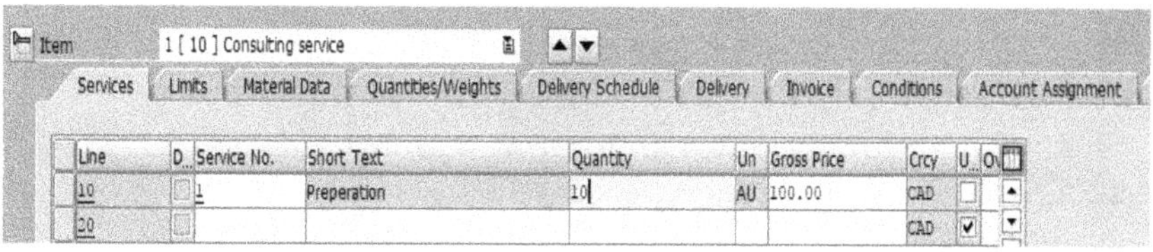

Figure 10: *Create Purchase Order – Service Tab*

Also, the cost center for the services must be assigned in the account assignment tab (Fig 10).

In the limits tab, we can enter the limit for unplanned services. When these limits get depleted as the year passes, SAP will give an error relating to the value exhaustion or validity period exhaustion.

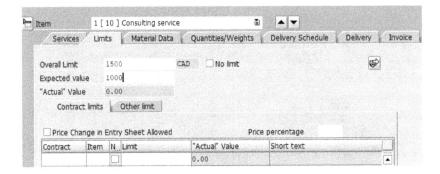

Figure 11: *Create Purchase Order – Limits Tab*

After that choose the Delivery tab and uncheck the Goods Receipt check box. Services do not have goods receipt as they are not relevant for inventory management (they don't have stock).

Figure 12: *Create Purchase Order – Delivery Tab*

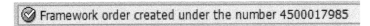

Figure 13: *Order Created message*

POSTING INCOMING UNDER/OVER PAYMENTS WITH AND W/O DISCOUNTS

For posting these payments, we must have our over/under and discount G/Ls in place along with employee tolerances set up in configuration. We can see the effects of the same via actual postings.

i) Effect of tolerance limits

For purpose of training, our tolerance limits on this demo system are $100 - deviation of more than $100 either way is considered out of limits for us to post.

Let us try to post an incoming payment *outside of tolerance limits* from a customer in t-code F-28:

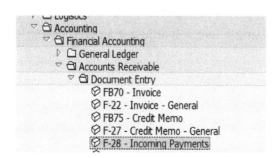

Figure 1: *Incoming Payments*

Ensure that account type D comes pre-entered. If not, enter it as 'D' – D represents customers. Enter the rest of the data on this familiar screen – Bank G/L account, amount, posting date, document date, value date, customer # etc:

Post Incoming Payments: Header Data

Process open items

Document Date	200516	Type	DZ	Company Code	SFE1
Posting Date	20.05.2016	Period	5	Currency/Rate	CAD
Document Number				Translatn Date	
Reference				Cross-CC no.	
Doc.Header Text				Trading part.BA	
Clearing text					

Bank data

Account	107000	Business Area	
Amount	1500	Amount in LC	
Bank charges		LC bank charges	
Value date		Profit Center	
Text		Assignment	

Open item selection

			Additional selections	
Account	601256		⦿ None	
Account Type	D	☐ Other accounts	○ Amount	
Special G/L ind		☑ Standard OIs	○ Document Number	
Pmnt advice no.			○ Posting Date	
☐ Distribute by age			○ Dunning Area	
☐ Automatic search			○ Others	

Figure 2: *Post Incoming Payments – Header Data*

Again, to select the appropriate line against which this amount needs to be adjusted (in our example, we will adjust it against line 3:

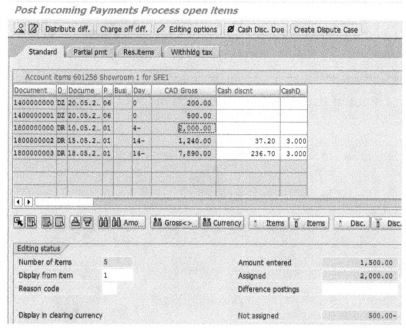

Figure 3: *Post Incoming Payments – Process Open Items*

Note the *Not assigned* amount, the difference of the actual and the amount being posted. This amount needs to now be posted to the under payment account as the customer has underpaid us by this amount. To verify if it will work, simulate the document:

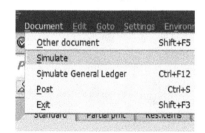

Figure 4: *Post Incoming Payments – Document options*

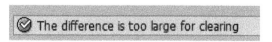

Figure 5: *Simulation error message*

This means we have not told SAP what to do with the difference of and it being outside of the employee's tolerance limits that we defined earlier to be only $100, it will not post automatically. We do have the option to post it as partial payment and throwing this difference amount back into the customer's AR.

ii) Posting an amount within the tolerance limits

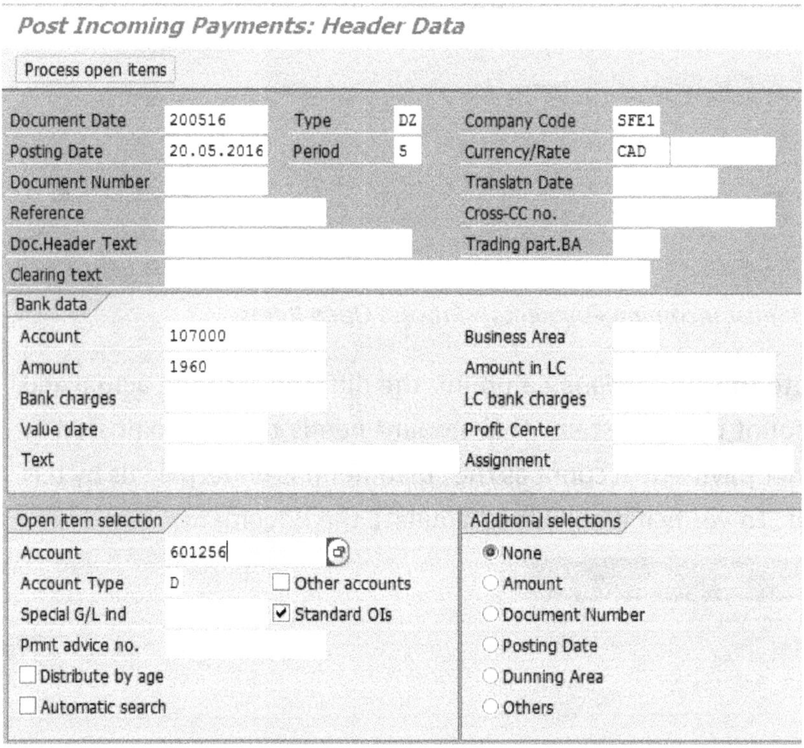

Post Incoming Payments: Header Data

Process open items

Document Date	200516	Type	DZ	Company Code	SFE1
Posting Date	20.05.2016	Period	5	Currency/Rate	CAD
Document Number				Translatn Date	
Reference				Cross-CC no.	
Doc.Header Text				Trading part.BA	
Clearing text					

Bank data

Account	107000	Business Area	
Amount	1960	Amount in LC	
Bank charges		LC bank charges	
Value date		Profit Center	
Text		Assignment	

Open item selection

Account	601256	
Account Type	D	☐ Other accounts
Special G/L ind		✔ Standard OIs
Pmnt advice no.		
☐ Distribute by age		
☐ Automatic search		

Additional selections

- ◉ None
- ○ Amount
- ○ Document Number
- ○ Posting Date
- ○ Dunning Area
- ○ Others

Figure 6: *Post Incoming Payments – Header Data*

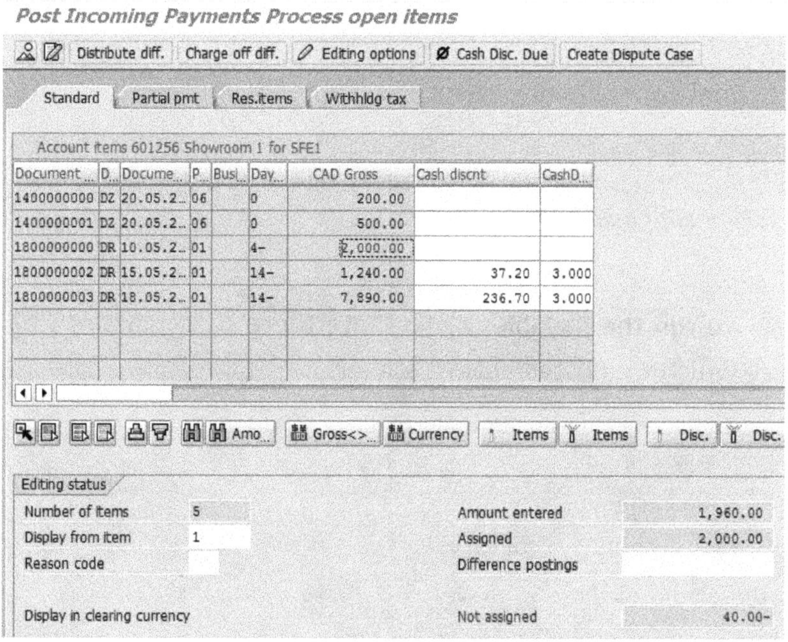

Figure 7: *Post Incoming Payments – Process Open Items*

When we try to simulate it this time, we find SAP determined the difference to post to the underpayment account from configuration as it is within $100:

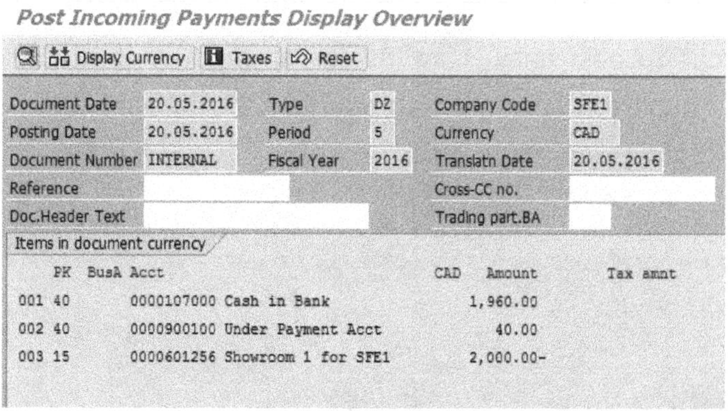

Figure 8: *Post Incoming Payments – Display Overview*

Had there been any cash discounts associated with this, it would have first posted to that cash discount and then the remaining balance (subject to being a max of $100, to this underpayment

319

account).

We can now post the document:

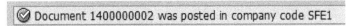
✅ Document 1400000002 was posted in company code SFE1

Figure 9: *Document posted*

When we run the payables again, note there is no balance for this invoice which we posted against earlier:

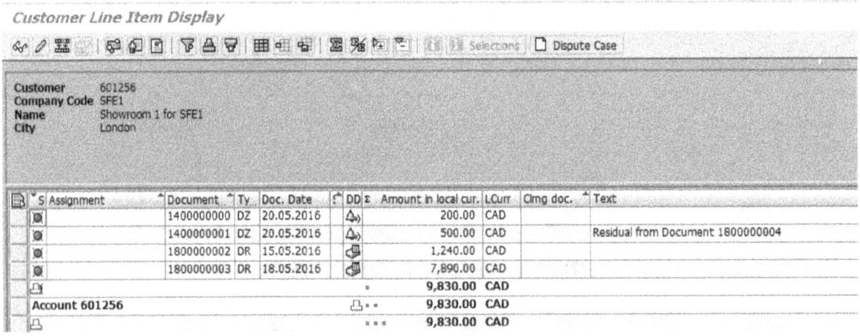

Customer Line Item Display

S	Assignment	Document	Ty	Doc. Date	DD	Σ	Amount in local cur.	LCurr	Clrng doc.	Text
		1400000000	DZ	20.05.2016			200.00	CAD		
		1400000001	DZ	20.05.2016			500.00	CAD		Residual from Document 1800000004
		1800000002	DR	15.05.2016			1,240.00	CAD		
		1800000003	DR	18.05.2016			7,890.00	CAD		
						*	9,830.00	CAD		
	Account 601256					**	9,830.00	CAD		
						***	9,830.00	CAD		

Customer 601256
Company Code SFE1
Name Showroom 1 for SFE1
City London

Figure 10: *Customer Line Item Display*

iii) Overpayment with cash discount

Let us attempt to post against an invoice an amount that will leave a difference more than the max permissible after the applicable cash discount is applied. See figure 11

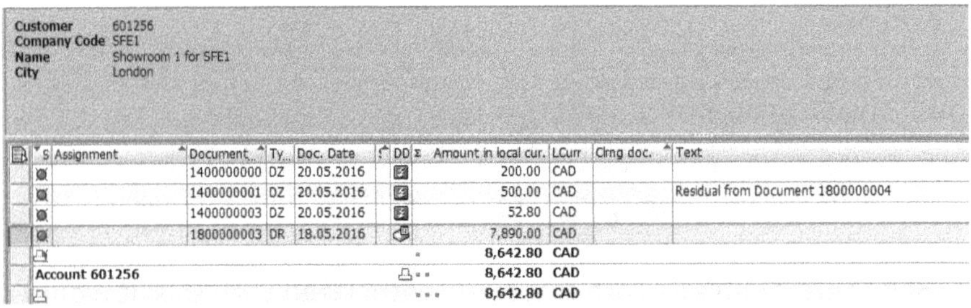

Customer 601256
Company Code SFE1
Name Showroom 1 for SFE1
City London

S	Assignment	Document	Ty	Doc. Date	DD	Σ	Amount in local cur.	LCurr	Clrng doc.	Text
		1400000000	DZ	20.05.2016			200.00	CAD		
		1400000001	DZ	20.05.2016			500.00	CAD		Residual from Document 1800000004
		1400000003	DZ	20.05.2016			52.80	CAD		
		1800000003	DR	18.05.2016			7,890.00	CAD		
						*	8,642.80	CAD		
	Account 601256					**	8,642.80	CAD		
						***	8,642.80	CAD		

Figure 11: *Customer Line Item Display*

Post Incoming Payments: Header Data

Process open items

Document Date	250516	Type	DZ	Company Code	SFE1
Posting Date	25.05.2016	Period	5	Currency/Rate	CAD
Document Number				Translatn Date	
Reference				Cross-CC no.	
Doc.Header Text				Trading part.BA	
Clearing text					

Bank data

Account	107000	Business Area	
Amount	7900	Amount in LC	
Bank charges		LC bank charges	
Value date		Profit Center	
Text		Assignment	

Open item selection

Account	601256
Account Type	D ☐ Other accounts
Special G/L ind	☑ Standard OIs
Pmnt advice no.	
☐ Distribute by age	
☐ Automatic search	

Additional selections

- ⦿ None
- ○ Amount
- ○ Document Number
- ○ Posting Date
- ○ Dunning Area
- ○ Others

Figure 12: *Post Incoming Payments – Header Data*

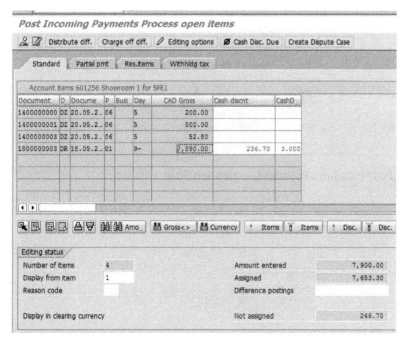

Post Incoming Payments Process open items

Distribute diff. | Charge off diff. | ⟋ Editing options | Ø Cash Disc. Due | Create Dispute Case

Standard | Partial pmt | Res.items | Withhldg tax

Account items 601256 Showroom 1 for SFE1

Document	D	Docume	P	Busi	Day	CAD Gross	Cash discnt	CashD.
1400000000	DZ	20.05.2...	06		5	200.00		
1400000001	DZ	20.05.2...	06		5	500.00		
1400000003	DZ	20.05.2...	06		5	52.80		
1800000003	DR	18.05.2...	01		9-	7,890.00	236.70	3.000

◀ ▶

🔍 📋 📑 📇 🖨 🔍 🔍 Amo. | Gross<> | Currency | ↑ Items | ⟱ Items | ↑ Disc. | ⟱ Disc.

Editing status

Number of Items	4	Amount entered	7,900.00
Display from item	1	Assigned	7,653.30
Reason code		Difference postings	
Display in clearing currency		Not assigned	246.70

Figure 13: *Post Incoming Payments – Process Open Items*

When we try to simulate this:

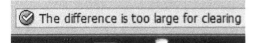

Figure 14: *Simulation error message*

Once again, the difference being over the employee tolerance we have defined, we cannot post this over payment.

We reduce the amount that is being paid so that the not assigned amount is reduced to under the tolerance: See figure 15

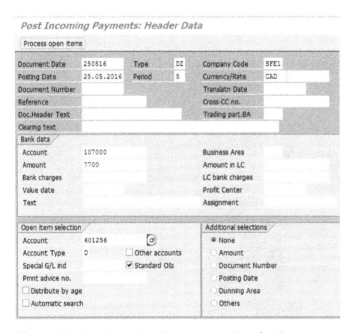

Post Incoming Payments: Header Data

Process open items				
Document Date	250516	Type	DZ	Company Code	SFE1
Posting Date	25.05.2016	Period	5	Currency/Rate	CAD
Document Number				Translatn Date	
Reference				Cross-CC no.	
Doc.Header Text				Trading part.BA	
Clearing text					

Bank data

Account	107000		Business Area	
Amount	7700		Amount in LC	
Bank charges			LC bank charges	
Value date			Profit Center	
Text			Assignment	

Open item selection			Additional selections	
Account	601256		◉ None	
Account Type	D	☐ Other accounts	○ Amount	
Special G/L ind		☑ Standard OIs	○ Document Number	
Pmnt advice no.			○ Posting Date	
☐ Distribute by age			○ Dunning Area	
☐ Automatic search			○ Others	

Figure 15: *Post Incoming Payments – Header Data*

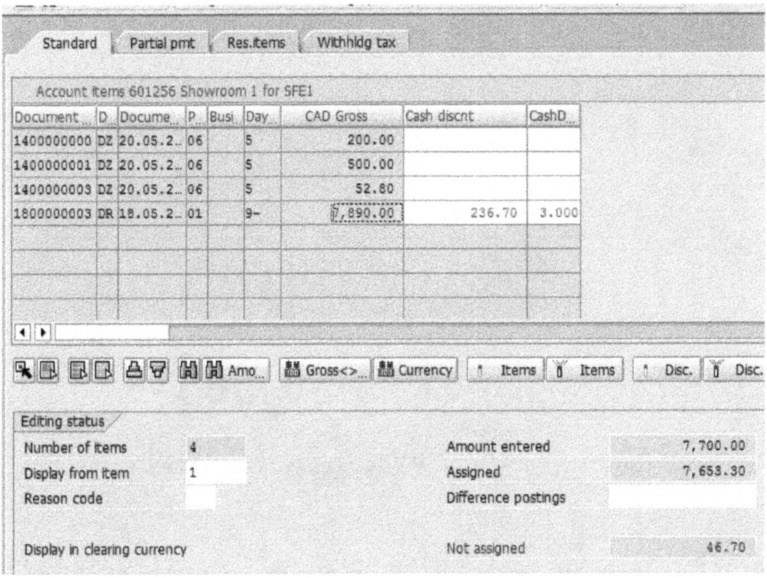

Figure 16: *Post Incoming Payments – Process Open Items*

We notice the unassigned difference after adjusting the cash discount is being posted to the over payment account

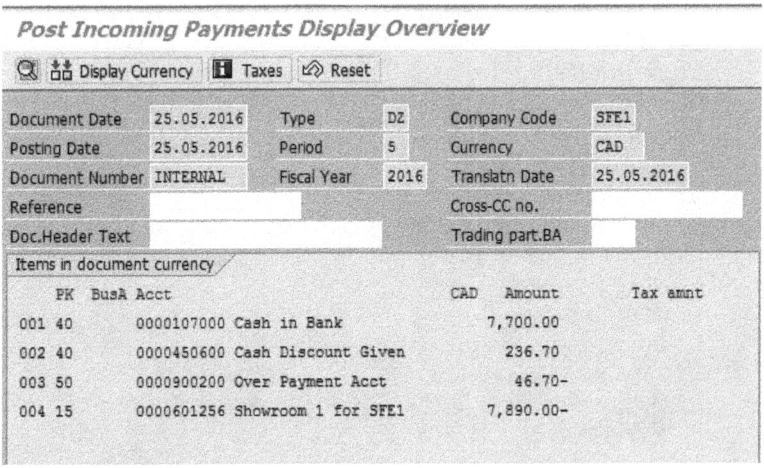

Figure 17: *Post Incoming Payments – Display Overview*

Figure 18: *Document posted message*

POSTING OUTGOING UNDER/OVER PAYMENTS WITH AND W/O DISCOUNTS

Let us now post an outgoing payment to a vendor within tolerance limits using F-53:

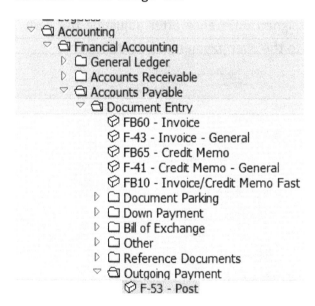

Figure 1: *Post Outgoing Payment*

i) Effect of tolerance limits

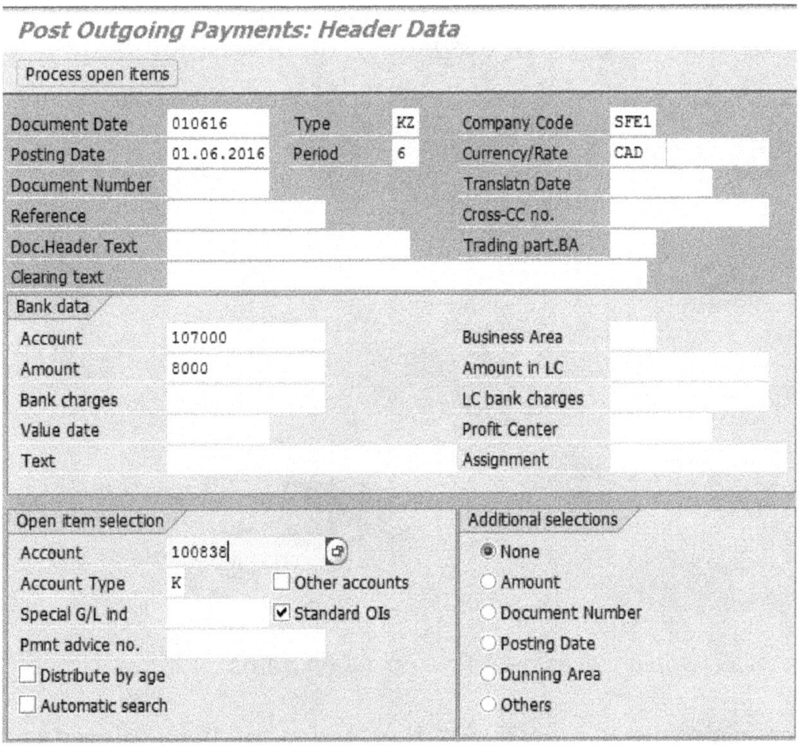

Post Outgoing Payments: Header Data

Process open items					
Document Date	010616	Type	KZ	Company Code	SFE1
Posting Date	01.06.2016	Period	6	Currency/Rate	CAD
Document Number				Translatn Date	
Reference				Cross-CC no.	
Doc.Header Text				Trading part.BA	
Clearing text					

Bank data

Account	107000	Business Area	
Amount	8000	Amount in LC	
Bank charges		LC bank charges	
Value date		Profit Center	
Text		Assignment	

Open item selection

Account	100838	
Account Type	K	☐ Other accounts
Special G/L ind		☑ Standard OIs
Pmnt advice no.		
☐ Distribute by age		
☐ Automatic search		

Additional selections

- ◉ None
- ○ Amount
- ○ Document Number
- ○ Posting Date
- ○ Dunning Area
- ○ Others

Figure 2: *Post Outgoing Payment – Header Data*

Click on __Process open items__ (Fig 2) and the vendor's open line items come up in the next screen:

Post Outgoing Payments Process open items

Distribute diff. | Charge off diff. | Editing options | Cash Disc. Due

Standard | Partial pmt | Res.items | Withhldg tax

Account items 100838 Wood vendor for SFE1

Document ...	D...	Docume...	P...	Busi...	Day...	CAD Gross	Cash discnt	CashD...
1900000000	KR	10.05.2...	31		12-	1,500.00-	30.00-	2.000
1900000001	KR	10.05.2...	31		12-	1,200.00-	24.00-	2.000
1900000002	KR	10.05.2...	31		12-	1,100.00-	22.00-	2.000
1900000004	KR	28.05.2...	31		28-	1,450.00-	30.81-	2.125
1900000011	KR	28.05.2...	31		28-	1,230.00-	26.14-	2.125
1900000016	KR	10.01.2...	31		143	8,500.00-		
1900000017	KR	20.01.2...	31		133	12,800.00-		
1900000018	KR	15.01.2...	31		138	4,500.00-		

Amo... | Gross<>... | Currency | Items | Items | Disc. | Disc

Editing status

Number of items	10	Amount entered	8,000.00-
Display from item	1	Assigned	35,847.05-
Reason code		Difference postings	
Display in clearing currency		Not assigned	27,847.05

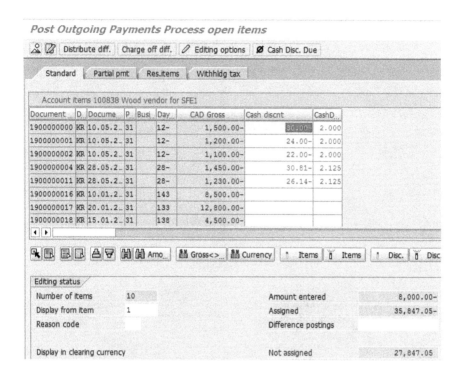

Figure 3: *Post Outgoing Payment – Process Open Items*

Once again, this is reflective of the vendor line item balance in FBL1N:

Vendor 100838
Company Code SFE1
Name Wood vendor for SFE1
City Oakville

S	Document	Doc. Type	Doc. Date	DD	Amount in doc. curr.	Curr.	Clrng doc.	PayT	Curr. cash disc. amt	Disc.1	Day1	Day2	Net	DD	Discount amount	Disc.2
	1900000000	KR	10.05.2016		1,500.00-	CAD		0003	30.00-	2.000	14	30	45		0.00	1.500
	1900000001	KR	10.05.2016		1,200.00-	CAD		0003	24.00-	2.000	14	30	45		0.00	1.500
	1900000002	KR	10.05.2016		1,100.00-	CAD		0003	22.00-	2.000	14	30	45		0.00	1.500
	1900000004	KR	28.05.2016		1,450.00-	CAD		0003	30.81-	2.125	14	30	45		0.00	1.500
	1900000011	KR	28.05.2016		1,230.00-	CAD		0003	26.14-	2.125	14	30	45		0.00	1.500
	1900000016	KR	10.01.2016		8,500.00-	CAD		0001	0.00	0.000	0	0	0		0.00	0.000
	1900000017	KR	20.01.2016		12,800.00-	CAD		0001	0.00	0.000	0	0	0		0.00	0.000
	1900000018	KR	15.01.2016		4,500.00-	CAD		0001	0.00	0.000	0	0	0		0.00	0.000
	1900000019	KR	20.01.2016		1,400.00-	CAD		0001	0.00	0.000	0	0	0		0.00	0.000
	1900000020	KR	25.01.2016		2,300.00-	CAD		0001	0.00	0.000	0	0	0		0.00	0.000

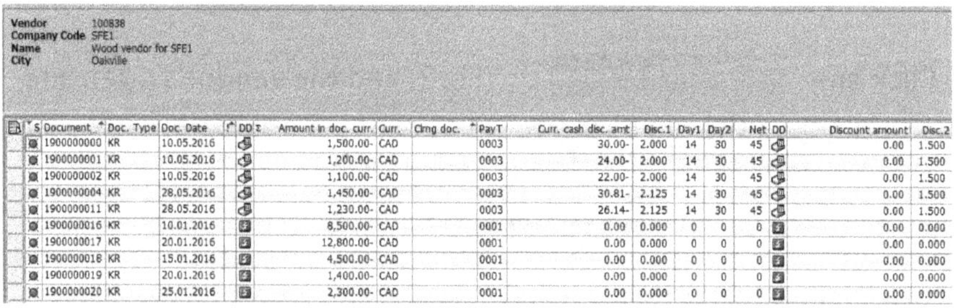

Figure 4: *Vendor Line Item Display*

As always, select, deactivate and activate the line we will post against, here the line that does not have a discount available for early payments:

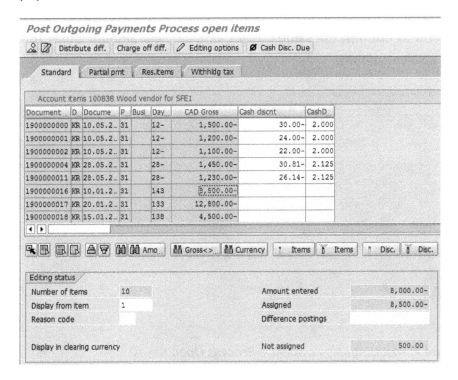

Figure 5: *Post Outgoing Payment – Process Open Items*

Since we are paying a lesser amount than the amount of the invoice, this must be an under payment. Let us confirm by trying to simulate the document:

Figure 6: *Simulation message*

The above message tells us we don't have the authorization to post this document because the difference between the vendor's invoice and the payment we are making is more than what we are authorized for.

ii) Posting an amount within the tolerance limits

Let us attempt the same posting with a bigger amount closer to the invoice amount:

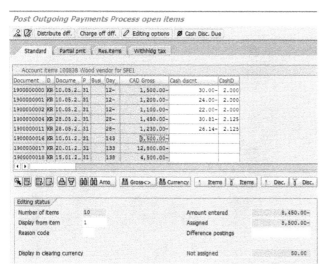

Figure 7: *Post Outgoing Payment – Process Open Items*

Similate the posting:

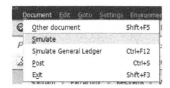

Figure 8: *Document options*

Post Outgoing Payments Display Overview

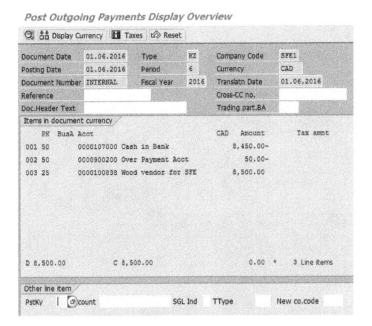

Figure 9: *Post Outgoing Payment – Simulation*

We see the difference is being posted to the over payment account as a credit (posting key 50) to the over payment account it determined from the configuration. This is counter intuitive – it hits the over payment account because it is a 'profit' to the customer.

Post the document and the vendor's payable report clears this document completely:

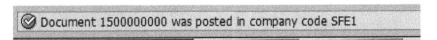

Figure 10: *Document posted message*

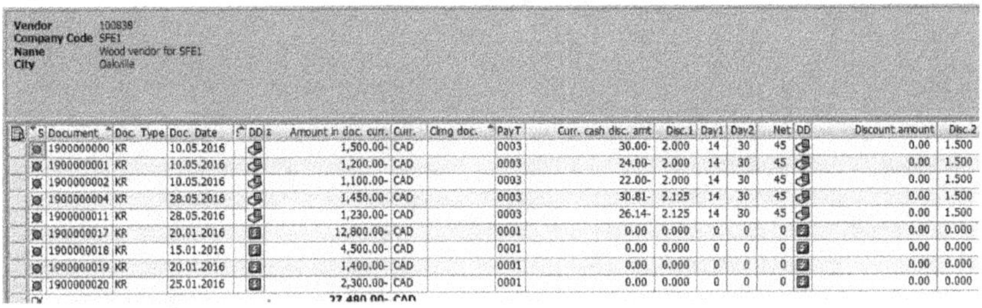

Figure 11: *Vendor Line Item Display*

iii) Overpayment with cash discount

In F-53 enter the amount we will pay the vendor:

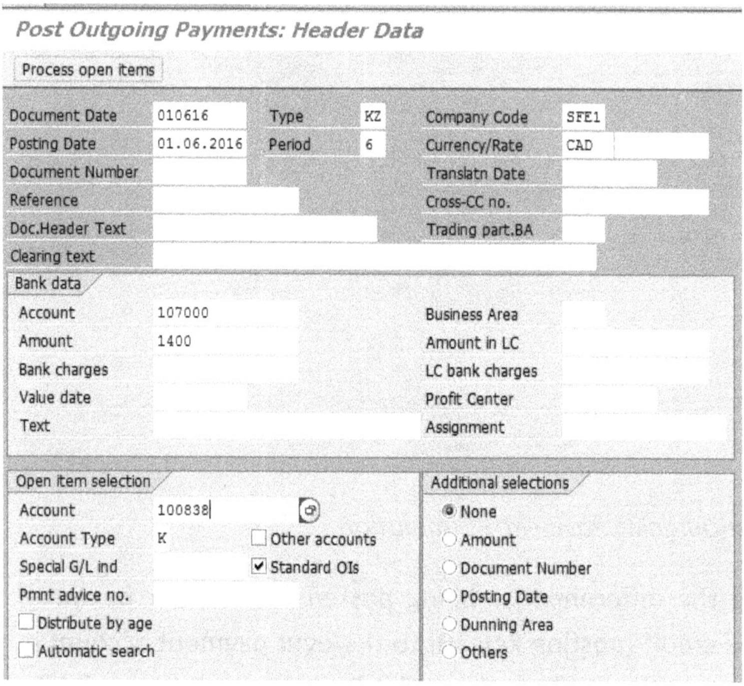

Post Outgoing Payments: Header Data

Process open items

Document Date	010616	Type	KZ	Company Code	SFE1
Posting Date	01.06.2016	Period	6	Currency/Rate	CAD
Document Number				Translatn Date	
Reference				Cross-CC no.	
Doc.Header Text				Trading part.BA	
Clearing text					

Bank data

Account	107000	Business Area	
Amount	1400	Amount in LC	
Bank charges		LC bank charges	
Value date		Profit Center	
Text		Assignment	

Open item selection

Account	100838
Account Type	K
Special G/L ind	
Pmnt advice no.	
☐ Distribute by age	
☐ Automatic search	

☐ Other accounts
☑ Standard OIs

Additional selections

◉ None
◯ Amount
◯ Document Number
◯ Posting Date
◯ Dunning Area
◯ Others

Figure 12: *Post outgoing payment – Header Data*

Process Open Items:

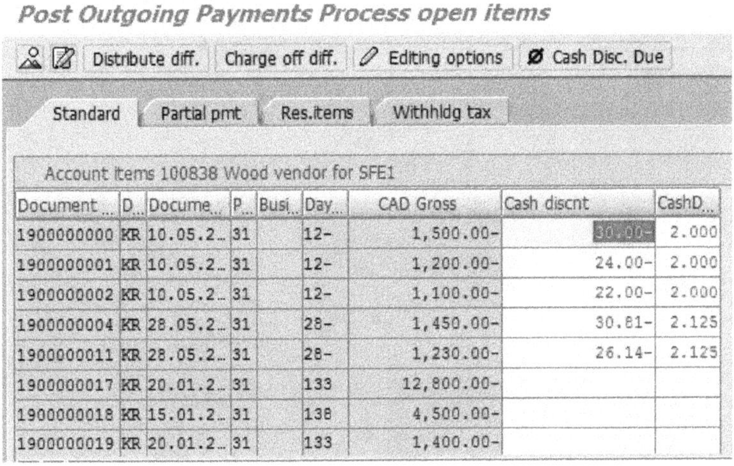

Document ...	D...	Docume...	P...	Busi...	Day...	CAD Gross	Cash discnt	CashD...
1900000000	KR	10.05.2...	31		12-	1,500.00-	30.00-	2.000
1900000001	KR	10.05.2...	31		12-	1,200.00-	24.00-	2.000
1900000002	KR	10.05.2...	31		12-	1,100.00-	22.00-	2.000
1900000004	KR	28.05.2...	31		28-	1,450.00-	30.81-	2.125
1900000011	KR	28.05.2...	31		28-	1,230.00-	26.14-	2.125
1900000017	KR	20.01.2...	31		133	12,800.00-		
1900000018	KR	15.01.2...	31		138	4,500.00-		
1900000019	KR	20.01.2...	31		133	1,400.00-		

Figure 13: *Post outgoing payment – Process open Items*

Let us assume the first invoice as in figure 14 is being paid off with this amount of $1,400 The invoice is $1,500 and since we are paying within 30 days, as per the terms, we are also entitled to a cash discount of 2 % = $30.

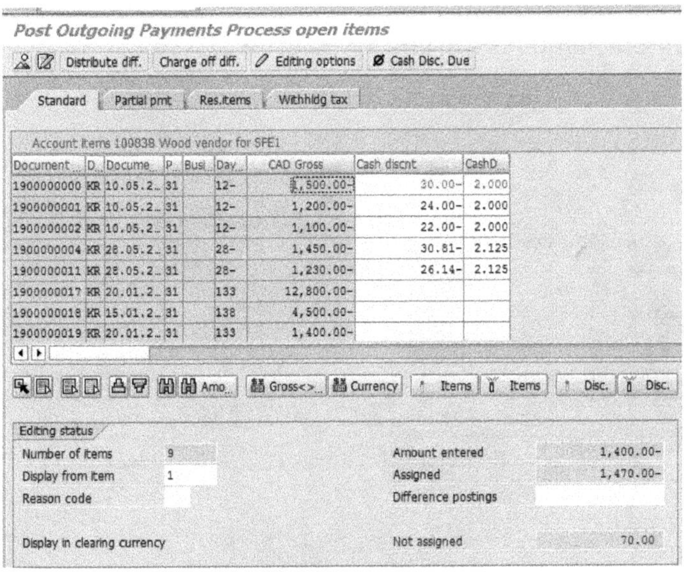

Document ...	D...	Docume...	P...	Busi...	Day...	CAD Gross	Cash discnt	CashD...
1900000000	KR	10.05.2...	31		12-	1,500.00-	30.00-	2.000
1900000001	KR	10.05.2...	31		12-	1,200.00-	24.00-	2.000
1900000002	KR	10.05.2...	31		12-	1,100.00-	22.00-	2.000
1900000004	KR	28.05.2...	31		28-	1,450.00-	30.81-	2.125
1900000011	KR	28.05.2...	31		28-	1,230.00-	26.14-	2.125
1900000017	KR	20.01.2...	31		133	12,800.00-		
1900000018	KR	15.01.2...	31		138	4,500.00-		
1900000019	KR	20.01.2...	31		133	1,400.00-		

Figure 14: *Post outgoing payment – Process open Items*

The Not Assigned amount of $70.00 will then be required to post to the over payment account. Let us simulate this event:

Post Outgoing Payments Display Overview

Document Date	01.06.2016	Type	KZ	Company Code	SFE1
Posting Date	01.06.2016	Period	6	Currency	CAD
Document Number	INTERNAL	Fiscal Year	2016	Translatn Date	01.06.2016
Reference				Cross-CC no.	
Doc.Header Text				Trading part.BA	

Items in document currency

PK	BusA	Acct		CAD Amount	Tax amnt
001	50	0000107000	Cash in Bank	1,400.00-	
002	50	0000460600	Cash Discount Taken	30.00-	
003	50	0000900200	Over Payment Acct	70.00-	
004	25	0000100838	Wood vendor for SFE	1,500.00	

Figure 15: *Post outgoing payment – Process open Items*

Post:

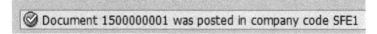

✅ Document 1500000001 was posted in company code SFE1

Figure 16: *Document posted message*

The AP statement removes the line all together:

Vendor	100838
Company Code	SFE1
Name	Wood vendor for SFE1
City	Oakville

S	Document	Doc. Type	Doc. Date	DD Σ	Amount in doc. curr.	Curr.	Clrng doc.	PayT	Curr. cash disc. amt	Disc.1	Day1	Day2	Net
	1900000001	KR	10.05.2016		1,200.00-	CAD		0003	24.00-	2.000	14	30	45
	1900000002	KR	10.05.2016		1,100.00-	CAD		0003	22.00-	2.000	14	30	45
	1900000004	KR	28.05.2016		1,450.00-	CAD		0003	30.81-	2.125	14	30	45
	1900000011	KR	28.05.2016		1,230.00-	CAD		0003	26.14-	2.125	14	30	45
	1900000017	KR	20.01.2016		12,800.00-	CAD		0001	0.00	0.000	0	0	0
	1900000018	KR	15.01.2016		4,500.00-	CAD		0001	0.00	0.000	0	0	0
	1900000019	KR	20.01.2016		1,400.00-	CAD		0001	0.00	0.000	0	0	0
	1900000020	KR	25.01.2016		2,300.00-	CAD		0001	0.00	0.000	0	0	0
					25,980.00-	CAD							
	Account 100838				25,980.00-	CAD							
					25,980.00-	CAD							

Figure 17: *Vendor Line Item Display*

INVOICE CORRECTION

Occasionally, we will have a situation when taxes were charged on an invoice when the customer was actually nontaxable due to their status and/or location or any other reason. If the invoice was created in the current open period, then the simplest way is to cancel and re-create a correct one without taxes. However this may not always be the case as such things often come to light only when the invoices become due for payment later. In SAP there is a process called 'invoice correction' whereby for the existing closed transaction we can re-do an invoice by netting off only the taxes if the period in which the original document was posted, is now closed.

Let's say we have an invoice on which we charged taxes in the highlighted invoice below. See figure 1

Customer	601256
Company Code	SFE1
Name	Showroom 1 for SFE1
City	London

	S	Assignment	Document...	Ty...		DD	Posting Date	Σ	Amount in local cur.	LCurr
			90036713	RV			08.06.2016		2,568.00	CAD
			90036719	RV			15.05.2016		160.50	CAD
			1400000003	DZ			20.05.2016		52.80	CAD
			1400000007	DZ			04.06.2016		50.00	CAD

Figure 1: *Customer Line Item Display*

Document Number	90036719	Company Code	SFE1	Fiscal Year	20:
Document Date	15.05.2016	Posting Date	15.05.2016	Period	5
Reference	0090036719	Cross-CC no.			
Currency	CAD	Texts exist	☐	Ledger Group	

Co	Itm	PK	S	Account	Description	Amount	Curr.	Tx	Co:
SFE1	1	01		601256	Showroom 1 for SFE1	160.50	CAD	09	
	2	50		451011	Revenue Stream 1	150.00-	CAD	09	
	3	50		216450	VAT A/R (Output)	10.50-	CAD	09	

Figure 2: *Display Document - Data Entry View*

The customer was in fact nontaxable and so will pay only the net amount instead of with taxes so we need to adjust the tax amount in SAP. One way of course, is to simply post a manual JE for this amount. However, since the transaction has actually originated from the SD side in SAP, the correct procedure would also be to originate the correction from SD. Besides, often tax authorities and auditors do not like to see manual JEs.

To originate this from SD, we create an order of type RK in transaction VA01 wrt this invoice: See figure 3

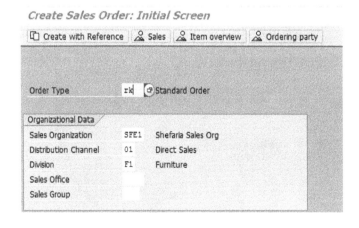

Figure 3: *Create Sales Order*

Click on ▢ Create with Reference (See Fig 3) and enter the reference invoice as below:

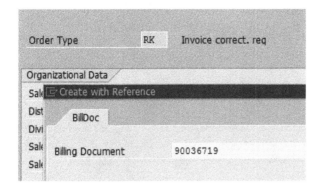

Figure 4: *Create Sales Order – Create with Reference*

Click on Copy:

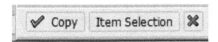

Figure 5: *Create Sales Order – Copy button*

We find that SAP pulls in 2 lines, one positive value and the other negative:

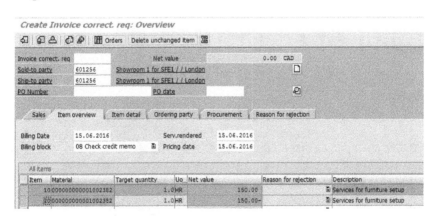

Figure 6: *Create Invoice correct. Req - Overview*

Left as it is, the system will create an invoice of 0 value. However, since we need to post a credit entry only for the taxes, we need to change the tax indicators at the line item level for the 2nd line on this order under the Billing tab (See figure 7). Note that SAP will not allow us to change anything on the first line anyway as that is a copy of what already occurred in the invoice and is thus, greyed out.

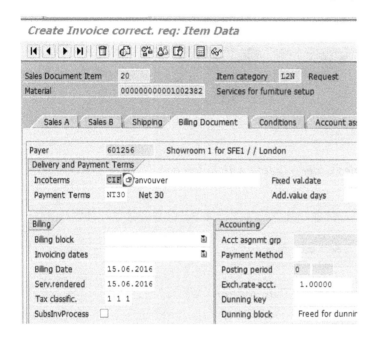

Figure 7: *Create Invoice correct. Req - Item Data*

The indicators in the Tax Classification fields need to be made to 0 as below:

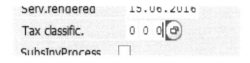

Figure 8: *Create Invoice correct. Req - Tax Classific field*

Since this is a credit, it requires us to enter an Order Reason on the main screen:

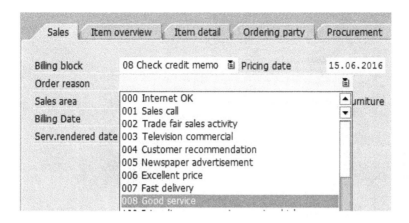

Figure 9: *Order reason*

Any reason can be given or a new one configured for such cases. We will also need to remove the Billing block we see in the print above and then bill this request:

Billing block	08 Check credit memo ▣ Pricir
Order reason	01 Calculation missing
	02 Compl Confirm Missng
Sales area	03 Prices incomplete
	04 Check terms of paymt
Billing Date	05 Check delivery terms
Serv.rendered da	08 Check credit memo
	09 Check debit memo
	41 not yet completed
	42 no price agreement
	43 new price as of....
	50 Authorisation Req
All items	51 Rejected
Item Materia	Target quantity

Figure 10: *Billing block*

337

Billing:

Credit Memo (G2) Create: Overview of Billing Items

📠 Billing documents 🔄

G2 Credit Memo	🖹 9000000001	Net Value		0.00	CAD
Payer	601256	Showroom 1 for SFE1 / / CA - London			
Billing Date	15.06.2016			🗐	

Item	Description	Billed Quantity	SU	Net value	Material	Tax amount
10	Services for furniture setup	1.0 HR		150.00	000000000001002382	10.50
20	Services for furniture setup	1.0 HR		150.00-	000000000001002382	0.00

Figure 11: *Credit Memo (G2) Create*

As we see above, SAP will be posting a credit memo for the tax amount dollars only. Save the document. The accounting document tells us the customer is being credited and tax G/L account being debited with this tax amount.

Data Entry View

Document Number	90036720	Company Code	SFE1	Fiscal Year	20
Document Date	15.06.2016	Posting Date	15.06.2016	Period	6
Reference	0090036719	Cross-CC no.			
Currency	CAD	Texts exist	☐	Ledger Group	

Co...	Itm	PK	S	Account	Description	Amount	Curr.	Tx	Co
SFE1	1	11		601256	Showroom 1 for SFE1	10.50-	CAD	**	
	2	40		451011	Revenue Stream 1	150.00	CAD	09	
	3	40		216450	VAT A/R (Output)	10.50	CAD	09	
	4	50		451011	Revenue Stream 1	150.00-	CAD		

Figure 12: *Display Document - Data Entry View*

The customer's AR statement now reads this tax amount being netted off. So, when the customer pays only the net amount the AR will be reflective of it too:

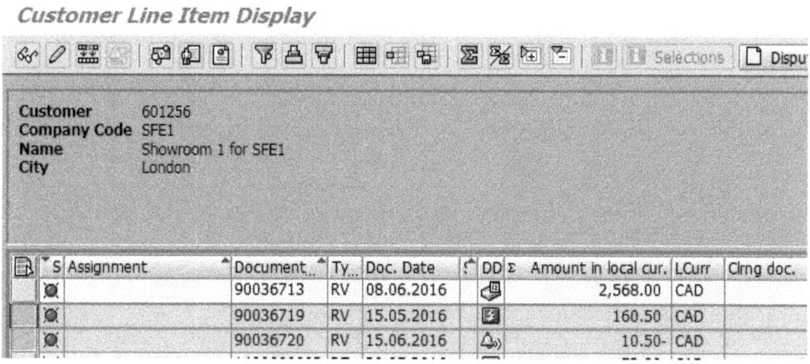

Customer Line Item Display

Figure 13: *Customer Line Item Display*

HANDLING DOWN PAYMENTS TO VENDORS

Down payments are often used to pay vendors for turnkey projects or asset purchases. These are treated differently in SAP compared to normal vendor payments for trade payables. Down payments made to vendors remain on the book as current assets till adjusted/cleared against the actual invoice.

    i.   Making the down Payment to Vendor
    ii.   Displaying the Balances for confirmation of postings
    iii.   Receiving/booking the Invoice against Down Payment made
    iv.   Clearing the Down Payment made
    v.   Displaying the Balances for confirmation of postings
    vi.   Clear the Vendor's Account

i) Making the down Payment to the Vendor

Now that we have configured the down payment account, we are ready to make a down payment to a vendor – that down payment will be held as a current asset till settled.

The t-code to make down payments is F-48 or the path:

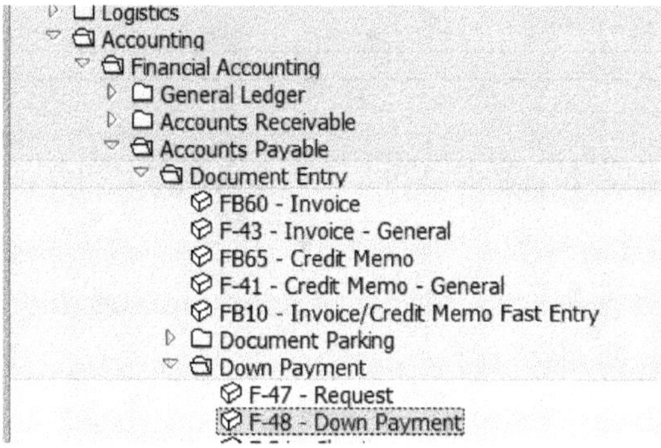

Figure 1: *Down Payment*

The screen opens like this:

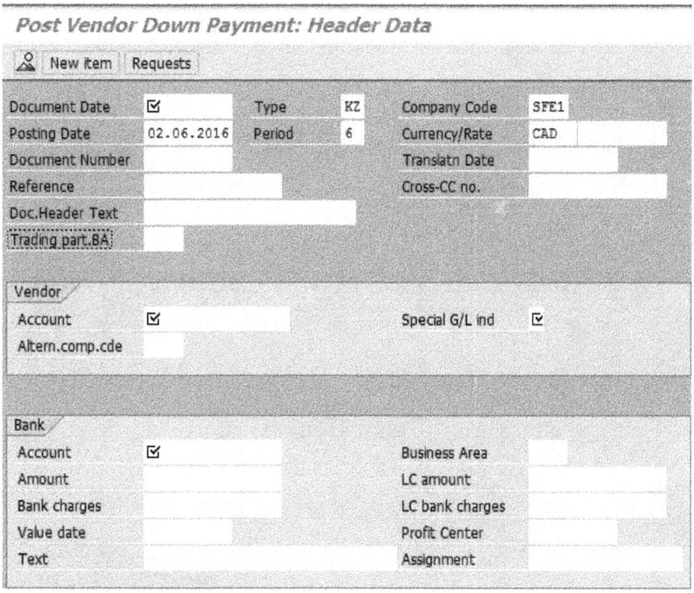

Figure 2: *Post Vendor Down Payment*

Enter the information:

- Date
- Vendor account #, we will use the same vendor as before 100838
- Bank GL account # which will hold this down payment and the value date
- CC
- Amount and currency
- The Spl acct indicator will be 'A' which is SAP standard for Down Payment:

Figure 3: *Spl acct indicator*

Enter the data as below to post this down payment:

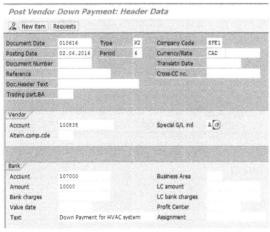

Figure 4: *Post Vendor Down Payment – Required data*

Hit Enter and the system takes us to the next screen:

Enter the amount or a * which is all this screen requires:

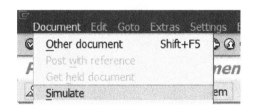

Figure 5: *Post Vendor Down Payment – Vendor item*

Note how SAP found the G/L account 213000 by itself to post to for reconciliation. It found it from the configuration we did earlier.

Now we have the option again to simulate this document for any errors before posting it:

Document	Edit	Goto	Extras	Settings
Other document			Shift+F5	
Post with reference				
Get held document				
Simulate				

Figure 6: *Document option*

If everything looks fine:

Post Vendor Down Payment Display Overview

Display Currency   Taxes   Reset

Document Date	01.06.2016	Type	KZ	Company Code	SFE1
Posting Date	02.06.2016	Period	6	Currency	CAD
Document Number	INTERNAL	Fiscal Year	2016	Translatn Date	02.06.2016
Reference				Cross-CC no.	
Doc.Header Text				Trading part.BA	

Items in document currency

	PK	BusA	Acct		CAD	Amount	Tax amnt
001	50		0000107000	Cash in Bank		10,000.00-	
002	29A		0000100838	Wood vendor for SFE		10,000.00	

Figure 7: *Post Vendor Down Payment Simulation*

Save the document and we get the number at the bottom:

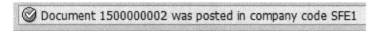

☑ Document 1500000002 was posted in company code SFE1

Figure 8: *Document posted message*

ii) Displaying the Balances for confirmation of postings

We can now display the balances in the vendor account via the transaction FK10N or the path:

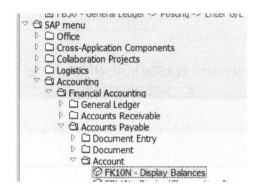

Figure 9: *Display Vendor Balances*

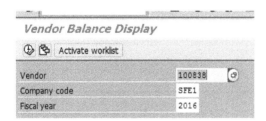

Figure 10: *Vendor Balances Display*

Execute and the results give all the balances against this vendor: The default screen will show the normal transaction balances:

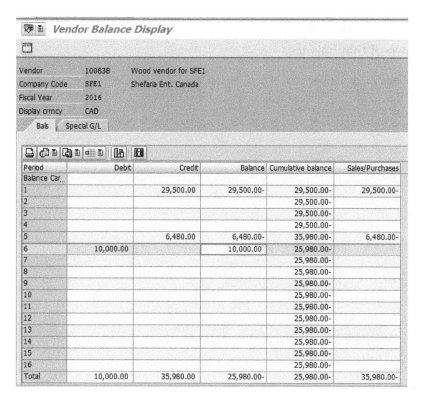

Figure 11: *Vendor Balance Display*

Clicking on the Special G/L tab - Bals Special G/L (Fig 12 below) will give us these advance payments made:

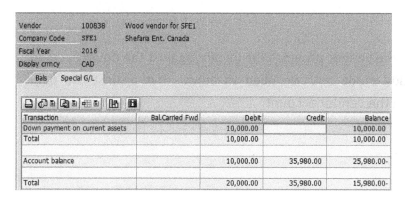

Figure 12: *Vendor Balance Display*

As usual, double click on the Totals line and you see the detailed breakdown of that balance:

Vendor	100838	Wood vendor for SFE1	
Company Code	SFE1	Shefaria Ent. Canada	
Fiscal Year	2016		
Display crrncy	CAD		

Bals / Special G/L

Transaction	Bal.Carried Fwd	Debit	Credit	Balance
Down payment on current assets		10,000.00		10,000.00
Total		10,000.00		10,000.00
Account balance		10,000.00	35,980.00	25,980.00-
Total		20,000.00	35,980.00	15,980.00-

Figure 13: *Vendor Balance Display*

Vendor	100838	
Company Code	SFE1	
Name	Wood vendor for SFE1	
City	Oakville	

S	Document	Doc. Type	Doc. Date	DD Σ	Amount in doc. curr.	Curr.	Clrng doc.	PayT	Curr. cash c
	1500000002	KZ	01.06.2016	A	10,000.00	CAD			
					10,000.00	CAD			
	1500000000	KZ	01.06.2016		8,500.00	CAD	1500000000		
	1500000001	KZ	01.06.2016		1,500.00	CAD	1500000001		
					10,000.00	CAD			
	Account 100838				20,000.00	CAD			
					20,000.00	CAD			

Figure 14: *Vendor Line Item Display*

Note the document # we just entered at the top as document type KZ. The letter A is symbolic of the Spl G/L indicator

iii) Receiving the Invoice against Down Payment made

Now, the vendor provides the invoice against the down payment we already made and we need to adjust that against the debit balance in the vendor account.

FB60 or follow the path below:

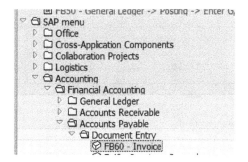

Figure 15: *Posting Vendor Invoice*

We debit the purchase account

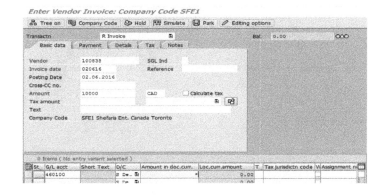

Figure 16: *Enter Vendor Invoice*

On hitting Enter, we get an information message:

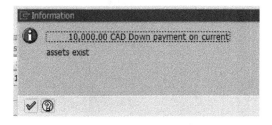

Figure 17: *information message*

*** This number in the message can be different if multiple

down payments have been posted to the vendor account which have not yet been cleared.

Hit Enter again:

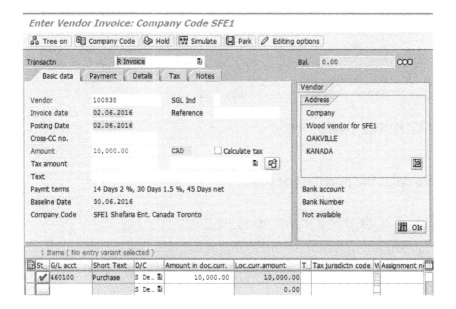

Figure 18: *Enter Vendor Invoice*

and save it:

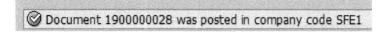

Figure 19: *Document posted message*

iv) Clearing the Down Payment made to vendor

F-54 or:

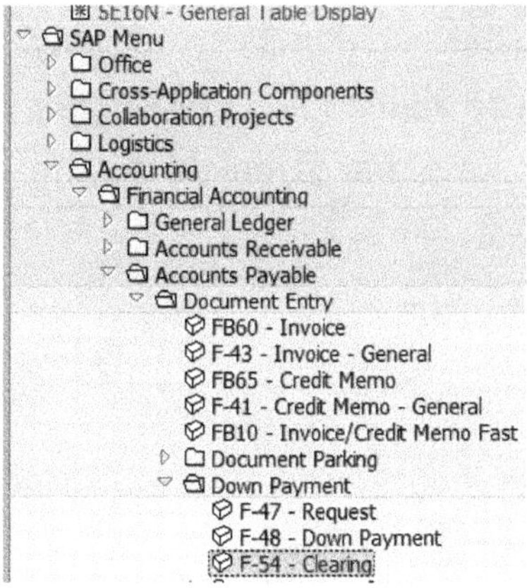

```
      SE16N - General Table Display
  ▽ 🗁 SAP Menu
      ▷ 🗀 Office
      ▷ 🗀 Cross-Application Components
      ▷ 🗀 Collaboration Projects
      ▷ 🗀 Logistics
      ▽ 🗁 Accounting
         ▽ 🗁 Financial Accounting
            ▷ 🗀 General Ledger
            ▷ 🗀 Accounts Receivable
            ▽ 🗁 Accounts Payable
               ▽ 🗁 Document Entry
                     ⊘ FB60 - Invoice
                     ⊘ F-43 - Invoice - General
                     ⊘ FB65 - Credit Memo
                     ⊘ F-41 - Credit Memo - General
                     ⊘ FB10 - Invoice/Credit Memo Fast
                  ▷ 🗀 Document Parking
                  ▽ 🗁 Down Payment
                        ⊘ F-47 - Request
                        ⊘ F-48 - Down Payment
                        ⊘ F-54 - Clearing
```

Figure 20: *Clear Vendor Down Payment*

Enter the relevant data:

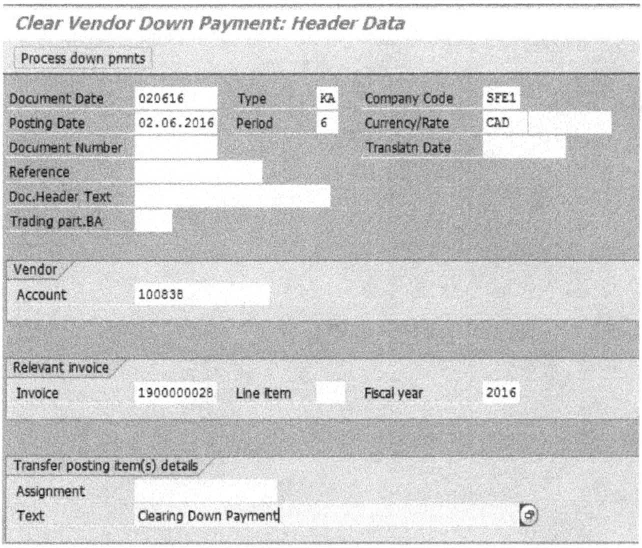

Clear Vendor Down Payment: Header Data

Process down pmnts

Document Date	020616	Type	KA	Company Code	SFE1
Posting Date	02.06.2016	Period	6	Currency/Rate	CAD
Document Number				Translatn Date	
Reference					
Doc.Header Text					
Trading part.BA					

Vendor
Account	100838

Relevant invoice
Invoice	1900000028	Line item		Fiscal year	2016

Transfer posting item(s) details
Assignment	
Text	Clearing Down Payment

Figure 21: *Clear Vendor Down Payment – Header Data*

Note the # we use – the posting # we got earlier to say that we will be clearing against this internal document #.

Click on the button 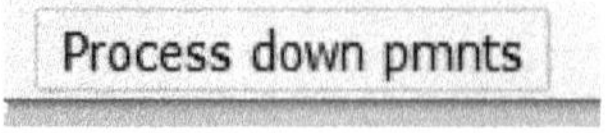 Process down pmnts (Fig 21) to display the down payments outstanding that can be adjusted – note SAP got the posting from the document # because that is linked to the original document #

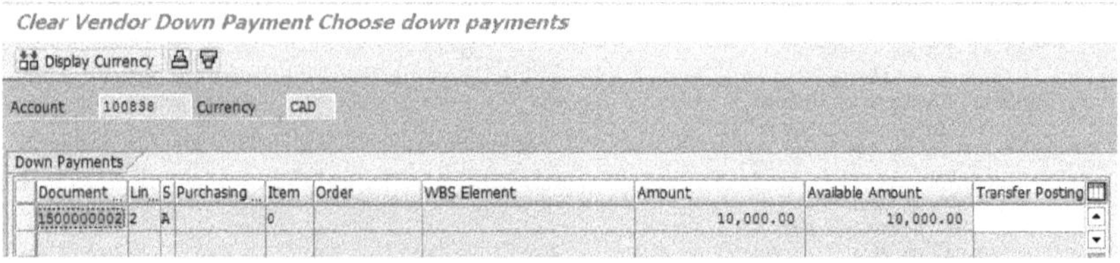

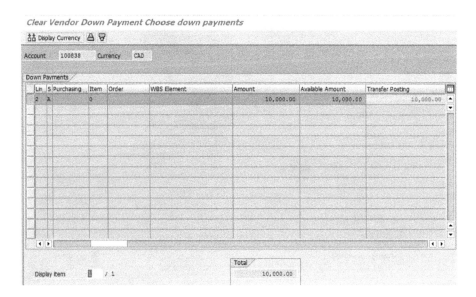

Figure 22: *Clear Vendor - Down Payment*

Enter the amount to clear in the Transfer posting column, press Enter and verify the bottom total changes to that same amount in blue:

Figure 23: *Clear Vendor - Down Payment*

Again, we can simulate the document:

Document Edit Goto Settings Environme
Other document Shift+F5
Post with reference
Get held document
Simulate

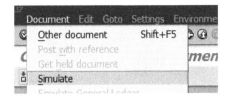

Figure 24: *Document options*

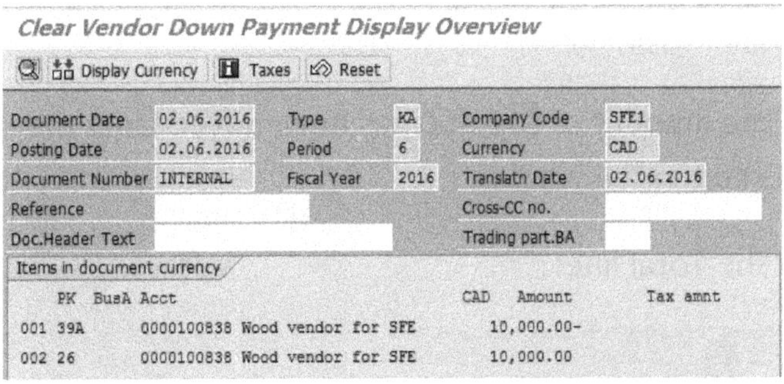

Clear Vendor Down Payment Display Overview
Display Currency
Taxes
Reset
Document Date 02.06.2016
Type KA
Company Code SFE1
Posting Date 02.06.2016
Period 6
Currency CAD
Document Number INTERNAL
Fiscal Year 2016
Translatn Date 02.06.2016
Reference
Cross-CC no.
Doc.Header Text
Trading part.BA
Items in document currency
PK BusA Acct
CAD Amount
Tax amnt
001 39A 0000100838 Wood vendor for SFE 10,000.00-
002 26 0000100838 Wood vendor for SFE 10,000.00

Figure 25: *Clear Vendor Down payment Display*

If everything looks right, post it by saving it:

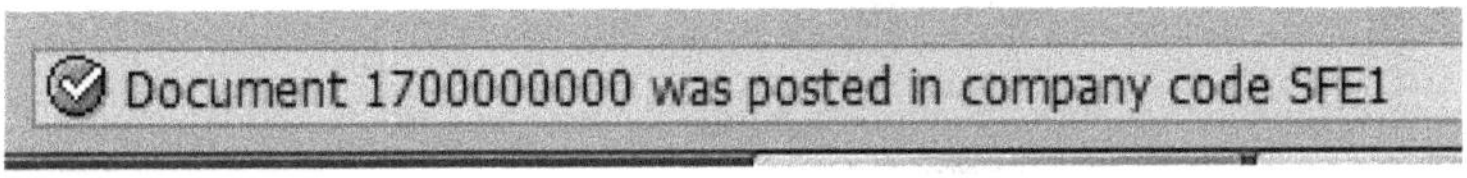

Document 1700000000 was posted in company code SFE1

Figure 26: *Document posted message*

v) Displaying the Balances

At this point if we check the balances in FK10N again:

Click on the tab Special G/L:

Vendor	100838	Wood vendor for SFE1			
Company Code	SFE1	Shefaria Ent. Canada			
Fiscal Year	2016				
Display crrncy	CAD				

Bals / Special G/L

Transaction	Bal.Carried Fwd	Debit	Credit	Balance
Down payment on curre		10,000.00	10,000.00	
Total		10,000.00	10,000.00	
Account balance		20,000.00	45,980.00	25,980.00-
Total		30,000.00	55,980.00	25,980.00-

Figure 27: *Customer Balance Display*

We notice that the amount of $10,000 has now moved from the column Balance to Credit in the vendor.

Double click on the Total line:

Vendor	100838		
Company Code	SFE1		
Name	Wood vendor for SFE1		
City	Oakville		

S Document	Doc. Type	Doc. Date	DD	E	Amount in doc. curr.	Curr.	Clrng doc.	F
1700000000	KA	02.06.2016			10,000.00	CAD		
					10,000.00	CAD		
1500000000	KZ	01.06.2016			8,500.00	CAD	1500000000	
1500000001	KZ	01.06.2016			1,500.00	CAD	1500000001	
1500000002	KZ	01.06.2016	A		10,000.00	CAD	1700000000	
					20,000.00	CAD		
Account 100838					30,000.00	CAD		
					30,000.00	CAD		

Figure 28: *Vendor Line Item Display*

The 2 highlighted cancelling entries of 10,000 each are revealed above. Note the reference of the clearing document 1700000000 in the document No 1500000002.

vi) Clearing the Vendor's Account

This is the last step in the process of down payments – to clear the vendor account. F-44 or follow the path:

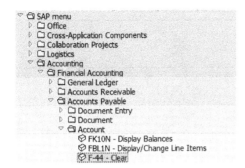

Figure 29: *Clear Vendor*

Clear Vendor: Header Data

Process open items

Account	100838	Clearing date	02.06.2016	Period	6
Company Code	SFE1	Currency	CAD		

Open item selection

Special G/L ind   A   ☑ Normal OI

Additional selections

- ◉ None
- ○ Amount
- ○ Document Number
- ○ Posting Date
- ○ Dunning Area
- ○ Reference
- ○ Collective invoice
- ○ Document Type
- ○ Business Area
- ○ Tax Code
- ○ Branch account
- ○ Others

Figure 30: *Clear Vendor – Header Data*

Enter the vendor account # as above and click on the tab

Process open items

.

To display all the invoices pending in the vendor account for clearing.

Clear Vendor Process open items

🛇 🖉	Distribute diff.	Charge off diff.	🖉 Editing options	🛇 Cash Disc. Due

Standard	Partial pmt	Res.items	Withhldg tax

Account items 100838 Wood vendor for SFE1

Assignment	Document	D	P	Posting	Docume	CAD Gross	Cash discnt	CashD
	1700000000	KA	26	02.06.2...	02.06.2...	10,000.00		2.000
	1900000001	KR	31	09.05.2...	10.05.2...	1,200.00–	24.00–	2.000
	1900000002	KR	31	09.05.2...	10.05.2...	1,100.00–	22.00–	2.000
	1900000004	KR	31	28.05.2...	28.05.2...	1,450.00–	30.81–	2.125
	1900000011	KR	31	28.05.2...	28.05.2...	1,230.00–	26.14–	2.125
	1900000017	KR	31	20.01.2...	20.01.2...	12,800.00–		
	1900000018	KR	31	15.01.2...	15.01.2...	4,500.00–		
	1900000019	KR	31	20.01.2...	20.01.2...	1,400.00–		

◄	►		

🖈🗈	🖻🗈	🖨🖝	🗐🗐 Amo.	🏧 Gross<>.	🏧 Currency	↑ Items	↓ Items	↑ Disc.	↓ Disc.

Editing status

Number of items	10	Amount entered	0.00
Display from item	1	Assigned	25,677.05–
Reason code		Difference postings	
Display in clearing currency		Not assigned	25,677.05

Figure 31: *Clear Vendor Process open Items*

Since there are many entries here, we first need to choose the correct ones that we want to clear. We know they are 1900000028 from the vendor's invoice reference document (FB60) and 1700000002 from clearing (F-54). So we need to select them first. Some items may be on the next screen and have to be found by scrolling in the right bar.

Select the ones you need to square off:

Account items 100838 Wood vendor for SFE1

Assignment	Document	D	P	Posting	Docume	CAD Gross	Cash discnt	CashD
	1700000000	KA	26	02.06.2...	02.06.2...	10,000.00		2.000
	1900000001	KR	31	09.05.2	10.05.2	1,200.00	24.00	2.000

Figure 32: *Clear Vendor Process open Items*

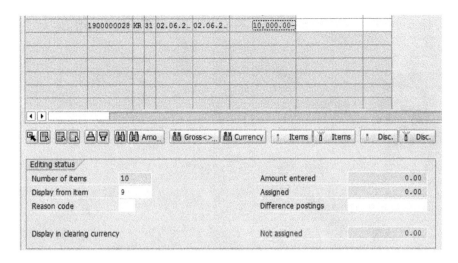

Figure 33: *Clear Vendor Process open Items*

Ensure that the not assigned amount is 0 as above.

At this point, we are ready to clear these 2 by saving the posting. This is a special posting which does not post any line item #s but merely takes them out of the pending reports. This clearing once done, can't be reversed either and the down payment process needs to begin again if required to. Again, SAP gives us the option to simulate the document:

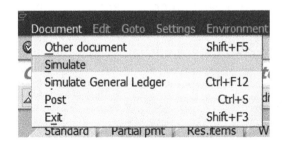

Figure 34: *Document options*

This simulation screen will have no line items unlike all others we saw:

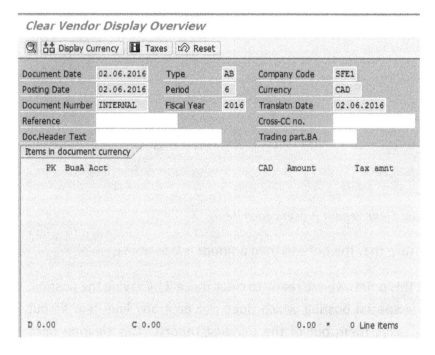

Figure 35: *Clear Vendor Display Overview*

This screen is blank because it creates no line items as the 2 lines are being netted off completely with each other. If there were to be differences of any kind, line items would be created for them. Since SAP showed no errors, we can now post the document by saving it. We get the posting number at the bottom:

Figure 36: *Document posted message*

Note from the # that this is a normal accounting document.

To verify the posting indeed took place and that the down payment was adjusted against the vendor invoice, we can look up FBL1N:

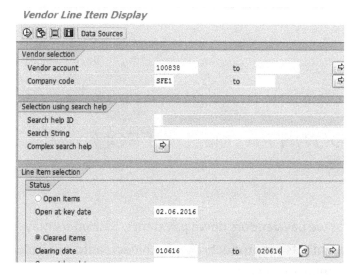

Figure 37: *Vendor Line Item Display*

And execute. We see both our documents here:

Vendor Line Item Display

S	Document	Doc. Type	Doc. Date	DD Σ	Amount in doc. curr.	Curr.	Clrng doc.	PayT	Curr
☐	1700000000	KA	02.06.2016		10,000.00	CAD	100000037	0003	
☐	1900000028	KR	02.06.2016		10,000.00-	CAD	100000037	0003	
☐	1500000000	KZ	01.06.2016		8,500.00	CAD	1500000000		
☐	1900000016	KR	10.01.2016		8,500.00-	CAD	1500000000	0001	
☐	1500000001	KZ	01.06.2016		1,500.00	CAD	1500000001		
☐	1900000000	KR	10.05.2016		1,500.00-	CAD	1500000001	0003	
				•	0.00	CAD			
Account 100838				••	0.00	CAD			
				•••	0.00	CAD			

Figure 38: *Vendor Line Item Display*

HANDLING DOWN PAYMENTS FROM CUSTOMERS

The same way as we pay vendors down payments, customers may also pay us down payments for products like machinery, automobiles etc., primarily the capital expense type purchases.

i.   Receiving/booking the down Payment from the customer
ii. Displaying the Balances for confirmation of postings
iii. Creating the Invoice against Down Payment received
iv. Clearing the Down Payment received
v.   Displaying the Balances for confirmation of postings
vi. Clear the Customer's Account

i) Receiving the down Payment from the customer

F-29 or follow the path below in Fig 1

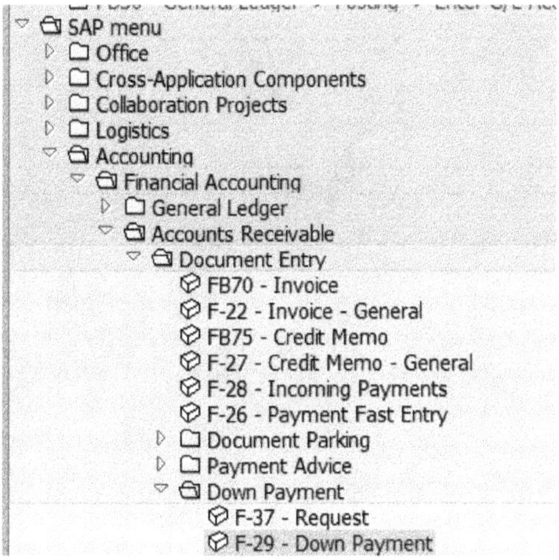

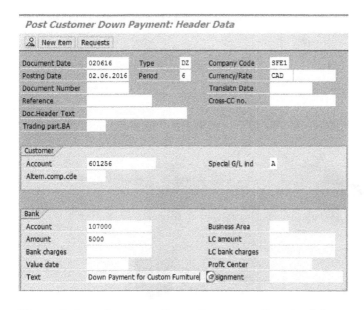

Figure 1: *Post Customer Down Payment*

Enter the necessary data as below, notes can also be entered:

Figure 2: *Post Customer Down Payment – Required data*

Hit Enter and on the next screen enter the amount again for the contra entry. Note how SAP fetches the G/L account 123000 on its own based on the configuration we did in the previous step:

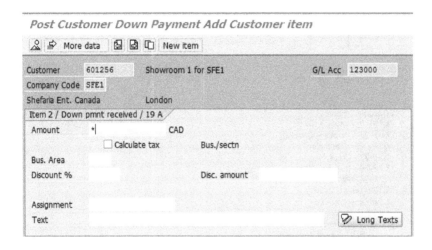

Figure 3: *Post Customer Down Payment – Add Customer Item*

As always, we can simulate the document before posting:

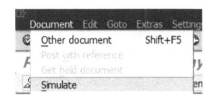

Figure 4: *Post Customer Down Payment – Document option*

Figure 5: *Post Customer Down Payment – Display Overview*

If the document looks good, post it by saving it to get the document #:

Figure 6: *Customer Down Payment – Posted message*

ii) Displaying the Balances for confirmation of postings

FD10N or:

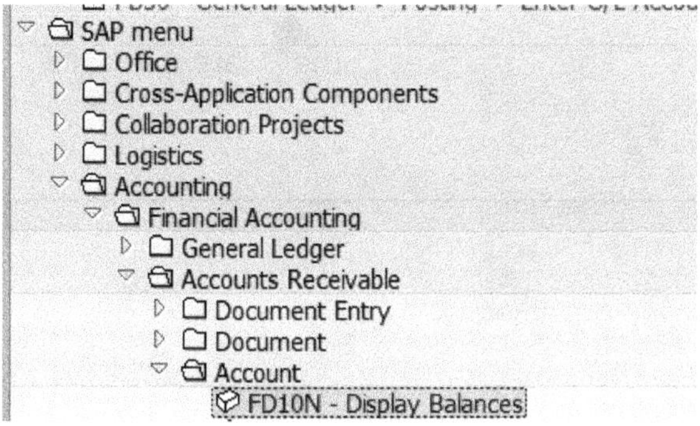

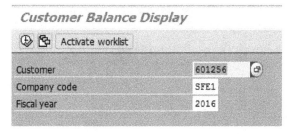

Figure 7: *Customer Balance Display*

Put the customer number and CC and the year and execute:

Customer Balance Display

⊕ 🗁 Activate worklist

Customer	601256
Company code	SFE1
Fiscal year	2016

Figure 8: *Customer Balance Display – Required information*

The down payment balances are under the special GL tab:

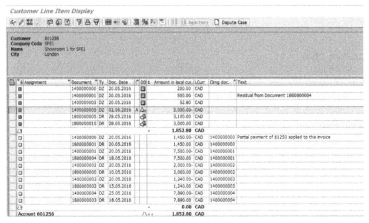

Figure 9: *Customer Balance Display*

Double click the Total line to see the latest entry:

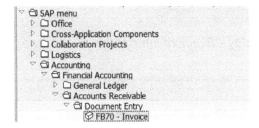

Figure 10: *Customer Line Item Display*

iii) Creating the Invoice against Down Payment received

FB70 or:

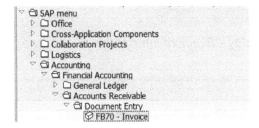

Figure 11: *Enter Customer Invoice*

Enter the important data as below to credit the appropriate G/L account for sales against this down payment received:

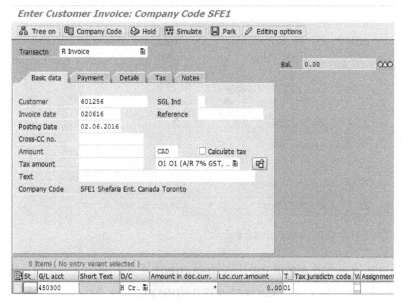

Figure 12: *Enter Customer Invoice – Basic data*

Hit Enter to ensure zero balance at top right in Green as in figure 14. An info message will pop up:

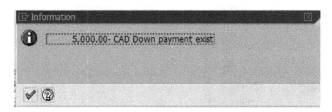

Figure 13: *Enter Customer Invoice – Information message*

Note: This amount could (and does) vary depending on how many other down payments exist in the system which have not been settled yet.

Remove the tax code if it appears in the line item.

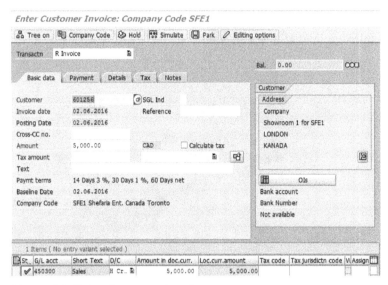

Figure 14: *Enter Customer Invoice*

Again, we can simulate this document if we wish to verify the entries or want to make corrections before posting: See figure 15

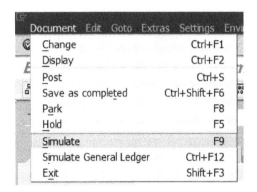

Figure 15: *Document option*

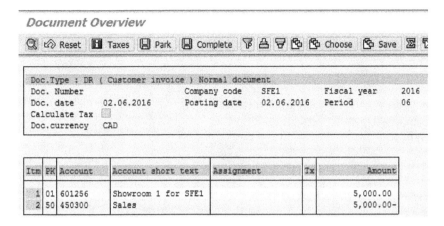

Figure 16: *Document Overview*

We can now save this document:

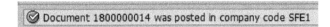

Figure 17: *Document posted message*

iv) Clearing down payment made by customer

F-39 or:

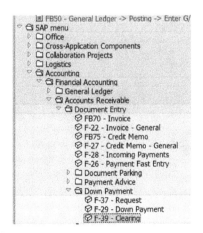

Figure 18: *Clearing Down payment from customer*

Enter the data as below including the invoice # which is being cleared:

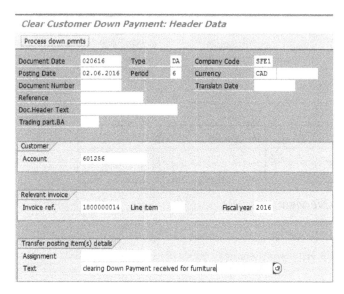

Figure 19: *Clear Customer Down Payment*

Click on **Process down pmnts** in Fig 19 above

Now choose the line (if multiple) and enter the amount being cleared in the last column:

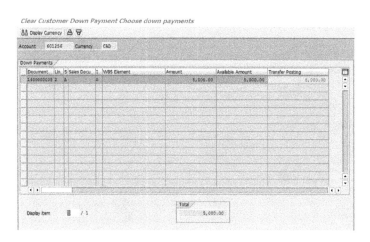

Figure 20: *Clear Customer Down Payment*

Ensure that the total at the bottom is same as the amount being cleared:

Again, we can simulate it:

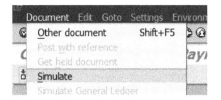

Figure 21: *Document option*

If it looks good, then save it:

Clear Customer Down Payment Display Overview

🔍 🔠 Display Currency | 🅸 Taxes | ✍️ Reset

Document Date	02.06.2016	Type	DA	Company Code	SFE1
Posting Date	02.06.2016	Period	6	Currency	CAD
Document Number	INTERNAL	Fiscal Year	2016	Translatn Date	02.06.2016
Reference				Cross-CC no.	
Doc.Header Text				Trading part.BA	

Items in document currency

PK	BusA	Acct		CAD	Amount	Tax amnt
001	09A	0000601256	Showroom 1 for SFE1		5,000.00	
002	16	0000601256	Showroom 1 for SFE1		5,000.00-	

Figure 22: *Clear Customer Down Payment*

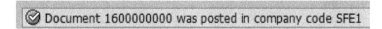
⊘ Document 1600000000 was posted in company code SFE1

Figure 23: *Document posted message*

v) Displaying the Balances

FD10N:

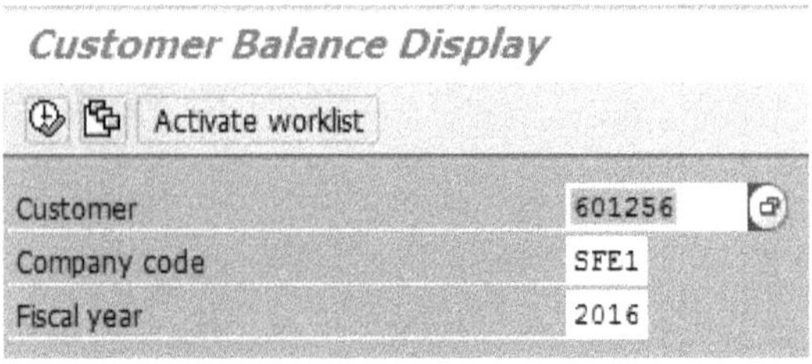

Customer Balance Display

		Activate worklist
Customer		601256
Company code		SFE1
Fiscal year		2016

Figure 24: *Customer Balance Display*

Customer	601256	Showroom 1 for SFE1
Company Code	SFE1	Shefara Ent. Canada
Fiscal Year	2016	
Display crrncy	CAD	

Balances / Special general ledger

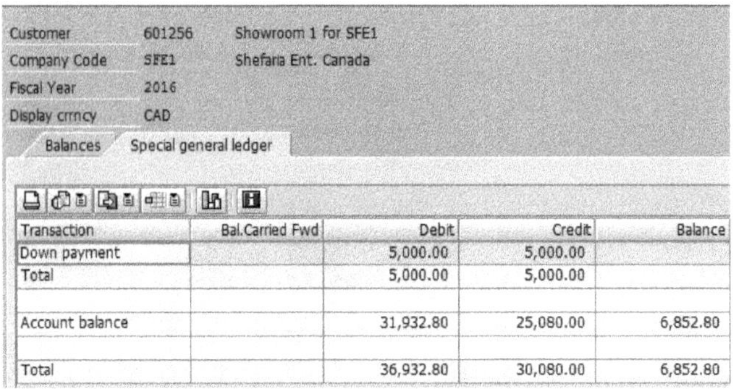

Transaction	Bal.Carried Fwd	Debit	Credit	Balance
Down payment		5,000.00	5,000.00	
Total		5,000.00	5,000.00	
Account balance		31,932.80	25,080.00	6,852.80
Total		36,932.80	30,080.00	6,852.80

Figure 25: *Customer Balance Display*

Double click on Total again to confirm the document is cleared:

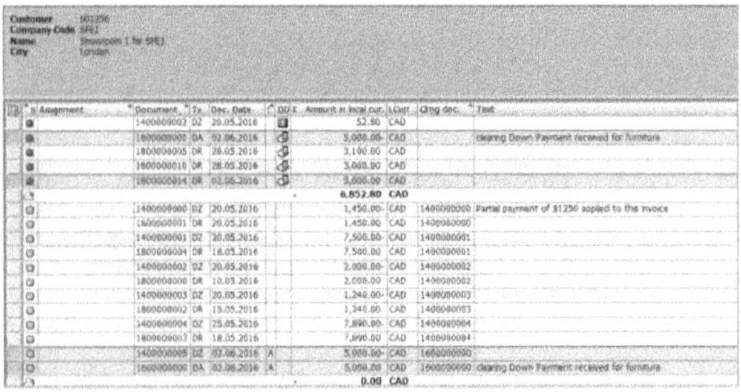

Figure 26: *Customer Line Item Display*

368

vi) Clearing the customer account

F-32 or:

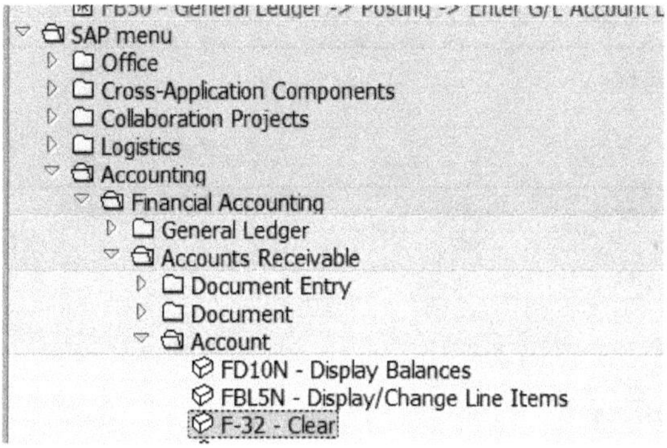

> 🔳 FB50 - General Ledger -> Posting -> Enter G/L Account L
> ▽ 🗁 SAP menu
>   ▷ 🗀 Office
>   ▷ 🗀 Cross-Application Components
>   ▷ 🗀 Collaboration Projects
>   ▷ 🗀 Logistics
>   ▽ 🗁 Accounting
>   ▽ 🗁 Financial Accounting
>   ▷ 🗀 General Ledger
>   ▽ 🗁 Accounts Receivable
>   ▷ 🗀 Document Entry
>   ▷ 🗀 Document
>   ▽ 🗁 Account
>   ⌑ FD10N - Display Balances
>   ⌑ FBL5N - Display/Change Line Items
>   ⌑ F-32 - Clear

Figure 27: *Clear Customer*

Enter the data as below:

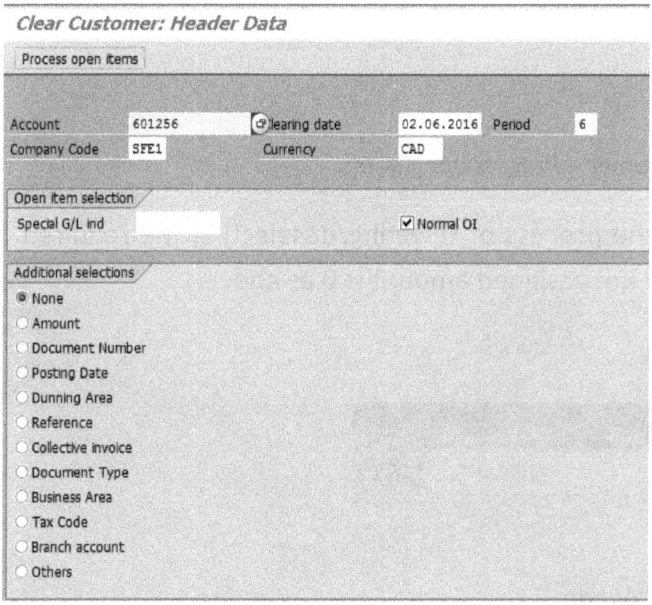

Clear Customer: Header Data

Process open items

Account	601256	Clearing date	02.06.2016	Period	6
Company Code	SFE1	Currency	CAD		

Open item selection

Special G/L ind		☑ Normal OI

Additional selections

- ⦿ None
- ○ Amount
- ○ Document Number
- ○ Posting Date
- ○ Dunning Area
- ○ Reference
- ○ Collective invoice
- ○ Document Type
- ○ Business Area
- ○ Tax Code
- ○ Branch account
- ○ Others

Figure 28: *Clear Customer – Header Data*

Click on 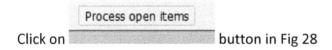 button in Fig 28

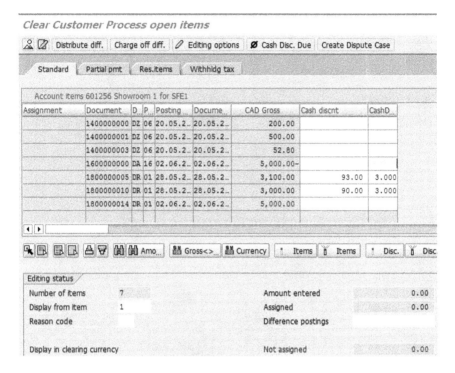

Figure 29: *Clear Customer – Process open items*

Again, follow the process of selecting/deselecting the required line and ensure the not assigned amount is 0 as above.

Simulate:

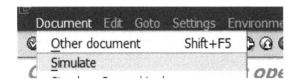

Figure 30: *Document option*

Clear Customer Display Overview

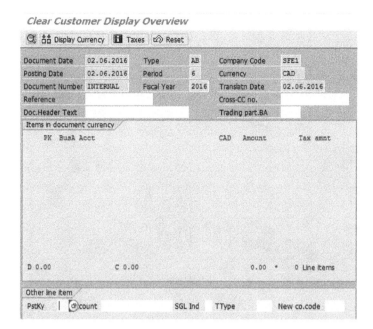

Figure 31: *Clear Customer Display Overview*

And if everything is good, Save it:

Document 100000038 was posted in company code SFE1

Figure 32: *Document posted message*

Check FD10N again:

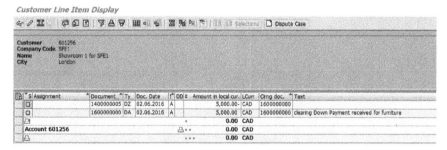

Figure 33: *Customer Line Item Display*

CUSTOMER STATEMENTS IN SAP

Most companies send customers' open AR statements at end of the month or quarter as the policy may be. Though for the most part, the feel and look of these statements will be specific to the company, with their logos, formatting, information etc, the basic process of running the transaction in SAP to generate statements will be the same. In most cases, the companies may also have their own transaction code to run statements en masse for all customers in a Co Code all together. However, standard SAP also does offer the ability to print an individual account statement or multiple statements. Since we will actually not be printing any, we can see the transaction that enables us to see an individual account statement as a pdf document within SAP.

Go to customer AR statement, FBL5N and enter the customer numbers and the date as on which you want to see the statements.

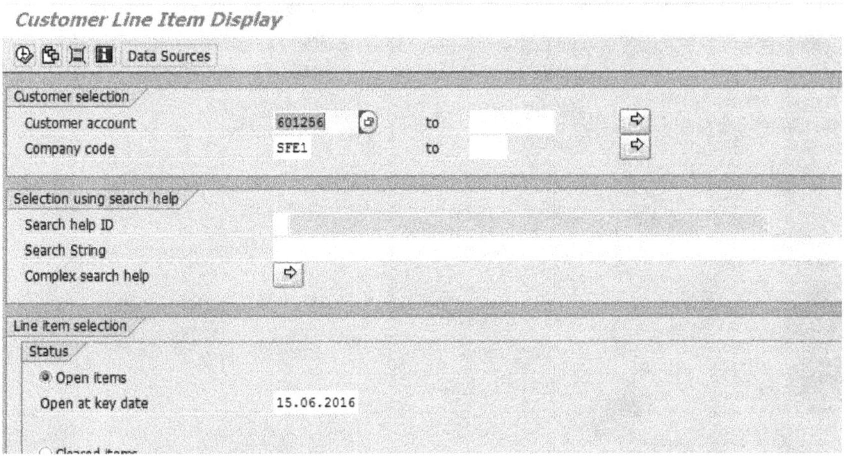

Figure 1: *Customer Line Item Display*

Execute to get to the detailed line items.

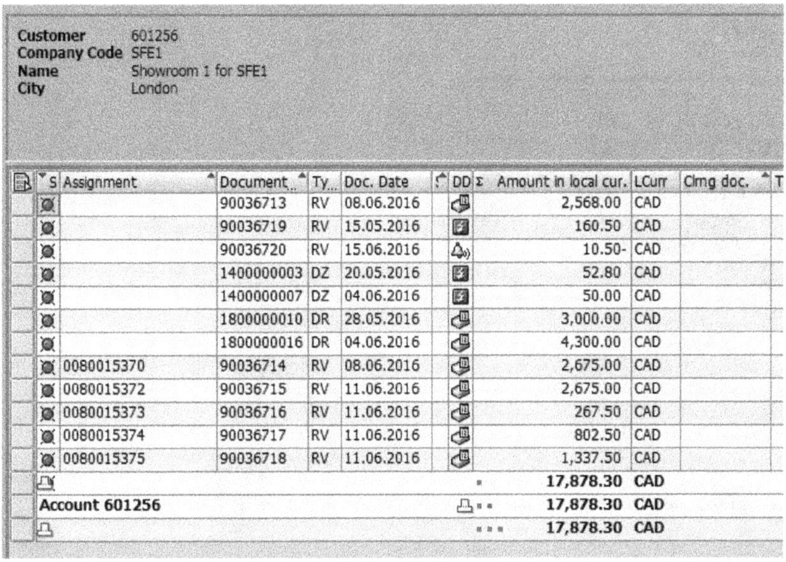

Figure 2: *Customer Line Item Display*

Click on any line item and follow the path below to request a statement:

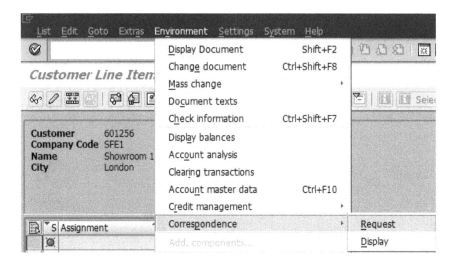

Figure 3: *Customer Line Item Display – Environment options*

Double click on the SAP06 option (can be different in different SAP systems)

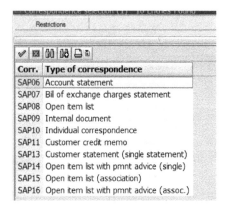

Figure 4: *Customer Line Item Display – Type of correspondence*

In the window that comes, enter the posting dates of the range of documents you need the statement for: See figure 5

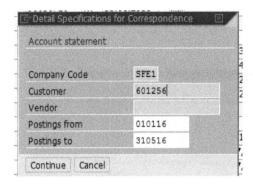

Figure 5: *Data Specification for Correspondence*

And click on the Continue Button.

A message at the bottom says:

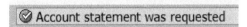

Figure 6: *Request message*

Go back to the same path, this time, asking to Display the statement:

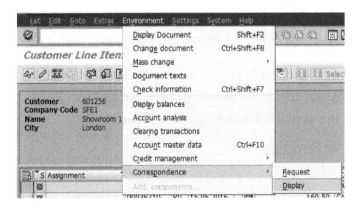

Figure 7: *Customer Line Item Display – Environment options*

Enter the Printer PDF1 when the window pops up and Click on continue:

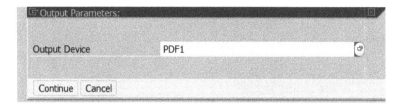

Figure 8: *Output Parameters*

The statement comes up as a Preview:

Figure 9: *Customer Statement*

You can scroll up and down the pages using the keys

In the real world, when printers are connected in SAP, we can print the statement out using the actual printer rather than PDF1. Scroll down to see the actual statement numbers, see Fig 10.

```
Account statement from 2016.01.01 to 2016.05.31

Doc.         Doc.          Trans-  Curr-              Amount      Clearing
Number       Date          action  ency

Balance carried forward 2016.01.01:              0.00
1800000000   2016.05.10 DR     CAD         2,000.00     1400000002
0090036719   2016.05.15 RV     CAD           160.50
1800000002   2016.05.15 DR     CAD         1,240.00     1400000003
1800000003   2016.05.18 DR     CAD         7,890.00     1400000004
1800000004   2016.05.18 DR     CAD         7,500.00     1400000001
1400000000   2016.05.20 DZ     CAD           200.00     1400000006
1400000000   2016.05.20 DZ     CAD         1,450.00-    1400000000
1400000001   2016.05.20 DZ     CAD           500.00     1400000014
1400000001   2016.05.20 DZ     CAD         7,500.00-    1400000001
1400000002   2016.05.20 DZ     CAD         2,000.00-    1400000002
1400000003   2016.05.20 DZ     CAD            52.80
1400000003   2016.05.20 DZ     CAD         1,240.00-    1400000003
1800000001   2016.05.20 DR     CAD         1,450.00     1400000000
1400000004   2016.05.25 DZ     CAD         7,890.00-    1400000004
1800000005   2016.05.28 DR     CAD         3,100.00     1400000015
1800000010   2016.05.28 DR     CAD         3,000.00

Final balance 2016.05.31:        CAD         7,013.30
```

Figure 10: *Customer Statement*

We could also choose all postings, not just open AR if in FBL5N, we choose the Posting Dates option instead of the Open as on option:

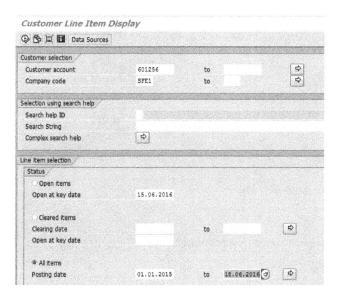

Figure 11: *Customer Line Item Display*

Executing it, we can see the same transactions as we see in the statement plus more though not in chronological order:

S	Assignment	Document	Ty	Doc. Date	DD	Σ	Amount in local cur.	LCurr	Clrng doc.	Text
		90036713	RV	08.06.2016			2,568.00	CAD		
		90036719	RV	15.05.2016			160.50	CAD		
		90036720	RV	15.06.2016			10.50-	CAD		
		1400000003	DZ	20.05.2016			52.80	CAD		
		1400000007	DZ	04.06.2016			50.00	CAD		
		1800000010	DR	28.05.2016			3,000.00	CAD		
		1800000016	DR	04.06.2016			4,300.00	CAD		
	0080015370	90036714	RV	08.06.2016			2,675.00	CAD		
	0080015372	90036715	RV	11.06.2016			2,675.00	CAD		
	0080015373	90036716	RV	11.06.2016			267.50	CAD		
	0080015374	90036717	RV	11.06.2016			802.50	CAD		
	0080015375	90036718	RV	11.06.2016			1,337.50	CAD		
						▪	17,878.30	CAD		
	0080015370	90000000	RV	08.06.2016			2,675.00	CAD	90036688	
	0080015370	90036688	RV	08.06.2016			2,675.00-	CAD	90036688	
	0080015370	90036689	RV	08.06.2016			2,675.00	CAD	90036690	
	0080015370	90036690	RV	08.06.2016			2,675.00-	CAD	90036690	
		90036692	RV	08.06.2016			2,407.50	CAD	90036695	
		90036695	RV	08.06.2016			2,407.50-	CAD	90036695	

Figure 12: *Customer Line Item Display*

They can be made to show up chronologically by sorting them by Doc. date as below. Place the cursor on that heading and click on the first button in the pair 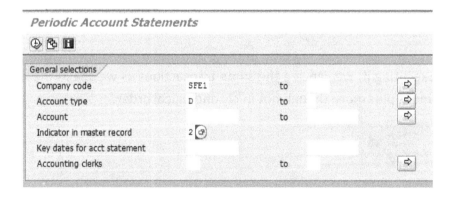 in the main menu to sort them by dates:

Customer	601256
Company Code	SFE1
Name	Showroom 1 for SFE1
City	London

S	Assignment	DocumentNo	Ty	Doc. Date	S	DD	Σ	Amount in local cur.	LCurr	Clng doc.	Text
☐		1800000000	DR	10.05.2016				2,000.00	CAD	1400000002	
☐		1800000015	DR	10.05.2016				1,500.00	CAD	1400000007	
✱		90036719	RV	15.05.2016	🗊			160.50	CAD		
☐		1800000002	DR	15.05.2016				1,240.00	CAD	1400000003	
☐		1800000004	DR	18.05.2016				7,500.00	CAD	1400000001	
☐		1800000003	DR	18.05.2016				7,890.00	CAD	1400000004	
✱		1400000003	DZ	20.05.2016	🗊			52.80	CAD		

Figure 13: *Customer Line Item Display*

Other than this, we can also use transaction F.27 to directly print or preview statements:

Periodic Account Statements

General selections				
Company code	SFE1	to		➪
Account type	D	to		➪
Account		to		➪
Indicator in master record	2			
Key dates for acct statement				
Accounting clerks		to		➪

Figure 14: *Periodic Account Statements*

The data in the above screen will get validated with the data in the customer master's correspondence tab and get pulled into the program to create the statements for example, this customer has WR as accounting clerk and 2 in the bank statement field:

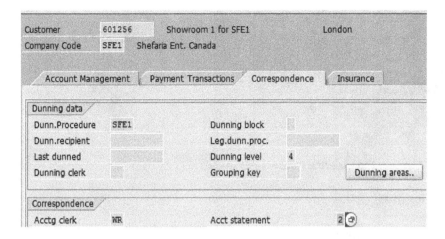

Figure 15: *Display Customer – Correspondence Tab*

So this customer will get pulled up in the statement (since the variant has asked for all accounting clerks). We could have restricted the data by specific accounting clerk/s.

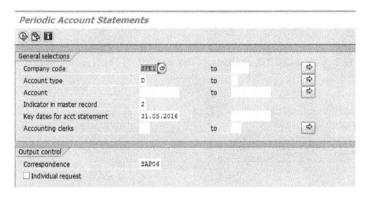

Figure 16: *Periodic Account Statements*

Executing on this screen, we get the message:

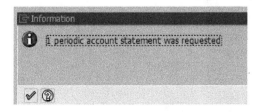

Figure 17: *Request Information*

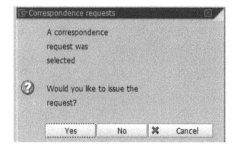

Figure 18: *Correspondence request*

Hit Enter:

Enter the output device in the new screen:

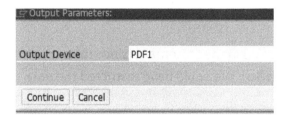

Figure 19: *Output Parameters*

When you see the screen below, you know statements have been generated:

CoCd	Type of correspondence	Spool no.	Name	Suf1	Suffix 2	Pages	Fax/e
SFE1	Account statement	22,334	SAP06		SFE1	1	

Figure 20: *Statement generated message*

They can be seen in transaction SP02:

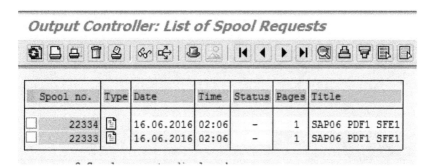

Figure 21: *List of Spool requests*

Click on 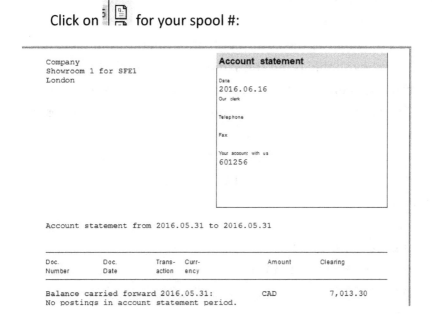 for your spool #:

Figure 22: *Account Statement*

DUNNING

Invoices and statements sometimes do not get payments from difficult customers. This is where dunning steps in. Simply stated, dunning is a reminder to the customer that payments from them are overdue and they should remit the same to the vendor. The dunning process can also keep track of a customer's payment habits which can be used in reporting and decision making on the credit policies a company should adopt to keep receivables in control. There may be customers who buy a lot, pay slow but do pay and do not default. In those cases, the company may want to retain the business, increase the prices marginally to cover for the lost interest and give more than normal credit so their receivables do not affect overdue AR. Further, this process can also be taken a step forward and this information sent to collection agencies. This is a useful feature for high volume mass product selling companies like cell phone providers, utility companies etc.

While the language on a dunning letter will be company specific like in statements, the process of generating dunning letters in SAP is the same. It involves some configuration set up and master data in the customer's CC data view.

The standard dunning system in SAP covers 4 different customer transactions:

    1. Open A/R invoices, including invoices that are partially credited or partially paid
    2. Invoices that include installments
    3. A/R credit memos
    4. Incoming payments that are not based on invoices

i)   Dunning the Customers as a job process

First we set up the appropriate master data. Go to transaction FD02 (change customer's CC data) and add the dunning procedure in the Correspondence tab:

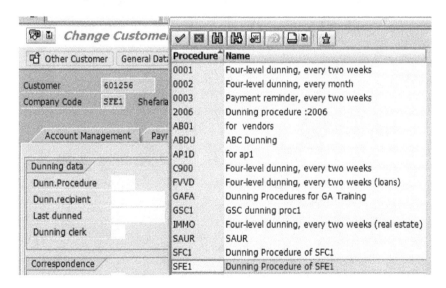

Figure 1: *Change customer – Correspondence Tab*

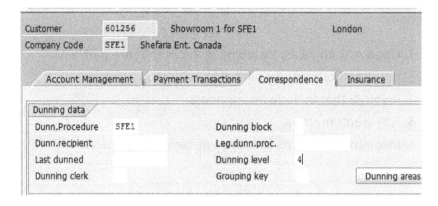

Figure 2: *Change customer – Correspondence Tab*

Save.

Once the customer is set up, we are ready to test the dunning process. The t code is F150 for setting up dunning runs for customers collectively or dun individually, or follow the path:

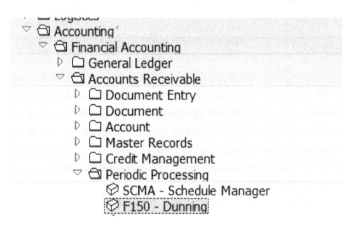

Figure 3: *Dunning*

Give the dunning run an ID and the date on which you want it to occur: See figure 4

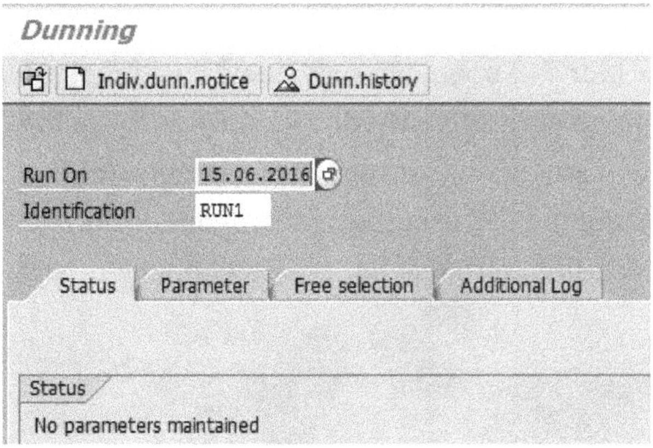

Dunning

Indiv.dunn.notice   Dunn.history

Run On   15.06.2016
Identification   RUN1

| Status | Parameter | Free selection | Additional Log |

Status
No parameters maintained

Figure 4: *Dunning – Necessary data*

Enter the other necessary data:

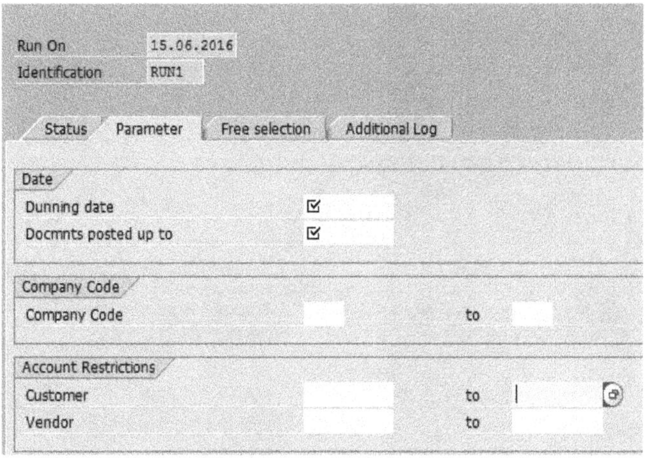

Run On   15.06.2016
Identification   RUN1

| Status | Parameter | Free selection | Additional Log |

Date
Dunning date   ☑
Docmnts posted up to   ☑

Company Code
Company Code   to

Account Restrictions
Customer   to
Vendor   to

Figure 5: *Dunning –Parameter Tab*

The dunning date is the date of issue and also the date from which the arrears are calculated. Documents posting date will include all the documents posted till that date.

Account restrictions enable you to exclude or include accounts that should not be dunned or should be dunned. This is different from the exclusions that occur due to data not set in the customer or vendor masters. SAP checks for both – those excluded in the customer master will be excluded as well as those listed here for exclusion will also be excluded. If you want only a few customers to be dunned, then set them up here and SAP will pick up only those for dunning provided they have been set up appropriately in the customer master to be dunned. If a customer is excluded in the customer master then inclusion here will not create dunning letters for them.

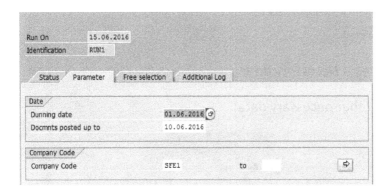

Figure 6: *Dunning –Parameter Tab, necessary data*

Save the run.

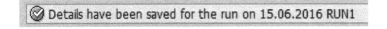

Figure 7: *Data saved message*

Now, a background job will kick in on 15.06.2016 in this case and create dunning notices for all the appropriately set up customers.

iii) Individual Dunning Notices

We can also see individual notices for any particular customer/s instead of all customers in one run.

Figure 8: *Individual Dunning Notice button*

Enter the PDF printer in the window that comes up:

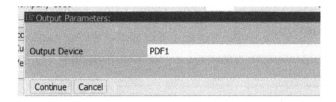

Figure 9: *Output parameters*

Enter data as:

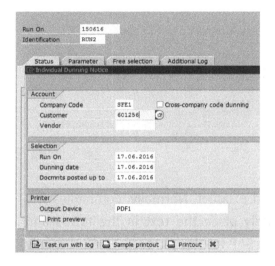

Figure 10: *Individual Dunning Notice – Necessary data*

Click on ⎙ Sample printout button

A very crude letter comes up:

```
 Dunning Data
FI Dunning - Modules
==================================================================
> Account D 0000601256 , company code SFE1 is being processed
>               Reading account data and document information — Phase 0 —
> Account D 0000601256 read items: 12
>               Processing and completing dunning lines — Phase I —
> Document 0090036713/2016/001 days in arrears 21- <= 0
> Document 0090036719/2016/001 has new dunning level 1 .
> Document 1400000003/2016/002 has new dunning level 1 .
> Document 1400000007/2016/002 has new dunning level 1 .
> Document 1800000010/2016/001 days in arrears 40- <= 0
> Document 1800000016/2016/001 days in arrears 47- <= 0
> Document 0090036714/2016/001 days in arrears 21- <= 0
> Document 0090036715/2016/001 days in arrears 24- <= 0
> Document 0090036716/2016/001 days in arrears 24- <= 0
> Document 0090036717/2016/001 days in arrears 24- <= 0
> Document 0090036718/2016/001 days in arrears 24- <= 0
>               Check legal dunning procedure and credit memos — Phase II -
> Credit memo 0090036720/2016/001 has new dunning level 1 . Without invoice refere
```

Figure 11: *Dunning - Modules*

This letter is not a finished product. Normally, companies will develop, align and appropriately place the text in the forms and layouts which will be created in SAP for this purpose. Here, it is only for demonstration purpose.

FINANCIAL STATEMENT VERSIONS

This is a very flexible functionality in SAP that enables us to set up the P&L and B/L by configuring the G/L accounts in the statements and then grouping them as needed. We will not go into much details of all here, but will get a good idea of the process involved. In standard SAP this is a configuration but it is likely that the company will implement this as a master data because of the high volume of activity. The path to set this up is via SPRO transaction. Look closely at the print below and get to the same point in your own training system:

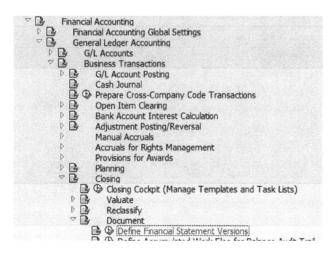

Figure 1: *Define Financial Statement Version*

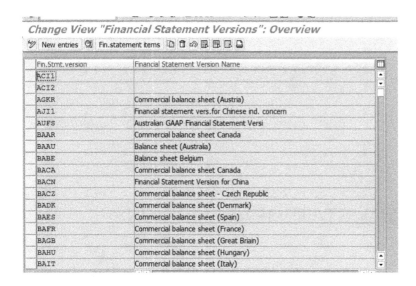

Figure 2: *Change view - Financial Statement Version*

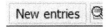

Figure 3: *New Entries button*

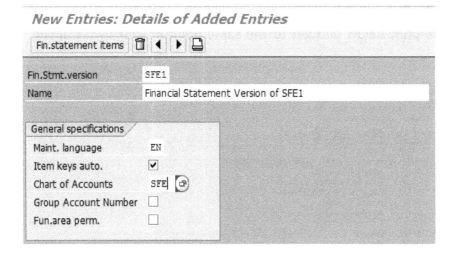

Figure 4: *New Entries – Details of added Entries*

Save the configuration.

Fin.statement items

Figure 5: *Save the configuration*

To configure the BS and P&L as you would like to, select the Fin Statement version and click on Fin. Statement items:

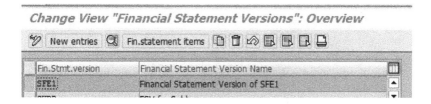

Figure 6: *Change view - Financial Statement Version*

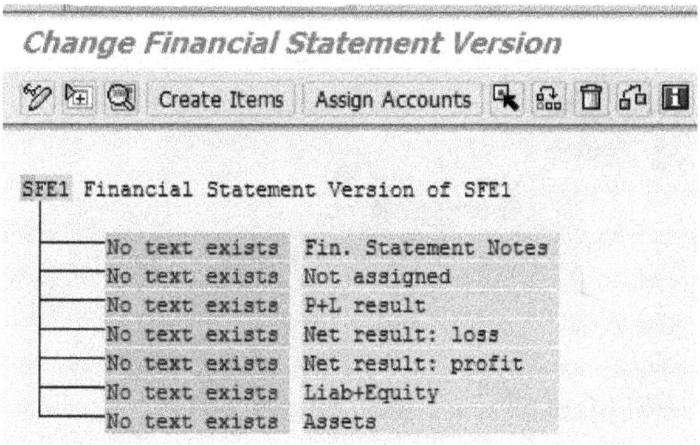

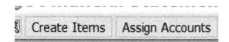

Figure 7: *Change Financial Statement Version*

Using the 2 keys:

Create Items   Assign Accounts

Figure 8: *Configuration keys*

We can create new headings and sub-headings by positioning the cursor at the required place via the key Create Items. E.g. if we want to create a new heading called Fixed Assets under Assets, we will Click on Assets and then on Create Items:

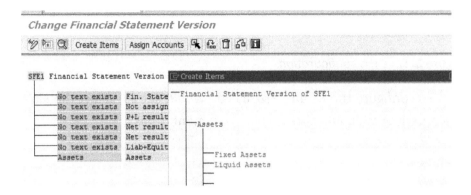

Figure 9: *Change Financial Statement Version*

Next, click on Create Items:

Hit Enter and Fixed Assets and Liquid Assets appear as a sub-headings of Assets:

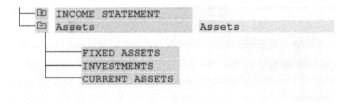

Figure 10: *Change Financial Statement Version*

Configuring G/Ls:

Next, we can configure the G/L accounts in each individual sub-heading/bucket. Click on the sub-heading you want to attach the corresponding G/L to, e.g. to Income Statement>Revenue> Revenue from Furniture Division. The click on Assign Accounts:

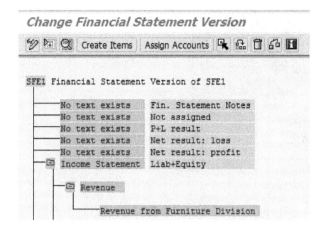

Figure 11: *Change Financial Statement Version*

And enter the G/L account e.g. 451011 for this :

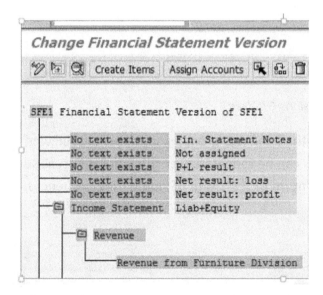

Figure 12: *Change Financial Statement Version*

Change Accounts
Item
Revenue from Furniture Division
ChAc
From Acct
To Account
D
C
SFE
451011
451011

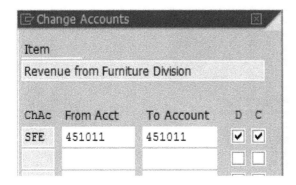

Figure 13: *Change Account*

Hit Enter and Save.

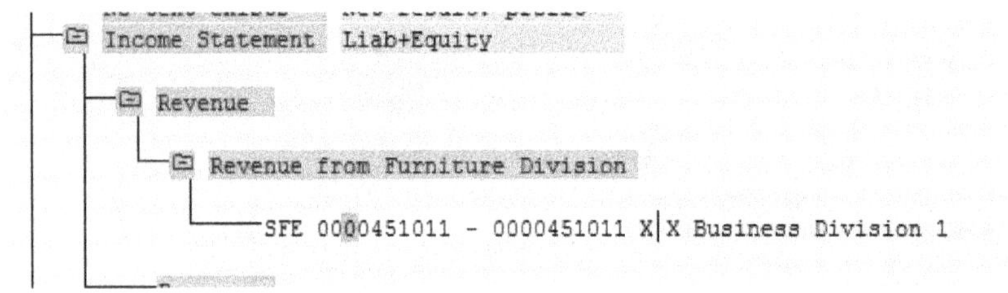

Income Statement
Liab+Equity
Revenue
Revenue from Furniture Division
SFE 0000451011 - 0000451011 X|X Business Division 1

Figure 14: *Display Fin Versions G/L Tree*

Similarly create all the headings/groups and assign the relevant G/Ls as above. The G/Ls can be repeated over the different areas so long as they follow the norm of P & L and BS numbering sequences. Save.

Executing the Financial Statement Version

Running the reports created in the financial statement versions is done via the transaction menu:

Accounting
▽ Financial Accounting
  ▽ General Ledger
    ▷ Posting
    ▷ Document
    ▷ Account
    ▷ Master Records
    ▷ Statistical Key Figures
    ▷ Periodic Processing
    ▷ Corrections
    ▷ Reporting
    ▽ Information System
      ▽ General Ledger Reports
        ▽ Balance Sheet/ Profit and Loss Statement / Cash Flow
          ▽ General
            ▽ Actual/Actual Comparisons
              ⊘ S_ALR_87012249 - Actual/Actual Comparison for Year
              ⊘ S_ALR_87012250 - Half-Year Actual/Actual Comparison
              ⊘ S_ALR_87012251 - Quarterly Actual/Actual Comparison
              ⊘ S_ALR_87012252 - Periodic Actual/Actual Comparison
              ⊘ S_ALR_87012269 - Balance Sheet Using Cost of Sales Approach (German Trade Law)
              ⊘ S_ALR_87012270 - Profit and Loss Statement Using Cost of Goods Sold (German Trade Law)
              ⊘ S_ALR_87012284 - Balance Sheet / Profit and Loss Statement
              ⊘ C_D00_07000220 CAD Minimal Variant

Figure 1: *Balance Sheet – Profit and Loss Statement*

Enter the details as needed:

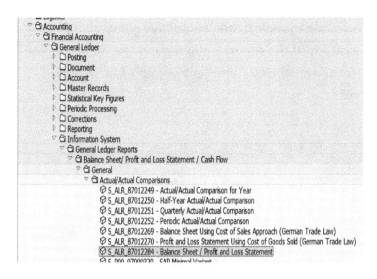

Figure 2: *Financial Statements*

Depending on how much has been configured, the amounts in

the G/Ls will be available to view in their respective headings and sub-headings at the bottom of the report – the data in the upper part is not a part of a formal financial statement version but is only G/L balances.

Financial Statements

Financial Statement Version of SFE1

OL	Ledger
10	Currency type Company code currency
CAD	Amounts in Canadian Dollar

FS Item	Text for B/S P&L Item	Tot.rpt.pr	tot.cmp.pr	Abs. difference	Pct.Diff.
2	460600 Discounts taken from vendors	90.00-	0.00	90.00-	
2	500000 Cost of Goods Sold (without Cost Element)	34,800.00	0.00	34,800.00	
2	530000 Gain/Loss Price Variances	5,522.00-	0.00	5,522.00-	
2	634000 Insurance	22,208.00	0.00	22,208.00	
2	665040 Depreciation Expense - Building	5,007.00	0.00	5,007.00	
2	665041 Depreciation Expense - Furniture & Fixture	909.00	0.00	909.00	
2	665042 Depreciation Expense - Machine & Equipment	1,125.00	0.00	1,125.00	
2	665043 Depreciation Expense - Low Value Assets	1,815.00	0.00	1,815.00	
2	700000 Write Off Fixed Assets	8,520.00	0.00	8,520.00	
2	700001 Clearing Account - Revenue from Account Sale	750.00	0.00	750.00	
2	700002 Gain & Loss Sale of Fixed Assets	950.00-	0.00	950.00-	
2	900100 Under Payment Account	346.00	0.00	346.00	
2	900200 Over Payment Account	341.70-	0.00	341.70-	
2		9,800.00	0.00	9,800.00	
4		9,800.00	0.00	9,800.00	
12	451011 Business Division 1	9,800.00-	0.00	9,800.00-	

Figure 3: *Financial Statements*

CASH JOURNAL – USER MANUAL

A Cash Journal can be created to represent a physical "Petty Cash Tin" and by entering and posting each Cash Payment or Cash Receipt, SAP will automatically update the Cash Balance thereby allowing an easy reconciliation of each Petty Cash "Box".

Each Cash Journal is linked to a GL Account via Configuration. This GL Account should be set to "Auto Postings only" so that postings can only be made using the Cash Journal and in this way the balance on the GL Account always agrees to Cash Journal balance. Postings are made according to pre-defined Business Transactions.

Transaction Code : FBCJ or follow the path below:

Figure 1: *Cash Journal*

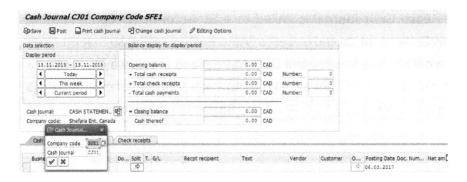

Figure 2: *Cash Journal*

Click 🖼 Fig 3 (below) in FBCJ to update Company Code : SFE1, Cash Journal : CJ01

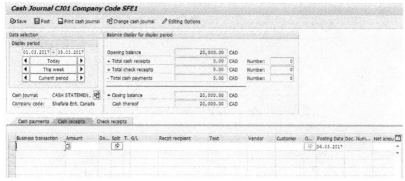

Figure 3: *Cash Journal*

Enter the Period for which you are going to run the cash journal

Figure 4: *Cash Journal - Period*

Based on the Period Opening and Closing Balance will be updated.

As an example, we are going to book Customer payment received in petty cash. Enter the following :

Under **Cash receipts** (Fig 3) Select Business Transaction via F4 function :

PAYMENT FROM CUSTOMER
Amount : 1500
Text : Description of Payment
Customer : 601288
Posting Date : Date e.g. 06.03.2017 [Date of payment received]

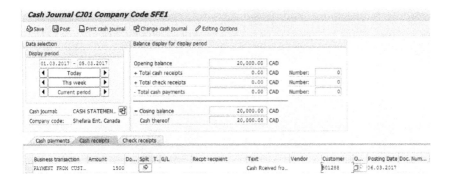

Figure 5: *Cash Journal*

Similarly for making payment to Vendor choose the following under ___ **Cash payments** ___ (Fig 3)

Business Transaction : Payment to Vendor

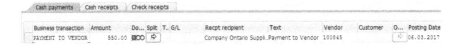

Figure 6: *Cash Journal entries*

After doing the necessary Cash Journal select the entry and Choose 🖫 **Post**

Entry will turn into Green showing it is posted successfuly.

Figure 7: *Posted entries*

Print Cash Journal : Choose 🖨 **Print cash journal**

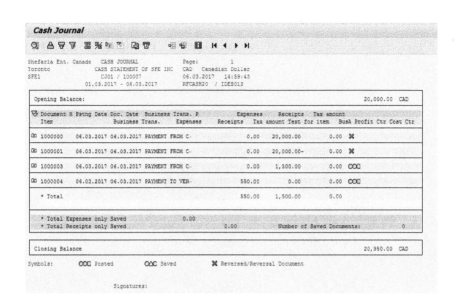

Figure 8: *Cash Journal*

Here you will see Opening / Closing Balance getting updated following Cash Journal Posting.

CROSS–APPLICATION, GENERAL COMPONENTS IN SAP

Strictly speaking, variants are variations of screens – both, input and output. They are not cross application components but 'common' components. Most of the screens in SAP behave similarly for the purpose of creating variants. The purpose of variants is twofold:

- To enable the user to save time by setting up screens with roughly the same data that may be needed every time the transaction is run
- To let different users who may be using the same transaction have their differentiation from each other in terms of inputs and outputs by naming their variants as suitable to them.

Variants are best explained by an example.

i)   Selection/Input Variants

Let us call a standard SAP transition to look up account balances FBL3N:

G/L Account Line Item Display

⊕ 🔁 🔳 🔲 Data Sources

G/L account selection

| G/L account | | to | | ⇨ |
| Company code | | to | | ⇨ |

Selection using search help

Search help ID

Search String

Complex search help   ⇨

Line item selection

Status

◉ Open items

Open at key date   07.08.2017

Figure 1: *G/L Account Line Item Display*

Let us assume you as an accounts person, is responsible for the company code SFE1 and for G/L accounts 100000 to 199999. A simple variant can be set up with these values:

G/L Account Line Item Display

⊕ 🔁 🔳 🔲 Data Sources

G/L account selection

| G/L account | 100000 | to | 199999 | ⇨ |
| Company code | SFE1 | to | | ⇨ |

Selection using search help

Search help ID

Search String

Complex search help   ⇨

Line item selection

Status

◉ Open items

Open at key date   07.08.2017

Figure 2: *G/L Account Line Item Display*

Save the values either by clicking on 🖫 or:

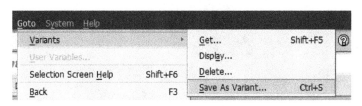

Goto	System	Help		
Variants		▸	Get...	Shift+F5	⑦
User Variables...			Display...	
Selection Screen Help		Shift+F6	Delete...	
Back		F3	Save As Variant...	Ctrl+S

Figure 3: *Variants options*

Give it a name:

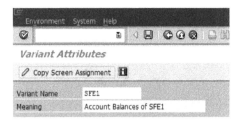

Figure 4: *Variant Attributes*

And save it:

Figure 5: *Variant Saved message*

Next time when you call the transaction FBL3N simply click on

the button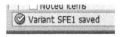

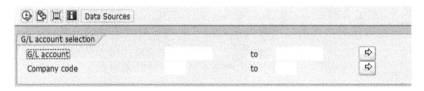

Figure 6: *Find Variant*

And enter the name of the variant if you know it:

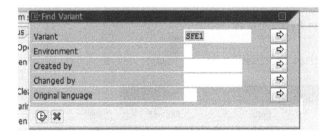

Figure 7: *Find Variant*

Or simply execute the above window to get a list of all and double click to choose the one you want:

| SFE1 | Account Balances of SFE1 | A | |

Figure 8: *Find Variant*

The figures you entered at the time of creating the variant will come on the screen so they don't have to be entered every time.

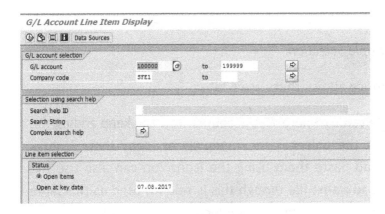

Figure 9: *G/L Account Line Item Display*

The above was a simple example of a variant. The inputs can be further defined using the feature of multiple values using the button

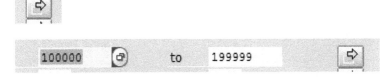

Figure 10: *Multiple Selection*

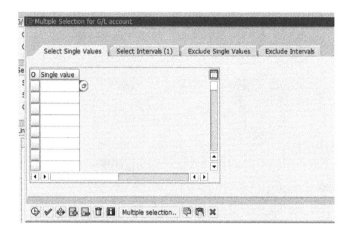

Figure 11: *Multiple Selection*

As you notice above, there are 4 tabs:

1. Select single values – here, G/L accounts. You can keep adding the G/Ls you want the balances for, manually or, copy them from a spreadsheet and paste them using the icon. You can also use the button to upload a text file though this is seldom used as the same objective can be achieved by the simpler copy/paste feature.

2. Select Intervals – this is what we have chosen in our variant:

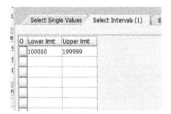

Figure 12: *Multiple Selection*

As seen above, multiple intervals of different ranges can be chosen.

3 and 4 – Exclude single values and exclude ranges – work exactly the same way as 1 and 2 except these are for excluding the G/L accounts while 1 and 2 were for including them.

ii)   Output/Display Variant

Let us stay with our variant and execute the report using the button Execute:

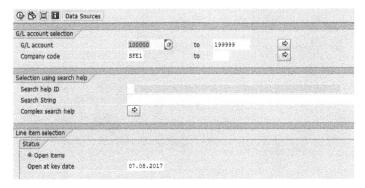

Figure 13: *G/L Account Line Item Display*

Some kind of a layout emerges:

S	Doc. Date	DocumentNo	Doc. Type	Cost Center	LCurr	Σ	Amount in local cur.	Texts	Text	Account	User Name	Reference
	30.07.2017	90036885	RV		CAD		350.00			105100	IDES0164	0090036885
		90036886	RV		CAD		150.00			105100	IDES0164	0090036886
	28.07.2017	5000000136	WE		CAD		135,000.00			134000	IDES014	
	22.07.2017	1400000153	DZ		CAD		20,250.00			105100	IDES014	
		1400000153	DZ		CAD		900.00-			105100	IDES014	
		1400000154	DZ		CAD		1,050.00			121000	IDES013	
		1400000157	DZ		CAD		50.00			121000	IDES0164	

Figure 14: *G/L Account Line Item Display*

The above is the display of the report based on some parameters. Let us see what they are and how this can be customized to our requirement.

The first is how to display. As seen above, this is an Excel friendly layout. It can be changed to a more generic layout using:

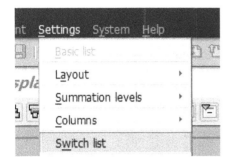

Figure 15: *Setting options*

G/L Balances
G/L Account
Company Code   SFE1

St	Doc. Date	DocumentNo	Type	Cost Ctr	LCurr	Amount in local cur.	Texts	Text	Account	User Name	Reference
☑	30.07.2017	90036885	RV		CAD	350.00			105100	IDES0164	0090036885
☑	30.07.2017	90036886	RV		CAD	150.00			105100	IDES0164	0090036886
✔	28.07.2017	5000000136	WE		CAD	138,000.00			134000	IDES014	
☑	22.07.2017	1400000153	DZ		CAD	20,250.00			105100	IDES014	
☑	22.07.2017	1400000153	DZ		CAD	900.00-			105100	IDES014	
☑	22.07.2017	1400000154	DZ		CAD	1,060.00			121000	IDES013	
☑	22.07.2017	1400000157	DZ		CAD	50.00			121000	IDES0164	
☑	22.07.2017	1800000224	DR		CAD	1,000.00			105100	IDES014	

Figure 16: *G/L Account Balances*

Most people will prefer the Excel type grid so we work with that:

Identify a few of these Windows based icons and work with them:

Figure 17: *Based Icons*

The SAP specific ones, refer to how the layouts can be created and saved:

As we notice, the columns currently available to us in this report are:

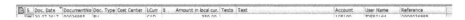

S	Doc. Date	DocumentNo	Doc. Type	Cost Center	LCurr	Σ	Amount in local cur.	Texts	Text	Account	User Name	Reference
	30.07.2017	90036885	RV		CAD		350.00			105100	IDES0164	0090036885

Figure 18: *Available columns*

The source of these columns are SAP tables – in this case, accounting tables (next section, ideally, to be visited once you have finished the rest of this book).

If you wish to add/delete or re-arrange any of these columns, click on . 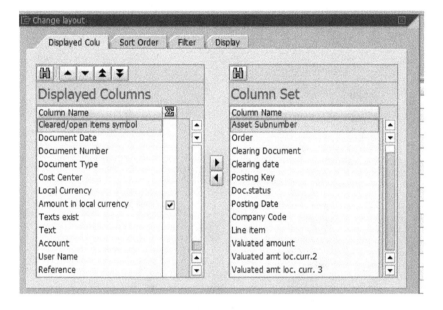 :

Figure 19: *Change Layout*

As you notice, the section on the left is the list of the columns displayed in the order from top to bottom > left to right in the report. The right section is the list of more fields/columns available though it is not necessary that all of them hold data. If you wish to see something new/additional or want to hide any, just double click on it and it flips from one column to the other as clicked.

The keys are useful to find, or move up or down the list.

Once you are satisfied with what you require in your report and want to save it with the ides of recalling it every time (same way as

the input variant), click on  :

Give it a name:

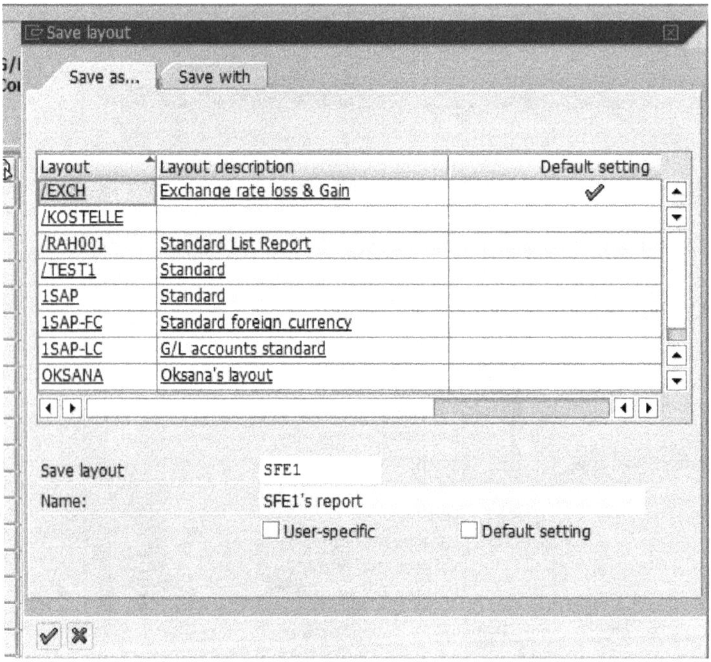

Figure 20: *Save Layout*

You can use the buttons:

Figure 21: *Save option*

To save as specific to you OR as a default layout. It is HIGHLY recommended NOT to save as a default layout otherwise everyone will see only that as a default and will have to change it to their requirements which will not be a very useful thing for other users. So we save this as user specific:

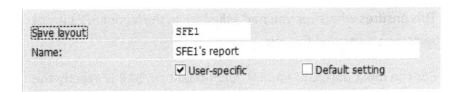

Figure 22: *Save Layout*

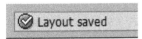

Figure 23: *Layout saved message*

Next time we run this report, we can call for our display variant

using the icon ![icon]: (See fig 17)

Click on the hyperlink SFE1 as below:

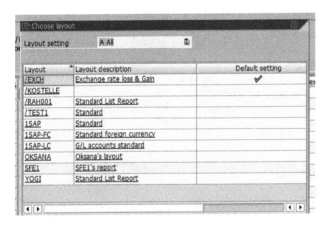

Figure 24: *Choose Layout*

The message displayed at the bottom is:

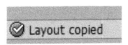

Figure 25: *Layout copied message*

This ensures whatever you had asked for in the layout SFE1 is not on the screen displayed for you.

For the most part, this variant functionality in SAP is exactly the same across all screens and all modules thereby making your life infinitely easier.

Not only do variants help you save time, they can also present you with data relating to the documents themselves e.g. by checking any particular line, you can go straight into the document and even change it for whatever is possible to be changed.

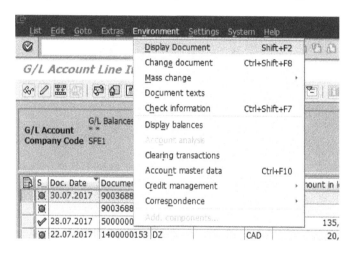

Figure 26: *Environment options*

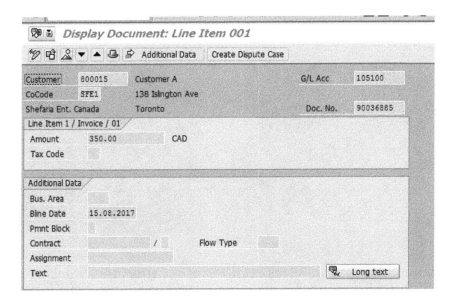

Figure 27: *Display Document*

Lots of other data is visible through the variants so you are saved the enormous amount of time in opening up different sessions to look up any transactions or documents.

TABLES IN SAP

Most of the data in SAP resides in tables and structures, primarily in the former. The latter can be read only by technically knowledgeable people but the former is available to all, subject to authorizations. We will take a peek into how the tables exist in SAP and how they can be read and data extracted from them.

Tens of thousands of tables exist in SAP well apportioned over the different modules. A few important ones related to Supply Chain are:

BKPF Accounting Document Header
BSEG Accounting Document Line items
LFA1 Vendor Master (General Section)
BSID Accounting: Secondary Index for Customers
BSIS Accounting: Secondary Index for G/L Accounts
BSIK Accounting: Secondary Index for Vendors
LFB1 Vendor Master (CC)
BSAK Accounting: Secondary Index for Vendors (Cleared Items)
BSAD Accounting: Secondary Index for Customers (Cleared Items)
LFBK Vendor Master (Bank Details)
BSAS Accounting: Secondary Index for G/L Accounts (Cleared Items)
SKAT G/L Account Master Record (CoA: Description)
AVIK Payment Advice Header

SKA1 G/L Account Master (CoA)
KNC1 Customer master (transaction figures)
KNBK Customer Master (Bank Details)
VBKPF Document Header for Document Parking
TTYP Object Types for Accounting
LFC1 Vendor master (transaction figures)
T052 Terms of Payment
BSIP Index for Vendor Validation of Double Documents
LFB5 Vendor master (dunning data)
KNB1 Customer Master – Co. Code Data (payment method,
       reconciliation acct)
KNB4 Customer Payment History
KNB5 Customer Master – Dunning info
KNKA Customer Master Credit Mgmt.
KNKK Customer Master Credit Control Area Data (credit limits)
KNVV Sales Area Data (terms, order probability)
KNVI Customer Master Tax Indicator
KNVP Partner Function key
KNVD Output type
KNVS Customer Master Ship Data
KLPA Customer/Vendor Link
VBUK Header Status and Administrative Data
VBAK Sales Document - Header Data
VBKD Sales Document - Business Data
VBUP Item Status
VBAP Sales Document - Item Data
VBPA Partners
VBFA Document Flow
VBEP Sales Document Schedule Line
VBBE Sales Requirements: Individual Records
LIPS Delivery Document item data, includes referencing PO
LIKP Delivery Document Header data
VBRK Billing Document Header
VBRP Billing Document Item
MARA   Material Master: General data
MAKT   Material Master: Description
MARM   Material Master: Unit of Measure
MAPE   Material master: Export control file

MARC   Material master: Plant data
MARD   Material master: Storage location
MAST   Material link to BOM
MBEW   Material valuation
MLGN   Material Master: WM Inventory
MLGT   Material Master: WM Inventory type
MDIP   Material: MRP profiles (field contents)
MKOP   Consignment price segment (old versions of SAP)
EBEW   Valuation of sales order stock
QBEW   Valuation of project stock
MVER   Material Master: Consumption <Plant>
DVER   Material Master: Consumption <MRP Area>
MVKE   Material Master: Sales <Sales Org, Distr Ch>
MLAN   Material Master: Tax indicator
EBAN   Purchase requisition: items
EBKN   Purchase Requisition: account assignment
EKKO   Purchasing document header
EKPO   Purchasing Document: Item

The transaction code to look up tables is SE16N as in Figure 1.

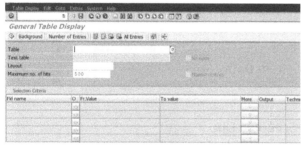

Figure 1: *General Table Display*

Enter the name of the table you want to look up and Hit Enter again:

| Background | Number of Entries | | | | All Entries | | |

Table	BKPF			Accounting Document Header
Text table				No texts
Layout				
Maximum no. of hits	500			Maintain entries

Selection Criteria

Fld name	O	Fr.Value	To value	More	Output	Technical name
Client						MANDT
Company Code	⊕			⇨	✓	BUKRS
Document Number	⊕			⇨	✓	BELNR
Fiscal Year	⊕			⇨	✓	GJAHR
Document Type	⊕			⇨	✓	BLART
Document Date	⊕			⇨	✓	BLDAT
Posting Date	⊕			⇨	✓	BUDAT
Period	⊕			⇨	✓	MONAT
Entered on	⊕			⇨	✓	CPUDT
Entered at	⊕			⇨	✓	CPUTM
Changed on	⊕			⇨	✓	AEDAT
Last update	⊕			⇨	✓	UPDDT
Translatn Date	⊕			⇨	✓	WWERT
User Name	⊕			⇨	✓	USNAM
Transaction Code	⊕			⇨	✓	TCODE

Figure 2: *General Table Display*

On the left are the names of the fields which are for most part, self-explanatory, on the right are their technical names for those who are more involved in using tables in programming. Enter input data you need to find the results for.

On the right, check the fields that you really want to see in your result as too much information can be clutter and also cause the program to take more time in executing. You can use the scroll bar on the right to look for more fields if required:

Figure 3: *Scroll bar*

Use the keys to select or deselect the all fields if needed and then select the ones you need individually.

417

The button [Number of Entries] tells you the # of entries in the table for the input data you have entered.

If the result is expected to take a long time, then this can also be run in the background using [Background] by setting up a job for it whose results can be downloaded later.

Unless you are sure the total will be less than 500, it is advisable to wipe out this number so you can get the entire list. The default can be changed in the option below though wiping it out is always the best option unless you are looking for only some sample data:

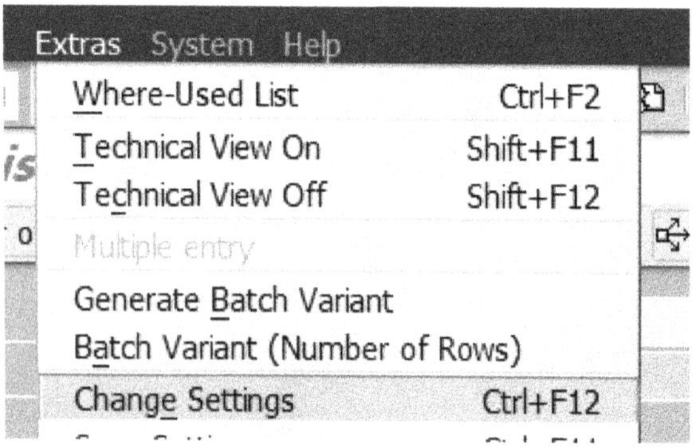

Figure 4: *Extras options*

Let's say we want to see only the company code, document number, date of posting and document type, so check only those boxes on the right as 'outputs'. If we want to look for all accounting entries made by any user ID for a certain period, enter these 2 data elements in their respective fields as in Fig 5.

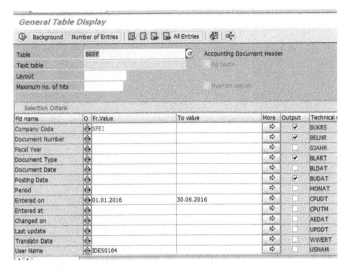

Figure 5: *General Table Display*

Execute (F8):

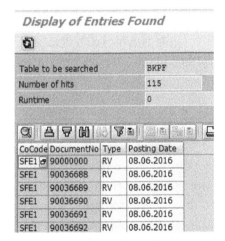

Figure 6: *Display of Entries Found*

We can either scroll through this list or download it using ![icon]. The rest of the screen icons should be familiar. In this way, all tables can be looked up for the required data.

QUERIES IN SAP

Queries in SAP link tables to give users results based off their unique requirements. There are 2 kinds of queries; one is a quick view (SQVI) which everyone has access to and the other is structured queries (SQ01) which require greater skills to develop and execute. Another main difference between the two is that a Quick viewer is available only to the person who creates it while the more structured queries can be made available to everybody using the appropriate user groupings.

In this training we will cover the Quick viewer as the access to the latter may be very limited in most organizations.

The concept of queries is simple – find one or more fields that are common to 2 or more tables and link the tables by those field/s to 'query' them. Then input your selection in one and get the outputs from that and the other table as desired in one single report instead of multiple lookups. However, this link needs to make sense in a few ways:

- The fields being linked must lead up to a unique value else SAP won't find a correct match or will find multiple matches
- There should not be any redundancy of data i.e. the data being linked must have consistency and clarity
- No unnecessary joins should exist between these tables or that can lead to inconsistent results or no results

As an example, we will use 2 tables from the previous section:

LFA1 - Vendor Master (General Section)
LFB1 - Vendor Master (CC)

The intent of our query is to find the vendor data in the CC section along with the vendor address. From our knowledge of the tables, we know the vendor address exists in LFA1 and the CC data in LFB1. Since the common key that holds them together is the vendor code itself, we will use it in the join.

To get to the quick viewer use transaction SQVI or the menu path:

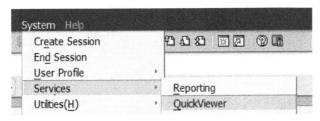

Figure 1: *System option*

Give it a short name till 15 characters:

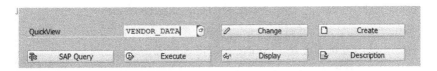

Figure 2: *QuickViewer*

Click on Create  button

Now you have the ability to give it a longer description/Title:

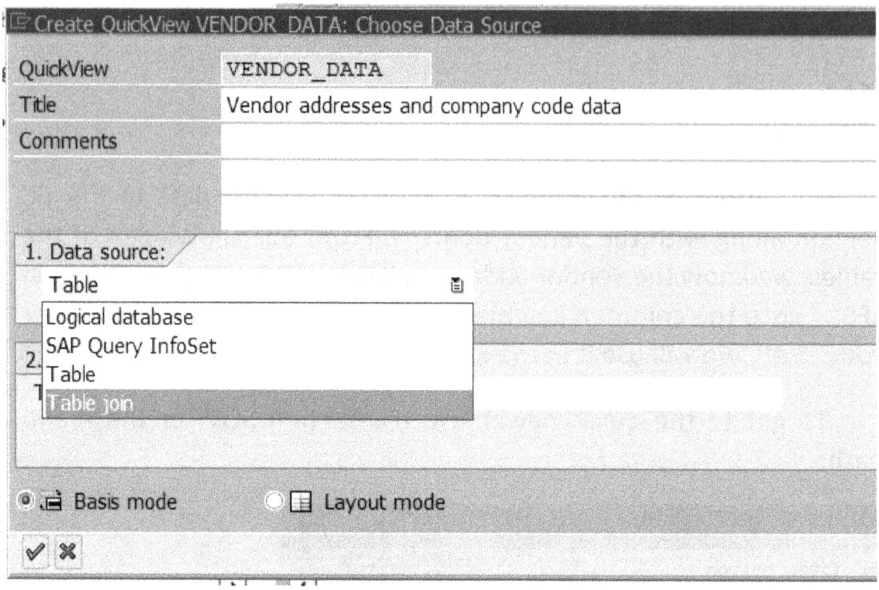

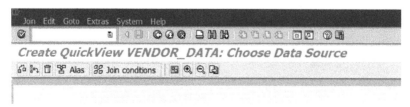

Figure 3: *Create QuickView Vendor Data*

Choose Data source as Table join.

(a) Logical database are complex data structures that have been provided by SAP for some important sub areas like pricing, purchasing, accounting documents etc and are normally used only by IT as they require more complexity to develop

(b) SAP Query Infoset is used in more structured queries mentioned in the beginning of this section

(c) Table read would be same as SE16N as in the previous section and using it as a query is meaningless if you have access to SE16N

(d) Table join – this is what we will use and is the most common way of creating a quick viewer

Say OK to come to this screen:

Figure 4: *Create QuickView Vendor Data*

There is a window that appears as a navigation pane which helps to see at a glance when many tables are being used for interconnection:

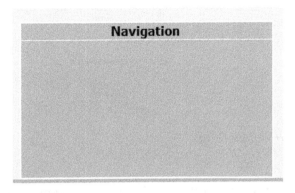

Figure 5: *Navigation window*

Our first task is to insert the tables we will be using. We use the icon ![icon] (see Fig 4) to do that:

Enter the name of the first table when the window comes up:

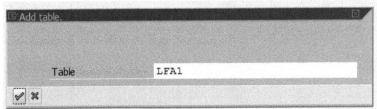

Figure 6: *Add Table window*

Hit Enter and it should be now available for use along with all its fields:

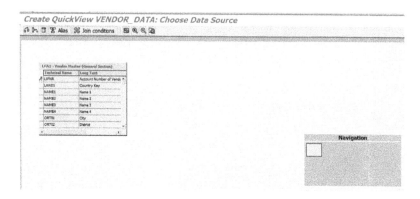

Figure 7: *Create QuickView Vendor Data*

Repeat the insert for the other table LFB1 and SAP will link them together automatically based on the most important field which is LIFNR (Vendor #):

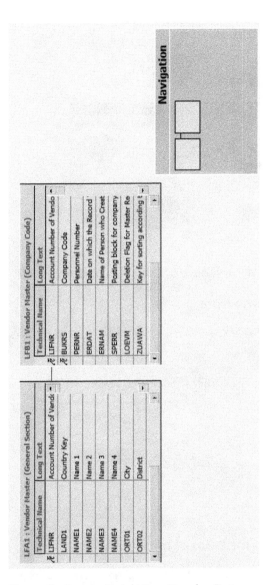

Figure 8: *Create QuickView Vendor Data*

The link between the 2 tables is now established. It is also possible to change this link to some other if there is any other field that can be more helpful.

Click on Green arrow to step back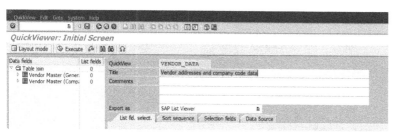

Figure 9: *QuickViewer*

Expand on the triangles on the left side of the screen to reveal all the fields in the 2 tables to choose from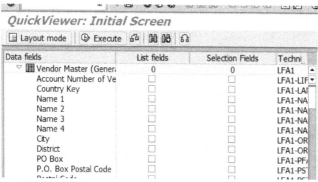

Figure 10: *QuickViewer*

We now have 3 options wrt the fields of these tables:

1. List fields i.e. show the value in this field in the result – List Field. Then check it.
2. Selection Fields i.e. we use a field to only input what we need as a selection criteria. Then check it.
3. Do both i.e. use it as a selection criterion and also have it's data it in the resulting report.

In our case we will use the following fields in the general area of the vendor:

Data fields	List fields	Selection Fields	Tec
▽ ⊞ Vendor Master (Gener:	5	1	LFA
Account Number of Ve	☑	☑	LFA
Country Key	☐	☐	LFA
Name 1	☑	☐	LFA
Name 2	☐	☐	LFA
Name 3	☐	☐	LFA
Name 4	☐	☐	LFA
City	☑	☐	LFA
District	☐	☐	LFA
PO Box	☐	☐	LFA
P.O. Box Postal Code	☐	☐	LFA
Postal Code	☑	☐	LFA
Region (State, Province	☑	☐	LFA

Figure 11: *Data fields*

and the following in the CC data:

QuickViewer: Initial Screen

☰ Layout mode ⊕ Execute ♋ 🗄 🗄 ♋

Data fields	List fields	Selection Fields	Te..
▽ ⊞ Vendor Master (Company	5	1	LFB1 ▲
Account Number of Vendo	☑	☐	LFB1 ▼
Company Code	☑	☑	LFB1
Personnel Number	☐	☐	LFB1
Date on which the Record	☑	☐	LFB1
Name of Person who Crea	☐	☐	LFB1
Posting block for company	☐	☐	LFB1
Deletion Flag for Master Re	☐	☐	LFB1
Key for sorting according t	☐	☐	LFB1
Reconciliation Account in G	☑	☐	LFB1
Authorization Group	☐	☐	LFB1
Interest calculation indicatc	☐	☐	LFB1
List of the Payment Metho	☐	☐	LFB1
Indicator: Clearing betweer	☐	☐	LFB1
Block key for payment	☐	☐	LFB1
Terms of Payment Key	☑	☐	LFB1
Our account number with t	☐	☐	LFB1

Figure 12: *QuickViewer*

Again, use the scroll bar at the right to see the other fields in the tables.

Save the query. It is common to get a window like this below and in which case, just hit Enter since it is only an info message in Yellow:

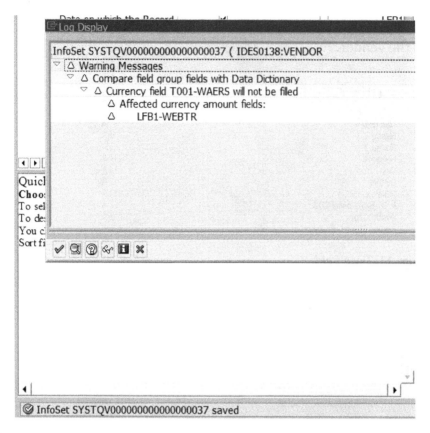

Figure 13: *Log Display*

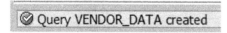

Figure 14: *Query created message*

Execute the query F8 or the icon ⊕ Execute

Alternatively, step out and go to SQVI again. This new query will now be available for you to use every time:

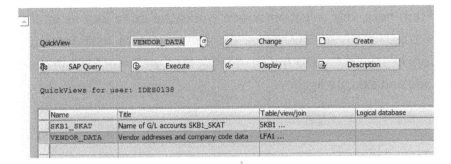

Figure 15: *QuickView*

Select and execute:

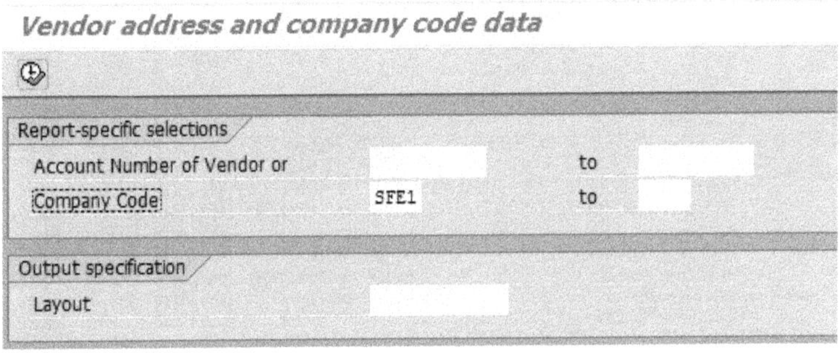

Vendor address and company code data

Report-specific selections			
Account Number of Vendor or		to	
Company Code	SFE1	to	

Output specification	
Layout	

Figure 16: *Input criteria*

Recall we had selected only 2 fields as input criteria – Vendor Number and the Company Code and so only those ones show up in the above selection screen.

From here, this selection screen works the same way as in all other transactions in SAP. Since we don't want to look for any vendors in any Co Code other than SFE1, then we enter SFE1 in the Co Code and execute again:

Vendor address and company code data

Vendor	CoCd	Acctg clerk	Name 1	City	PostalCode	Rg	Vendor	Date	Recon.acct	PayT
100863	SFE1	WR	GreenLand Corporation Ltd.	TORONTO	M6N 1B4	ON	100863	06/18/2016	211000	0008
100864	SFE1	WR	Concor Corporation Ltd.		M6N 1B4	ON	100864	06/20/2016	211000	0003
100865	SFE1	WR	Suculant Ltd.		M6N 1B4	ON	100865	06/20/2016	211000	
100844	SFE1	WR	FA Property Canada	Ontario		ON	100844	05/28/2016	211000	0003
100845	SFE1	WR	Ontario Supplier	Ontario		ON	100845	05/28/2016	211000	0003
100846	SFE1		Bolt Supply Company vendor for SFE1				100846	05/28/2016	211000	0003
100847	SFE1		Dubak Electric				100847	05/28/2016	211000	0001
100848	SFE1		Val Electric			ON	100848	05/28/2016	211000	0001
100849	SFE1		Data Enterprise for Devika	Toronto			100849	05/28/2016	211000	0003
100850	SFE1		SP Plus				100850	05/28/2016	211000	0001
100851	SFE1		Jazmin				100851	05/28/2016	211000	0001
100852	SFE1		STONE VENDOR FOR SFE1	TORONTO			100852	05/28/2016	211000	0003
100853	SFE1		xyz company	TORONTO	M6N 1B4	ON	100853	06/02/2016	211000	0003
100854	SFE1		ABC for sfe1	Toronto			100854	06/03/2016	211000	0003
100855	SFE1		Wood for SFE1				100855	06/03/2016	211000	0003
100856	SFE1		QQQ Company Ltd.	TORONTO	M6N 1B4	ON	100856	06/04/2016	211000	0003
100857	SFE1		WEY Company Ltd.		M8N 7Y6	ON	100857	06/05/2016	211000	0003
100858	SFE1		Burn Company			ON	100858	06/11/2016	211000	0003
100859	SFE1	WR	Free Polution Corporation Ltd.		M6N 1B4	ON	100859	06/14/2016	211000	0008
5000000085	SFE1		Health Corporation Ltd.		M6N 1B4	ON	5000000085	06/15/2016	211000	0008
100860	SFE1	WR	BGW Corporation Ltd		M6N 1B4	ON	100860	06/16/2016	211000	0003
100838	SFE1	WR	Wood vendor for SFE1	Oakville			100838	05/10/2016	211000	0003

Figure 17: *Vendor address and company code data Query*

This list can be now downloaded the same way as we have done at other times. It can be modified to hide columns you don't need and it helps to save the layout if you will use the query frequently. Queries can also be modified the same way by adding/deleting fields or even adding tables using the Change Query button from the main SQVI screen.

GLOSSARY OF TERMS

BOM	Bill of Material
CC	Company code
CoA	Chart of Accounts
CS01/02/03	Create, Change, display Bill of Material
DC	Distribution Channel - the way goods are sold - e.g. retail, wholesale etc
DIV	Division, represents a business area/segment in a company
F.27	Look up, generate or print customer statements
F-02	Reclass entries
F1	Help Key
F150	Dunning customers
F-28	Posting customer payments
F-29	Receiving down payment from customer
F-30	Transfer AR between customers
F-32	Clear customer account of down payment
F-39	Clearing down payment received from customer
F-44	Clear vendor account of down payment
F-48	Make down payment to vendor
F-49	Noted Items

F-53	Post payments to vendors
F-54	Clearing down payment made to vendor
FAGLB03	Display G/L account balances
FB03	Display Accounting Document
FB08	Reverse accounting document
FB50	Post journal entry
FB60	Post vendor invoice in accounting
FB70	Post customer invoice in accounting
FBCJ	Cash Journal
FBL1N	Look up Vendor Payables
FBL3N	Display line items of accounting documents
FBL5N	Look up Customers' receivables
FBV0	Post parked document
FBV3	List of parked Documents
FD01/02/03	Create, change, display customer master from FI perspective
FD10N	Display customer balance
FI	Financial Accounting
Financial statement Versions	SAP terminology for P&L and Balance Sheet
FK01/02/03	Create, change, display vendor master from FI perspective

FK10N	Display vendor balance
FS00	Area Menu for creating G/L accounts
FSG	Field Status Group
FTXP	Set up tax codes and rates
FV50	Park document
G/L	General ledger
GR	Goods Receipt
IR	Invoice Receipt
JE	Journal entry
LIV	Logistics Invoice Verification
MB03	Display material document
MB1C	Post initial stocks directly
ME01/03	Maintain (includes create and change) and display source list
ME11/12/13	Create, Change, display Purchasing Info records
ME21N/22N/23N	Create, Change, display Purchase Orders
ME41/42/43	Create, Change, Display RFQ
ME47	Enter vendor quotations in the system
ME49	Compare Quotations from vendors
ME51N/52N	Create, change Purchase Req

MI01/02/03	Create, change and display physical inventory document
MI05	Change inventory count
MI07	Post inventory recount document
MI10	Enter count w/o physical count document
MI11	Recount inventory
MI20	Compare physical with book stock
MIGO	Post Goods Receipt
MIR4	Display accounting document of LIV Material document
MIRO	Invoice Receipt
MK01/02/03	Create, change, display vendor master from MM perspective
MM	Materials Management
MM01/02/03	Create, change or Display material respectively
MMBE	Overview of Stocks
MRRL	Evaluated Invoice Receipt (to auto create payables)
P.Org	Purchasing Org; the highest object in MM, responsible for purchases on behalf of the c. code
PIR	Purchasing Info record
Posting Key	Key used by SAP to segregate based on customer or vendor, type of posting, debit or credit
PP	Production Planning
PR	Purchase Requisition

QM	Quality Management
RFQ	Request for Quotation
Sales Area	A unique combination of SO, DC and DIV
SAP	Pronounced ess-aye-pee, formerly called Systems, Applications, Products in Data Processing
SCM	Supply Chain Management
SD	Sales & Distribution
SE16N	Look up tables
SFE1	Company code being used in this manual for demo/training
SO	Sales Organization: Representing the company code, it is the highest object in SD
Source List	Listing of approved vendors for a certain product
SP02	Look up spools generated by yourself
SQ01	Central query - visible to all users
SQVI	Quickview visible only to the user who creates it
T-code	Transaction Code
VA01/02/03	Create, Change, Display Sales Order
Variant	A variation of input and output screen as desired by the user to simplify information
VB11/12/13	Create, change, display material determination
VD01/02/03	Create, change, display customer master from SD perspective
VD51/52/53	Create, Change, display customer-material info record

VF01/02/03	Create, Change, display Billing Document
VF11	Cancel Billing document
VK11/12/13	Create, Change, display pricing record
VL01N/02N/03N	Create, Change, display Delivery
VL09	Reverse Goods Issue from delivery
VT01N/02N/03N	Create, Change, display Shipment
XD01/02/03	Create, change, display customer master Centrally (all views)
XK01/02/03	Create, change, display vendor master Centrally (all views)

MAIN SYMBOLS

Symbol	Meaning	Extended meaning/ Function
/n	New	Before the t-code, replaces the existing screen with the new t-code
/o	Another	Before the t-code, replaces opens up a new screen with the new t-code
	Session key	Opens up a new session – up to 6 can be opened simultaneously in the latest version, at the time of writing
	Execute button or F8	Executes the program to give results based on what the user has selected on the input screen
	Navigation keys	Goes one step back (also F3), goes completely out of the transaction and cancels the current screen, respectively
	Page scroll	First page, previous page, next page and last page respectively
	Find on current page	Find and find again respectively, useful when you have long lists of documents and want to find any particular one

Menu — Restore, Move, Size, Minimiz, Maxim, Close, Create, Stop T	Click on top extreme left to get to this window	Creates new session or stops current transaction. Very useful if you started a transaction but forgot to use /o and want another window open to run another transaction. Also useful to cancel the current transaction if you gave incorrect input parameters and it is taking too long to fetch the results.
F1	Help	
F4	To look up values	For configurable objects, we can choose only what is available. Pressing F4 enables us to look up this list to choose from it.

ABOUT THE AUTHOR

Yogi Kalra has worked in the SAP field for over 25 years across multitudes of industries and with big 4 Consulting experience. Based in Canada, he has done projects all over Europe and North America. Prior to entering the SAP space, he was in Business handling Sales, Distribution, Depots, Purchasing and Accounting across Chemicals and Computer hardware industries for over 12 years. He is a CGA and MBA in Finance from University of Toronto, Canada and has been instrumental in training clients during and after SAP implementations in most of the SAP modules including but not limited to, FI, MM, SD, PP and QM.

This book is the first in the series of SAP books in configuration and user training in all these modules. SAP FI (Configurations & Transactions) and SAP SD-LE (Configurations & Transactions) are also available at most book stores.

www.ingramcontent.com/pod-product-compliance
Lightning Source LLC
Chambersburg PA
CBHW071231050326
40690CB00011B/2068